Mainstreaming in Early Childhood Education

Mainstreaming in Early Childhood Education

K. EILEEN ALLEN

20 19 18 17 16 15 14 13 12 11

LIBRARY OF CONGRESS CATALOG CARD NUMBER: 78-74838
ISBN: 0-8273-1692-5

Printed in the United States of America
Published simultaneously in Canada
by Nelson Canada,
A division of The Thomson Corporation

DELMAR PUBLISHERS INC. • **ALBANY, NEW YORK**
2 COMPUTER DRIVE, WEST — BOX 15-015
ALBANY, NEW YORK 12212

PREFACE

MAINSTREAMING IN EARLY CHILDHOOD EDUCATION is an informative, easy-to-read text focusing on developmental, social, educational, legal, and a variety of other issues related to the education of young handicapped children. Practical information is given on the early identification and assessment of young children at risk or potential risk in the population. The role of the preschool teacher in identifying, assessing, and individualizing educational programs for the young handicapped child in a mainstreamed setting is discussed in detail. This text presents a comprehensive picture of the field of early childhood education for handicapped children in a least restrictive (integrated or mainstreamed) setting.

The book is divided into twenty-one units, grouped into six sections. Included in these six sections are units on the following topics: the meaning of the term handicapped, causes and classifications of handicapped conditions, legislation for the handicapped, implications of the term mainstreaming, early identification and screening, Individualized Education Programs, teaching the handicapped and nonhandicapped (teacher skills, working with specialists), curriculum approaches, managing special needs, and home-community-school relations. Some of the major issues dealt with are: the developmental curriculum and its relationship to the delayed or disabled child; specific disabling conditions that the preschool teacher in the integrated setting is likely to encounter; and insights that family and community can provide into the child's present and future environments.

Each unit starts with a set of well-organized objectives intended to guide the student's study of the unit. Accompanying the text material are numerous illustrations showing young handicapped and nonhandicapped children in a variety of learning situations. The unit material also includes such features as practical examples of how to teach specific skills to children, student activities, discussion topics, unit summaries, and review questions.

The author of this text, K. Eileen Allen, is a Professor of Human Development at the University of Kansas. She is a widely recognized authority on mainstreaming who has published extensively in the field of early childhood education. One of the first articles on mainstreaming was published by this author in 1972. Continuing to research and write on the subject, she presented a paper on mainstreaming at an international conference on special education at the University of Stirling in Scotland (1978). Recently, Professor Allen conducted a series of training institutes on early childhood mainstreaming in various cities under the auspices of the Council of Exceptional Children. As part of her extensive past experience, she served as Director of the Developmental Disabilities program at the University of Washington. Currently, Professor Allen is involved in teaching graduate and undergraduate courses, teacher-training, service and research at the University of Kansas. She is also one of the principal investigators in a major grant from the Bureau of Education for the Handicapped focusing on early intervention with young handicapped children.

A current catalog including prices of all Delmar educational publications is available upon request. Please write to:

**Catalog Department
Delmar Publishers Inc.
2 Computer Drive, West
Box 15-015
Albany, New York 12212**

NOTICE TO THE READER

CONTENTS

SECTION 1
PERSPECTIVES ON THE HANDICAPPED

Unit 1 HANDICAPPED: WHAT DOES IT MEAN?

OBJECTIVES

After studying this unit, the student will be able to

- State why there is disagreement about the definition of the terms normal and handicapped.
- Specify, in order, at least ten developmental milestones.
- Explain why a developmental deviation may or may not be a handicap.

It has been estimated that between three and fifteen percent of the people in the United States are handicapped. No two sources agree on the exact figure. This is because no two groups or agencies agree on a definition of the word handicapped, especially where young children are concerned.

The handicapped child is one who may be easy to recognize or difficult to recognize, figure 1-1. It depends upon how obvious the handicap is and who is viewing the child. A child may be considered handicapped in one setting but not in another. For example, a preschooler who speaks only Spanish may be considered handicapped in a classroom where only English is spoken. On the other hand, the same child may be very capable in a Spanish-speaking environment. Note, too, that the child's preschool teacher may be considered "handicapped" in the child's native environment, if the teacher speaks only English.

Fig. 1-1 The handicapped child may or may not be easy to recognize.

MANY MEANINGS

It seems that the term handicapped can have many meanings. This was not always so. In the past, the term usually referred to individuals who were noticeably "different" either physically or mentally. These children were usually thought of as the crippled or the mentally retarded. In line with this there were "crippled children's homes," and homes for the "feeble-minded" as the mentally retarded were commonly called at one point. These were just about the only service facilities provided for such children.

Today, the term handicapped covers a much broader range. It includes a variety of defects and deficiencies, and many kinds of abnormal and atypical developmental

Fig. 1-2 The term handicapped carries a broad meaning.

patterns. As indicated earlier, there is some disagreement about the meaning of the term. In this book, the term handicapped has a broad meaning, figure 1-2. It refers to one or more instances of the following:

- any condition which delays a child's normal growth and development

- any condition which distorts (makes abnormal or atypical) a child's normal growth and development

- any condition which has a severe negative effect on a child's normal growth and development or adjustment to life

WHAT IS NORMAL?

To fully understand the definition just given for handicapped, it is necessary first to understand the term normal. Here again, there is disagreement about the meaning of the word. What is normal for one child may be quite abnormal for another child. No two children are exactly alike. No two children grow and develop at exactly the same rate. Some children walk at eight months, others do not walk until eighteen months. Most children begin walking somewhere in between eight and eighteen months. All children within this range, however, are normal with respect to walking. The same is true for every other area of development. Normalcy, therefore, can have great variation and great differences among individuals.

There are, however, certain principles of normal development that serve as guides. One is that the order of stages of development is usually the same for all children. Each child, however, moves at a different rate throughout the developmental sequence, figure 1-3. Certain children are a little more skilled or a little less skilled than most others of their own age. For example, most five- or six-year-olds can draw fairly recognizable houses, trees, and

Fig. 1-3 **Each child moves through the developmental sequence at an individual rate.**

people. Only a few of these children, however, produce outstanding paintings in high school.

All normally developing children move step by step through each stage of development. Each preceding step is necessary before the next one can be taken. Regardless of how old the child is, an earlier stage usually must be mastered before the child can move into the next stage. There are exceptions to this principle, however. Most infants crawl before they walk, but some do not. Some pretoddlers move about by propelling themselves on their bottoms. Others lie flat on their backs and push with their feet, figure 1-4. Such methods of getting around before walking are quite appropriate for these children. It must be remembered, too, that no child grows uniformly, or all at the same time. Developmental progress is never smooth and flowing; it is usually quite uneven. In fact, a child may

seem to stop working on one skill or even slide backwards (regress) when beginning to work on a new one.

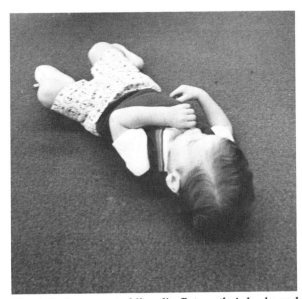

Fig. 1-4 **Some pretoddlers lie flat on their backs and propel with their feet.**

3

DEVELOPMENTAL MILESTONES

In spite of this great variation, there are certain behaviors or skill sequences that can be seen at specific times in almost every normally developing child. These are considered significant points or events in development. They are often referred to as *developmental milestones*. It is of concern if a child does not reach, or is seriously delayed in reaching, one of these milestones. This usually indicates that something is amiss in the child's development. Only a brief description of these milestones is given here. More detailed profiles are provided in the units on physical, social, language, and intellectual development.

Infancy

In the past, the newborn baby was thought to be able to do little except eat and sleep. Research in the past ten years has shown that this is far from true. Very young babies are interested in many things in their environment. They follow a moving object with their eyes. They will turn their heads in an effort to locate a noise.

From earliest infancy, the human face (especially the face of the major caregiver) is a source of great interest for the baby. At about six weeks of age, or between four and ten weeks, the baby begins social or responsive smiling, figure 1-5. The social smile is considered a major developmental milestone. If the twelve- to fourteen-week-old infant has not yet begun social smiling, it may be a clue to a potentially serious developmental problem.

Between two and three months of age, the infant is making social kinds of sounds. These sounds are considered social for two reasons: (1) they are made in response to another person's voice, and (2) they may cause another person to respond to the baby. Both are important to future language development. By this time, the infant is smiling readily at people. Infants also smile at things, and even at their own noises and actions. By three months of age, infants display some eye-hand coordination, allowing them to reach and grasp objects that attract them.

At about five or six months of age, the infant shows some rolling over behavior. At about seven months, many infants can sit without support. By nine months, most infants are crawling or showing signs of readiness to crawl. Cruising (holding onto a low table or chair or some other stable piece of furniture) comes next in motor development for most children. Then comes walking! The average walking age is about twelve months, although there is a great difference among individual babies. The "normal" range is from seven or eight months to eighteen months, as mentioned earlier.

The baby's mental or cognitive development is closely tied to physical development. The infant pokes, pats, touches, tastes, crawls,

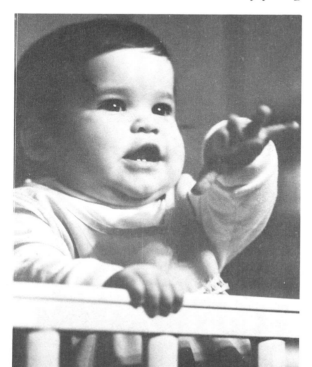

Fig. 1-5 The social smile is a major developmental milestone.

Fig. 1-6 The older infant seems to be moving every waking moment.

or walks almost every waking moment, figure 1-6. This kind of exploring enables infants to learn many things about the world around them. The majority of research suggests that this is a very important period in a baby's cognitive development.

Between two and three years of age most children are moving about freely. In fact, they are moving about almost too freely, it sometimes seems, at least to parents trying to keep up with them. A number of other behaviors can be observed in the normally developing child during this year. These behaviors include the ability to

- manipulate small toys and other objects quite skillfully
- understand much of what is said
- speak in simple, sentencelike language
- imitate the behavior of others (a skill needed especially to learn language)

- exhibit some of the social skills which society demands
- function on the toilet or at least exhibit certain readiness traits for toilet training

The Preschool Years

By the time the child is three, most of the basic motor skills are developed. The child runs, jumps, and climbs with assurance. Many behaviors are acquired that help the child become more independent. The child is growing more slowly. The amount of food needed is greatly reduced. Unfortunately, few parents understand this. They may think their child has suddenly become a picky eater. Unwittingly, they try to force the child to eat more than is required during this reduced growth period. This often causes serious conflicts between parents and child. Such conflicts can create tensions that have an unhappy effect on the whole parent-child relationship.

Language skills are developing rapidly during this preschool period. Many children, however, become nonfluent for awhile, that is, they may stutter and stammer. Usually this nonfluency disappears if adults do not try to "correct" the child. By the age of six, the child's vocabulary usually averages about 2,500 words. All of the grammatical forms in the child's native language are present.

The three-to-five period also marks strong social and emotional development. Children begin to share and take turns. They begin to understand how others feel. This is sometimes referred to as developing *empathy.* The development of self-concept also emerges during these years. That is, children begin to realize that each is a separate person with a separate identity from everyone else. They form a number of strong social attachments. The idea of having "best friends" is taking hold, figure 1-7. Children are acquiring the social behaviors that will make them

acceptable members of the community in which they are growing up.

During all of these early years, the child is like a sponge, able to absorb seemingly endless learnings. Children learn to count and classify objects, and to name colors and shapes. They begin to name and even write letters.

If all goes well, the developing child passes one milestone after another. This still does not lead to a final definition of normalcy for a number of reasons.

A child may be developing normally in some areas and be quite delayed, even handicapped, in others. A child who has a severe physical problem that prevents running, jumping, and climbing behaviors may be quite normal, even advanced, in language and intellectual development. The opposite may be equally true.

Thus, it can be seen how difficult it is to say absolutely what is meant by the words "handicapped" and "normal." It can also be seen how important it is for the observer to

Fig. 1-7 The idea of "best friends" is developing.

know normal growth and development in order to spot problems in development.

DEVELOPMENTAL PROBLEMS

It may be useful to think of developmental problems as having two basic forms, delays and deviations. A *delay* is when a child is performing like a normal child of a younger age in one or more areas of development. A *deviation* is when some aspect of the child's development is different from what is *ever* seen in a normally developing child. It must be remembered, however, that deviations in development are not necessarily handicapping. For example, individuals with six toes are rare. Therefore, six-toed individuals are "deviant," but they are not classified as handicapped when that is their only deviation. On the other hand, what may seem to be a minor problem can be a handicap if it is a source of anxiety to the individual. Such things as facial blemishes, birthmarks, missing fingers, or one short leg might be a handicap for some individuals, but of little concern to others. It depends upon how well the child, especially in the very early years, is helped to handle the deviation.

There are, of course, a number of developmental delays or deviations which can be specified. Each of these will be discussed in unit 2.

SUMMARY

There is no one single agreed-upon definition for the word handicapped. Over the past several years, however, it has come to mean any individual who has delays or deficiencies that interfere seriously with normal growth and development.

The term normal must be defined in order to understand the word handicapped. Again, there is no absolute definition of the word normal. Normal development implies that a child goes through specific stages of development in a specific order. In other words, a normally developing child does what the child development norms specify as being appropriate for the average child to do at approximately each given age. These are often referred to as developmental milestones.

It is important to remember that there is a wide range of individual differences among normal children. Normal growth and development must be understood in order to understand the growth patterns of children who are not developing normally. With this kind of understanding, it is possible to better evaluate the abnormal child's abilities and problems. It is also possible to better identify those areas where the handicapped child's needs and abilities are the same as those of the normal child. Finally, it must be understood that what may be handicapping for one child may not be handicapping for another child.

STUDENT ACTIVITIES

- Find out about the kinds of institutions or homes for the handicapped in your community.

- Observe a group of preschool children. List developmental deviations that you see which do *not* appear to be handicapping.

- Locate an infant over three months of age. Observe for at least one hour while the baby is awake. Note where the infant is in terms of developmental milestones.

- Explain why a teacher of handicapped preschoolers must have an understanding of normal growth and development.

REVIEW

A. Briefly answer each of the following.

1. How many handicapped individuals are there in the United States? (percentage)

2. Why can no exact figure be given for the number of handicapped?

3. Is a child who does not speak English considered handicapped?

4. Give a broad definition for the term handicapped.

5. Define developmental milestones.

6. Why be concerned if a baby does not engage in early social smiling?

7. Why might children two and one-half years of age begin to eat considerably less than they had been eating earlier?

8. What is meant by the development of self-concept?

9. Name and explain two basic forms of developmental problems.

10. Why might the same type of deviation be handicapping for one child and not for another?

B. Select the best answer from the choices offered to complete each statement.

1. The term handicapped has
    a. many meanings.
    b. few meanings.
    c. only one meaning.

2. A child who speaks a different language than the preschool group
    a. is always handicapped.
    b. is never handicapped.
    c. may or may not be handicapped.

3. Normal development means
    a. all children walk at the same age.
    b. all five-year-olds speak grammatically.
    c. there is great variation among children.

4. Very young babies
    a. can only eat and sleep.
    b. are not interested in their environment.
    c. will turn their heads to locate a noise.

5. By three years of age all normal children
    a. are toilet trained.
    b. understand much of what is said to them.
    c. use compound sentences.

6. Developmental delay means the child
   a. is behind in all areas of development.
   b. can never catch up to other children of the same age.
   c. is performing like a much younger normal child.

7. Any young child who can run, jump, and climb
   a. is never considered handicapped.
   b. may be handicapped in some other developmental areas.
   c. is perfectly normal.

8. A child with six toes is considered
   a. deviant.
   b. delayed.
   c. handicapped.

C. Match each phrase in Column I with the correct ending in Column II.

Column I	Column II
1. In earlier times, the term handicapped referred to	a. adults do not try to "correct" the child
2. The term handicapped covers many kinds of	b. will follow a moving object with their eyes
3. Most children walk between	c. abnormal and atypical developmental patterns
4. Normally developing children move or pass	d. is the child's reduced appetite and need for less food
5. Infancy research of the past ten years indicates that very young babies	e. step by step through each stage of development
6. If the twelve- to fourteen-week-old infant has not begun social smiling, this may be	f. children who were noticeably different, physically or mentally
7. Stuttering or stammering in young children usually disappears if	g. eight and eighteen months old
8. A frequent source of conflict between children two and one-half years old and their parents	h. understand abnormal growth and development
9. Birthmarks or missing fingers	i. a clue to a potentially serious problem
10. It is necessary to understand normal growth and development in order to	j. may be handicapping for some and not for others
	k. two and three years old

D. Define the following terms.

1. developmental milestone
2. nonfluency
3. empathy
4. deviation
5. developmental delay

Unit 2 CAUSES OF HANDICAPS

OBJECTIVES

After studying this unit, the student will be able to

- Explain and give examples of the three major factors that are responsible for both a handicapped and a nonhandicapped individual.
- List six common but preventable causes of mental retardation and other kinds of handicaps.
- Discuss the Milwaukee Project, focusing on why these findings are important.

In the United States, there are about eight million handicapped children and youths. Approximately one million are infants and preschoolers. They represent many kinds of deviations, deficiencies, and delays. Some of these children receive educational services; others do not. Figure 2-1 shows the approximate number of children in the United States, served and unserved, who have various kinds of handicaps.

	1975–76 Served (Projected)	1975–76 Unserved	Total Handicapped Children Served and Unserved	Percent Served	Percent Unserved
TOTAL: Age 6–19	3,860,000	2,840,000	6,700,000	58	42
TOTAL: Age 0–5	450,000	737,000	1,187,000	38	62
TOTAL: Age 0–19	4,310,000	3,577,000	7,887,000	55	45
SPEECH IMPAIRED	2,020,000	273,000	2,293,000	88	12
MENTALLY RETARDED	1,350,000	157,000	1,507,000	90	10
LEARNING DISABLED	260,000	1,706,000	1,966,000	13	87
EMOTIONALLY DISTURBED	255,000	1,055,000	1,310,000	19	81
CRIPPLED AND OTHER HEALTH IMPAIRED	255,000	73,000	328,000	78	22
DEAF	45,000	4,000	49,000	92	8
HARD OF HEARING	66,000	262,000	328,000	20	80
VISUALLY HANDICAPPED	43,000	23,000	66,000	65	35
DEAF-BLIND AND OTHER MULTIHANDICAPPED	16,000	24,000	40,000	40	60

Taken from the 1976 Annual Report of the National Advisory Committee on the Handicapped

Fig. 2-1 Estimated number of handicapped children served and unserved, by type of handicap.

Handicapping conditions may show up at different times in a child's development. Sometimes the handicap is apparent at the time of birth. At other times, it is not detected or does not develop until much later. Generally, the more severe the handicap, the earlier it can be recognized, figure 2-2. There are exceptions, however. A very disabling hearing loss, for example, may not be discovered until the child is in public school.

Causes of handicapping conditions can be explained in a variety of ways. One way is to look at the makeup of all individuals in terms of three major factors:

genetic - inherited characteristics from the mother and father
biological - the physical processes of life
environmental - the people, places, and things which surround the child

All three of these factors are operating in combination in every individual. At this time, however, they will be examined one by one.

Fig. 2-2 The more severe the handicap, the earlier it can be recognized.

Genetic

The genetic inheritance of each child is determined at conception. The father contributes 23 chromosomes, each containing millions of genes. The mother also contributes 23 chromosomes. In a process called *mitosis*, the chromosomes divide and recombine. This process, at the time of conception, determines every hereditary trait of the baby to be. Thus, normal characteristics such as the color of the eyes, the shape of the nose, and body build are determined. Any genetically abnormal characteristics that may occur are determined at this time, too.

The most widely known chromosomal mishap results in the Down's syndrome or Mongoloid child, figure 2-3. These children represent one of the most common, easily identified forms of mental retardation. They can usually be recognized at birth because of particular features, referred to as *stigmata*, which are characteristic of all Down's children. In most cases, these children look more like each other than they look like their own family members. Examples of stigmata include:

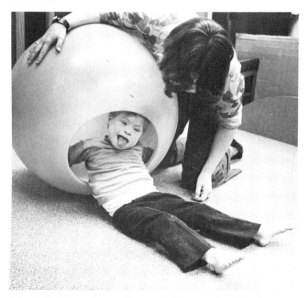

Fig. 2-3 Down's syndrome is the result of a chromosomal mishap.

- small, round head
- epicanthic folds (vertical folds of skin at the inner angle of the eyelid)
- low set, unusually shaped earlobes
- protruding tongue
- broad hand with stubby fingers
- very short, incurved little finger
- widely spaced big toe

There are, of course, many other conditions resulting from genetic factors. These range from the inconsequential (such as the six-toed individual mentioned earlier), to the severely mentally retarded.

There are other factors, too, which must be taken into account. The metabolism of each individual is one of these, figure 2-4. Metabolism refers to the sum total of chemical and physical activity which both creates and destroys living cells. There can be errors in this process, also. In some cases, these metabolic errors are tied in, in some complex way, with genetic inheritance of the individual. Two of the more common metabolic disorders will be discussed.

One such metabolic disorder is *PKU* (*phenylketonuria*). In earlier times, PKU always resulted in mental retardation. Today, through routine screening of newborn babies, retardation can be avoided. A special diet is required, starting in very early infancy.

Hypoglycemia is another fairly common metabolic disorder. It is characterized by an abnormally low level of blood sugar in the system. This can lead to poor mental functioning. It can also lead to convulsions in some children. Hypoglycemia, unfortunately, is a term that is used too loosely, and often incorrectly. Teachers and parents must be alert to its misuse, especially when applied to a child who is not functioning well in school. There is no evidence that hypoglycemia

Fig. 2-4 Metabolic errors may account for some developmental irregularities.

Fig. 2-5 Good maternal health is important in producing healthy children.

causes hyperactivity or any other kind of learning disability.[1]

BIOLOGICAL FACTORS

Regardless of genetic input, biological processes take over completely at the moment of conception. In nine months' time, these processes change a microscopic "egg" into a human baby. There are many things, good and bad, that influence biological development during this nine month gestation or *in utero* period. In fact, the cause of most developmental abnormalities is biological rather than genetic.

What happens to the mother during this gestation period is very important. General good health, adequate nutrition, and freedom from disease are important factors in producing

a healthy baby, figure 2-5. It is also important for the mother to avoid X rays and drugs, in fact, medications of all kinds, unless specifically prescribed by a competent professional. Infections or viruses that the mother experiences can also have a damaging effect on the unborn child. *Rubella*, also called German or three-day measles, is one such virus. Contracted during early pregnancy, maternal rubella can result in a child born with one or more severely handicapping conditions.

There are a number of other conditions which can also lead to mental retardation or a handicap of one kind or another. Among the more common of these are

- maternal diabetes

- maternal iron deficiency

- maternal malnutrition and protein deficiency

[1] Harvey P. Katz, M.D., "Important Endocrine Disorders of Children," eds. Robert A. Halsam and Peter J. Valettuti, *Medical Problems in the Classroom,* (Baltimore: University Park Press, 1975) p. 77.

- drug addiction during pregnancy
- lack of prenatal care
- premature birth
- very young adolescent mothers or elderly mothers

Prevention measures can be used to correct all of these conditions. Rarely need a child be born handicapped for any of the above reasons. Most of these handicaps can be prevented if mother and child receive appropriate care both before and after the child's birth.

BIRTH TRAUMA

The events at the time of birth may also explain certain deviations or disabilities. A number of infants experience *birth trauma*, figure 2-6 (also called birth injury). One common traumatic experience is *anoxia* or insufficient oxygen getting to the brain. This can result in severe mental retardation in what was a normal, healthy baby right up until the time of birth. On the other hand, many babies come through what appeared to be a severe birth experience without damage.

During the baby's early months, illnesses or accidents that occur can lead to serious developmental problems. One example is lead poisoning from eating or licking objects painted with a lead-based paint. Other problems that can occur are diseases such as meningitis and encephalitis. *Meningitis* has to do with infection of the brain and the membranes covering the brain. *Encephalitis* is an acute inflammation of the same area. Either of these may result in serious damage, especially if they occur in the first few months after birth.

ENVIRONMENTAL FACTORS

Genetic and biological factors account for many handicapping conditions. A poor environment is also a major contributing factor. This is especially true where mental retardation is concerned. A number of studies, including reports of the President's

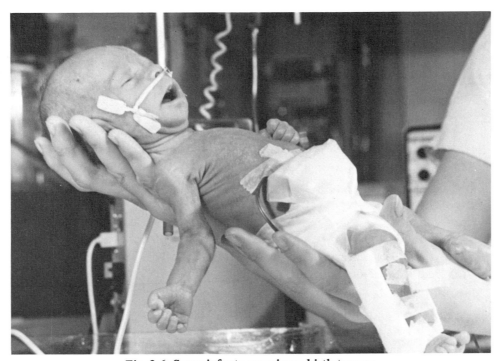

Fig. 2-6 Some infants experience birth trauma.

Committee on Mental Retardation, verify this. These reports indicate that between 50 and 75 percent of retarded children in the United States come from the poverty level in society. Most developmental disabilities also appear to be related to poverty.

Both of these conditions are preventable, if the environment is changed. The most important environmental changes, in terms of prevention, are to make available

- universal prenatal care

- universal medical care for infants and young children

- better nutrition for mothers and infants

- improved and additional day care and preschool centers

- assistance in family planning and location of services

THE MILWAUKEE PROJECT

The Milwaukee Project demonstrates how important the environment is in producing healthy children instead of retarded and otherwise handicapped children. For that reason it is discussed briefly in this unit on causes of handicaps.

A preliminary survey by the Milwaukee group of behavioral scientists revealed a most significant fact. Children whose mothers functioned as retarded had 14 times a greater chance of being retarded themselves. To put it another way, mothers with IQs lower than 80 made up less than half the total surveyed. They accounted, however, for about four-fifths (80 percent) of the children with IQs under 80. Their children were considered "high risk" or most likely to be mentally or physically impaired.

With the cooperation of the mothers whose IQs were 70 or below, the newborn infant was put into a highly structured

program. A staff member of the Milwaukee Project visited the home daily. This person played with, fondled, and talked to the infant. At about four months of age, the baby was brought each day to a child care center sponsored by the project. Here the infant was provided with a variety of structured and unstructured learning experiences.

The intellectual gains that the project babies achieved were impressive. This was particularly true when they were compared with the babies in the control group. The babies in the control group were the same ages and from the same poverty environment. The main difference was that the control group babies did not have the stimulating experiences that the project babies were having. The following is a report on the results given by the President's Commission on Mental Retardation (1972).

By 43 months, the children in the enriched environment are scoring an average of 33 IQ points higher than the control group, with some scoring an IQ of 135. Their intellectual development on the average is exceeding the norms generally established by peer groups of the majority culture.

The superior performance is even more noticeable in language development. Children at the Infant Education Center are building an impressive vocabulary by 25 months, some even speaking in sentences. The control group has virtually no vocabulary at that age. A few of the control children are not speaking at all by 28 months.

Both groups are composed of children who, because of their circumstances, were almost certain to be classified as mentally retarded during their school years.

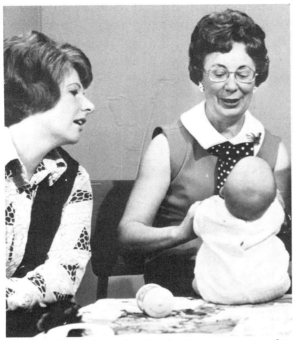

Fig. 2-7 Babies in early stimulation programs tend to make impressive developmental gains.

SUMMARY

There are many causes for the conditions that handicap one million preschool children in the United States. The basic causes are genetic, biological, and/or environmental in origin. Usually these three factors operate together to produce the handicapped individual.

A large number of the conditions that may cause a child to be handicapped are preventable. The mother's good health during pregnancy is very important. Good medical care and nutritional support of the mother and baby is another significant preventive factor.

Poverty is a major environmental factor in producing children who are developmentally disabled or mentally retarded. Such retardation can often be prevented through very early intervention with high-risk babies, figure 2-7.

STUDENT ACTIVITIES

- Find out all you can about genetic counseling available in your community. Report to the class.
- Visit the Maternal and Infant Care (MIC) program in your community. List the kinds of services provided. If there is no MIC program, try to find out if there are or have been efforts made to establish such a center.
- Check with a pediatrician or pediatric nurse in your community regarding screening for PKU. Describe the screening procedure.

REVIEW

A. Match each term in Column I with the correct item in Column II.

Column I	Column II
1. genetic	a. in utero period
2. biological	b. birth shock or injury
3. mitosis	c. phenylketonuria
4. Down's syndrome	d. German measles
5. gestation period	e. chromosome division
6. PKU	f. Mongoloid
7. hypoglycemia	g. infection of the brain
8. birth trauma	h. inherited characteristics
9. meningitis	i. low blood sugar
10. rubella	j. physical processes of life

B. Briefly answer the following.

   1. Approximately how many handicapped children (age 6-19) were there in the United States in 1975-76?
   2. How many handicapped preschoolers (age 0-5) were there?
   3. In that year (1975-76), how many handicapped children ages 0-19 years were receiving services?
   4. In the same year, how many such children were unserved?
   5. In that same year, how many preschool children were unserved?

C. Select all of the correct answers from the choices offered to complete each statement.

   1. Basic origins of handicapping conditions can be
       a. genetic.   d. a combination of a, b, and c.
       b. biological.   e. only a and b.
       c. environmental.
   2. A child's genetic inheritance is determined
       a. after the mother's third month of pregnancy.
       b. at the moment of birth.
       c. by the merging of chromosomes from both parents.
       d. at the moment of conception.
       e. during the baby's first year.
   3. Fairly common metabolic and nutritional disorders are
       a. Down's syndrome.   d. PKU.
       b. mitosis.   e. hypoglycemia.
       c. meningitis.
   4. There are a number of conditions in the pregnant woman that might contribute to a mentally retarded baby such as
       a. diabetes.
       b. rubella.
       c. being near a retarded person.
       d. iron deficiency.
       e. going up and down too many steps.
   5. Poverty is a contributing factor in
       a. 50 to 75 percent of the retarded children in the United States.
       b. less than 20 percent of the retarded children in the United States.
       c. 35 to 50 percent of the retarded children in the United States.
       d. all of the retarded children in the United States except the Down's syndrome children.
       e. less than half of the retarded children in the United States.

D. Briefly explain each of the following.

   1. mitosis   5. anoxia   8. control group
   2. stigmata   6. prenatal care   9. biological factors
   3. in utero   7. high-risk infants 10. encephalitis
   4. metabolism

Unit 3 CLASSIFICATIONS OF HANDICAPPING CONDITIONS

OBJECTIVES

After studying this unit, the student will be able to

- List six major categories of handicapping conditions.
- Define mental retardation according to AAMD specifications and explain why this new definition is important.
- Give the rationale for combining developmental and learning disabilities into one category.

Handicapping conditions, as noted in unit 2, include many different kinds of abnormalities and disabilities, figure 3-1. These can be put into separate categories, that is, grouped or classified in various ways. The medical profession may group them one way, special education another, and federal agencies still another. The classifications thought to be most useful to teachers, parents, and child care people are described in this unit. In Section 5 these handicapping conditions are discussed in much greater detail.

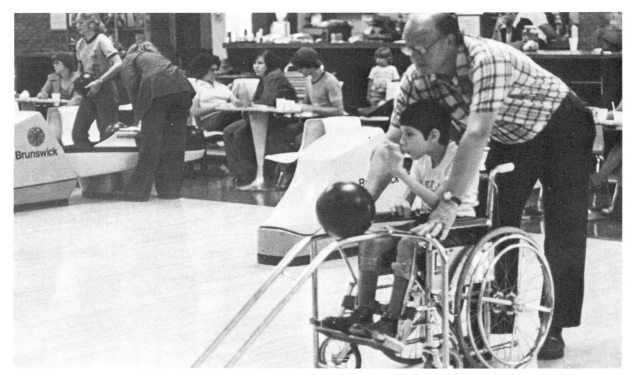

Fig. 3-1 Handicapping conditions include many kinds of disabilities.

Fig. 3-2 Children's adaptive behavior includes playing socially with others.

MENTAL RETARDATION

The American Academy of Mental Deficiency (AAMD) defines mental retardation in the following way:

Mental retardation refers to significantly sub-average general intellectual functioning existing concurrently with deficits in adaptive behavior, and manifested during the developmental period.

This is a complicated definition which requires some redefining. The best way to do this is to look at each concept individually.

intellectual functioning - usually refers to the score that the individual gets on an IQ test such as the Stanford-Binet or the Wechsler

significantly subaverage - usually refers to an IQ score of 70 or below achieved on the IQ test that was given

adaptive behavior - how well the children or youths take care of their own needs and carry out the social responsibilities expected of people their age, figure 3-2

developmental period - the period from birth to 18 years of age

This definition is a most important advancement in the field of mental retardation. No longer can an individual be labeled as mentally retarded on the basis of a low IQ score alone. If individuals are functioning adequately in the community, whether they can or cannot do school work well or pass IQ tests, they are not to be labeled mentally retarded.

VISUAL IMPAIRMENT

Some children are totally blind, having no sight at all. These individuals are relatively few in number. A larger number of children have limited vision. These children are often referred to as partially sighted or visually impaired. They may be labeled as legally blind, however, because of the degree of vision loss.

The American Medical Association (AMA) gives a definition of the legally blind. This is a person whose central visual acuity (keenness of vision) does not exceed 20/200 in the better eye with correcting lenses. (Normal vision is 20/20.) For educational purposes a somewhat different definition is given. A person is considered blind who has no measurable vision, or vision so limited that it cannot serve as a channel for learning. The partially sighted are those who have a serious visual disability. They can, however, rely somewhat on visual aids (filmstrips, movies, etc.) and can read print.

Abnormal conditions of the eyes that interfere significantly with a child's vision can usually be detected at birth or very soon after. *Cataracts*, a clouding of the lens of the eye, is one such condition. Early surgery is almost always necessary if any vision is to be saved. Often, however, a child with severely damaged eyes may have a surprising amount of vision.

HEARING IMPAIRMENT

Individuals with hearing impairments are usually classified in one of two ways. One is according to the severity of the loss. The other involves *when* the impairment occurred. Educationally and socially, the deaf are those individuals whose hearing loss is so severe at birth or during the language development period that it prevents them from acquiring normal language comprehension or expression.

Partially hearing individuals have a less drastic loss. They have insufficient hearing but enough so that they are able to develop some language skills during the critical period for acquiring language.

Hearing impairments are often very difficult to detect in infants and young children. Partial hearing losses and even deafness may go undetected for years. Deaf children have often been incorrectly diagnosed as mentally retarded. Many have spent their whole lives in institutions for the mentally retarded.

NEUROLOGICAL IMPAIRMENT

This condition describes individuals who have specific and identifiable central nervous system (CNS) disorders or damage. Unfortunately, there is no general agreement about what kinds of problems should be included under this heading, figure 3-3. Sometimes the hyperactive or hyperkinetic child is thought of in this way. However, in most cases, the overly active child is *not* neurologically impaired.

There are two conditions which can be attributed to a CNS disorder. These are also ones that teachers are likely to encounter. One is cerebral palsy (CP) and the other is epilepsy. These are discussed separately.

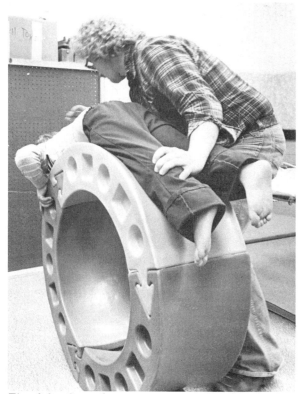

Fig. 3-3 Central nervous system disorders lead to different kinds of problems.

Cerebral Palsy

Cerebral palsy is the result of damage (or insult, as it is more commonly called) to a certain portion of the brain. The portion affected is called the motor cortex. This is the gray matter of the brain which controls movement and posture. CP is a nonprogressive disorder; that is, it does not get worse as the child grows older.

The motor or movement dysfunction is not the only way the child is affected. Usually it results in some impairment of intellectual and perceptual development. There are many degrees and many types of CP. Some of the most common types are listed. These are often found in combination in one child.

spasticity - increased muscle tone

athetosis - slow, writhing movements

rigidity - extreme stiffening of legs and arms

ataxia - muscle incoordination due to balance disturbance

tremor - involuntary shaking movements

atonia - limpness and lack of muscle tone

Epilepsy

Epilepsy, also caused by damage to the CNS, is characterized mainly by convulsions. While there are several classifications of epilepsy, the ones most likely to be encountered by teachers and child care personnel are either the grand mal seizure or the petit mal seizure, figure 3-4.

Grand mal seizures are the most common form. They can be frightening to anyone who has not witnessed such seizures. The child loses consciousness and falls to the floor. There are shaking movements and rigidity of the arms and legs. Even the most violent grand mal usually lasts only a few moments. Children who are on an appropriate medication program function very well in a regular school setting.

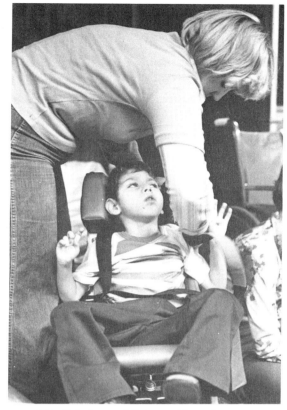

Fig. 3-4 Some children suffer seizures.

Petit mal attacks are much milder. They may occur so often, however, that they interfere with a child's learning. Brief staring episodes, and sometimes fluttering of the eyelids or lapses in speech fluency, are the major signs of a petit mal attack. Often petit mal epilepsy is referred to as a nonconvulsive epileptic condition.

EMOTIONAL DISTURBANCES

Once again, there is no common agreement about what constitutes emotional disturbance, figure 3-5. "Disturbed" children often exhibit a number of behaviors which are also seen in nondisturbed children:

* self-destructive behavior (head banging, for example)

* cruelty to animals

Fig. 3-5 There is little agreement as to what characterizes emotional disturbance.

- temper tantrums
- inability to tolerate frustration
- moodiness and withdrawal
- difficulty in making friends
- school phobia (an unfounded fear of going to school)

The major difference between the normal and the disturbed child is how often the behaviors occur and under what conditions. The child who has a temper tantrum once in a great while when very frustrated is seldom cause for concern, figure 3-6. On the other hand, the child who tantrums several times a day over every minor frustration may well be cause for great concern.

Sometimes the hyperactive or hyperkinetic child is classed as emotionally disturbed. The terms refer to children who seem to be in constant motion, disturbing everyone and everything. However, these terms are overworked and misused. Many young children have been so labeled incorrectly.

Two conditions that are often classified as emotional disturbances are autism and

Fig. 3-6 The child who has a tantrum once in a while is not cause for concern.

schizophrenia. These are clinical terms. They are discussed here simply because they are so often used and misused.

Autism

In young children, this condition is usually called infantile autism. These children exhibit extremes of withdrawal from any kind of normal social interaction. Such withdrawal extends even to their own parents and siblings (brothers and sisters). It is as if these children lived in a closed-off, private, self-centered world of their own. They often exhibit unusual or bizarre behaviors. Some, for example, twirl a small object very rapidly close to their eyes for many minutes at a time. Others may flap their hands continuously, or fixate their eyes on a light while rotating their bodies.

Schizophrenia

This represents a cluster of psychotic, or severely inappropriate or deranged behaviors. These individuals are said to be cut off from

reality. They may insist that they are someone else. The schizophrenic person may also have flights of fancy, strange ideas, or disordered reasoning processes.

A word of caution is in order before leaving this very brief discussion of emotional disturbances. It must be remembered that most young children exhibit a number of the behaviors mentioned, figure 3-7. This may be especially true when the child first enters preschool, day care, or kindergarten. In small amounts or for short periods of time, most of these behaviors are quite normal for young children. It is only when a maladaptive behavior continues week after week with no sign of lessening, that the teacher should ask for consultation.

LEARNING DISABILITIES AND DEVELOPMENTAL DISABILITIES

Learning Disabilities (LD)

Again, there is no agreed-upon definition for this condition. In the preschool child, the term may refer to imperfect ability to listen, think, or speak, figure 3-8. During the school

Fig. 3-7 Most young children exhibit some inappropriate behavior.

Fig. 3-8 Learning disabilities take many forms.

Fig. 3-9 Efforts should be directed at what to do for children.

years, the term may refer to imperfect ability to read, write, spell, or do arithmetic. Many labels have been assigned to conditions that are thought to contribute to LD. The following are a few of the more commonly used:

- brain injury
- perceptual-motor impairment
- minimal brain dysfunction or damage (mbd)
- dyslexia
- developmental aphasia

LD children are mainly those whose handicaps are said *not* to be due to visual, hearing, or physical handicaps; mental retardation; or emotional disturbance.

Developmental Disabilities (DD)

There is also a lack of agreement as to what constitutes a DD child. There has, however, been federal legislation (1969) which specifies particular conditions. For program funding purposes, these conditions must exist:

- mental retardation, cerebral palsy, epilepsy, or other adverse neurological condition
- treatment needed similar to that required for the mentally retarded
- evidence of the disability before the child turned 18
- the expectation that the disability is long term and will continue indefinitely, substantially handicapping the child

It has been suggested by John Meier that it is useless to try to separate learning disabilities from developmental disabilities[1]. Instead, because there is so much overlap between the two conditions, developmental and learning disabled (DLD) is a more appropriate description for children so involved. In this way, effort could be directed at what to do for such children instead of what to call them, figure 3-9.

[1]John H. Meier, *Developmental and Learning Disabilities* (Baltimore: University Park Press, 1976).

Fig. 3-10 Labeling the handicapped child is not the important issue.

There are many other types of handicapping conditions as well as labels for them. Mostly, however, they are combinations, offshoots, or subparts of the conditions discussed in this unit. To list other classifications would only add to the confusion and disagreement which already exists. What must be remembered is that it is *not* the label that is important, figure 3-10. What is important is how the child is treated and helped to learn in spite of a handicap.

SUMMARY

There are six major categories of handicapping conditions with which the student should be familiar.

- mental retardation
- vision or hearing impairments
- neurological disorders
- emotional disturbances
- developmental disabilities
- learning disabilities

There is much professional disagreement surrounding the causes and the meaning of each of these conditions. For some conditions, such as mental retardation and developmental disabilities, there are "official" definitions which are useful.

Labeling the handicapped child is not the most important issue. What *is* important is what is done for the child.

STUDENT ACTIVITIES

- Visit a school that has blind and vision-impaired children. Find out all you can about the materials used for teaching these children.

- Talk to a teacher who works with deaf or hearing-impaired children about helping a child to adjust to a hearing aid. What suggestions does the teacher make that you think might be most useful if you were to help a child make such an adjustment?

- Observe a group of preschool children. Note any children that you think might be developmental and learning disabled (DLD). Give your reasons.

REVIEW

A. Define each of the following terms.

   1. adaptive behavior
   2. legally blind
   3. cataracts
   4. insult to the brain
   5. nonprogressive disorder
   6. school phobia

B. Match each item in Column I with the correct definition in Column II.

Column I	Column II
1. intellectual functioning	a. no vision whatsoever
2. developmental period	b. hyperkinetic
3. totally blind	c. insufficient hearing to learn language
4. normal visual acuity	d. developmental and learning disabilities
5. deaf	e. 0 to 18 years
6. CNS	f. extreme stiffening of arms and legs
7. motor cortex	g. usually refers to the score a person gets on an IQ test
8. hyperactive	h. petit mal
9. rigidity	i. controls movement and posture
10. nonconvulsive epileptic	j. classification
11. DLD	k. 20/20
12. category	l. central nervous system

C. Briefly answer each of the following.

   1. For educational purposes, how is blindness defined?

   2. In what two ways are the hearing impaired classified?

   3. The classroom teacher may encounter two forms of epilepsy. Name and describe each form.

   4. Both normal children and emotionally disturbed children may have temper tantrums. What indicates that the problem may be serious?

   5. Why combine learning disabilities (LD) and developmental disabilities (DD) into a single heading of developmental and learning disabilities (DLD)?

D. Select the three best answers from the choices offered to complete each statement.

1. According to the AAMD definition, a retarded person
    a. cannot manage in the community.
    b. has an IQ of 70 or below.
    c. carries out social expectations appropriately.
    d. cannot function in a school setting.

2. The deaf are those individuals who
    a. have a drastic hearing loss.
    b. were not able to develop expressive language at the appropriate time.
    c. were not able to develop comprehensive language at the appropriate time.
    d. always perform better with a hearing aid.

3. The hyperkinetic child
    a. is not neurologically impaired, generally speaking.
    b. has suffered insult to the motor cortex.
    c. is not emotionally disturbed, generally speaking.
    d. is very often mislabeled as neurologically impaired or emotionally disturbed.

4. CP children may have the following conditions that cause problems in controlling their bodies:
    a. dyslexia.
    b. ataxia.
    c. spasticity.
    d. tremors.

5. A grand mal seizure is characterized by
    a. loss of consciousness.
    b. rigidity of arms and legs.
    c. brief staring episodes.
    d. violent shaking movements.

SECTION 2
THE CHANGING SCENE

Public Law 94-142
94th Congress, S. 6
November 29, 1975

An Act

To amend the Education of the Handicapped Act to provide educational assistance to all handicapped children, and for other purposes.

Be it enacted by the Senate and House of Representatives of the United States of America in Congress assembled, That this Act may be cited as the "Education for All Handicapped Children Act of 1975".

STATEMENT OF FINDINGS AND PURPOSE

Sec. 3. (a) Section 601 of the Act (20 U.S.C. 1401) is amended by inserting "(a)" immediately before "This title" and by adding at the end thereof the following new subsections:

"(b) The Congress finds that—

"(1) there are more than eight million handicapped children in the United States today;

"(2) the special educational needs of such children are not being fully met;

"(3) more than half of the handicapped children in the United States do not receive appropriate educational services which would enable them to have full equality of opportunity;

"(4) one million of the handicapped children in the United States are excluded entirely from the public school system and will not go through the education process with their peers;

"(5) there are many handicapped children throughout the United States participating in regular school programs whose handicaps prevent them from having a successful educational experience because their handicaps are undetected;

"(6) because of the lack of adequate services within the public school system, families are often forced to find services outside the public school system, often at great distance from their residence and at their own expense;

"(7) developments in the training of teachers and in diagnostic and instructional procedures and methods have advanced to the point that, given appropriate funding, State and local educational agencies can and will provide effective special education and related services to meet the needs of handicapped children;

"(8) State and local educational agencies have a responsibility to provide education for all handicapped children, but present financial resources are inadequate to meet the special educational needs of handicapped children; and

"(9) it is in the national interest that the Federal Government assist State and local efforts to provide programs to meet the educational needs of handicapped children in order to assure equal protection of the law.

"(c) It is the purpose of this Act to assure that all handicapped children have available to them, within the time periods specified in section 612 (2) (B), a free appropriate public education which emphasizes special education and related services designed to meet their unique needs, to assure that the rights of handicapped children and their parents or guardians are protected, to assist States and localities to provide for the education of all handicapped children, and to assess and assure the effectiveness of efforts to educate handicapped children."

Unit 4 FEDERAL LEGISLATION

OBJECTIVES

After studying this unit, the student will be able to

- Define landmark legislation and give two examples that affect handicapped children.
- Name four presidents who signed laws that aid the handicapped, and briefly describe the specific law that each signed.
- Explain why the Education for All Handicapped Children Act is considered important legislation on behalf of the handicapped.

Most federal laws and federally sponsored activities for the handicapped have occurred within the past few years. A number of special-interest groups have persistently expressed interest in such legislation. One of the earliest and most influential of these groups is the National Association for Retarded Children (NARC). This organization has been renamed The National Association for Retarded Citizens, figure 4-1. It is an organization made up of parents of retarded children and other concerned citizens.

NARC did a great deal of persistent lobbying, that is, pressuring of legislators. These efforts began to get results in the early 60s. This was during John F. Kennedy's administration. There was much sympathy within the government for the handicapped at that time. This may have been because one of the president's sisters was mentally retarded.

Fig. 4-1 NARC - a powerful citizen's group working for retarded persons.

As a result, the Kennedy family devoted much effort and money to bettering conditions for all handicapped persons.

LANDMARK LEGISLATION

One piece of landmark legislation was passed during President Kennedy's time in the White House. This historic bill, Public Law (PL) 88-164, was called "Facilities for the Mentally Retarded." For the first time, the United States Government would provide funding for the handicapped. The bill sponsored and funded service, training, and research activities in the field of mental retardation. Passage of the bill was aided by the efforts of parents and private citizens. They banded together to form the Association for Children with Learning Disabilities.

Another important piece of federal legislation was passed when Lyndon B. Johnson was president. This was Public Law 89-10, the Elementary and Secondary Education Act. Within this bill there were various types of funding for children with learning

disorders. Once more, sympathy of the president may have been a favorable influence in getting the bill passed. The story is that a member of President Johnson's family had a learning disability called dyslexia. Dyslexia is a kind of reading disability.

Public Law 89-313 was a difficult one to administer, however. This was mainly because of the Title VI part of the Act. This part had to do with handicapped children. One reason for the difficulty was the existence of many special-interest groups. Each wanted money for programs to serve their own particular interests. Another difficulty was the lack of clear-cut definitions. Who were the learning disabled? What were the symptoms associated with learning disabilities? These were some of the questions; there were no agreed upon answers, however, figure 4-2. Also, there were few trained personnel to carry out programs. Finally, and most unfortunate of all, was the lack of research. In other words, no one knew what kinds of programs might be effective.

HEAD START

At about this time Head Start came into being, figure 4-3. It was a part of President Johnson's war on poverty under the Economic

Fig. 4-2 Clear-cut definitions of "learning disabled" are lacking.

Fig. 4-3 Bettye Caldwell has been a prime figure in Head Start since its beginning.

Opportunity Act. Head Start lead to the discovery of many young children who tested out as mentally retarded. In most cases, the diagnosis of mental retardation was not real. It was due to a lack of opportunity to learn the kinds of things that IQ tests tested for. These children were referred to as the culturally deprived or disadvantaged. They were also called the "six-hour retarded children." They were so labeled because they functioned well in their own environments, but performed poorly or not at all in the middle-class school environment.

At the time of Head Start, the appropriate use of funds under Public Law 89-313 became even more difficult to administer. Also, there were some bad side effects. Large amounts of money were inadvertently used in such a way as to further segregation. This was a serious setback for the handicapped and for members of various racial and ethnic groups. (Meier, 1976)

In 1966, PL 89-750 mandated the U.S. Office of Education to establish a special bureau. It was to administer all federal authorities involved in the education of the handicapped. Thus, Congress established the Bureau of Education for the Handicapped (BEH). BEH operates within the Office of Education. BEH has been an effective agent for many years. Most important is the Bureau's administration of programs for all kinds of disabled and handicapped children.

In 1968, Congress passed the Handicapped Children's Early Education Assistance Act, Public Law 90-538. This law, signed by President Johnson, established experimental demonstration centers. These centers were set up for the education of preschool handicapped children. This was the first legislation for handicapped children not attached to other legislation. This program is sometimes known as the First Chance Network. The purpose of PL 90-538 is to develop experimental projects to serve as demonstration models. These are to demonstrate how to provide special help to handicapped children and their families.

Another important piece of legislation, PL 91-230, has to do with integration of the handicapped. Title VI, Part C, provides money (through grants or contracts) to establish model preschool programs. Several major goals underlie this legislation:

Fig. 4-4 The Down's syndrome programs at the University of Washington serve as major training and demonstration sites.

- To provide early education and services to young handicapped children and their families.

- To integrate handicapped children into regular education systems; or to help them to need less intensive special education services.

- To stimulate model preschool projects of national significance that will be accepted and duplicated in local communities.

This funding has resulted in a variety of excellent programs for young handicapped children. Several of these are now validated (officially sanctioned) models. As such, they serve as major training and demonstration sites, figure 4-4.

DEVELOPMENTAL DISABILITY ACT

When PL 88-164 went out of existence, it was replaced by PL 91-517 (the Developmental Disability Act). It was to serve not only the mentally retarded but also the epileptic, cerebral palsied, and other neurologically impaired children. *Neurologically impaired* refers to specific damage to the central nervous system. A later bill, PL 94-103, allowed for other types of disabilities. This was to include children who showed no clear-cut evidence of neurological disorders, but were experiencing learning difficulties.

HANDICAPPED IN HEAD START

In 1972 an important piece of legislation focused on mainstreaming young handicapped children. This was an amendment to the Head Start portion of the Economic Opportunity Act titled Public Law 92-924. It requires that at least 10 percent of Head Start funds be used to serve young handicapped children. Head Start had always kept an open door policy. Open door means that Head Start has always welcomed handicapped children into their program. The new legislation,

however, was to insure that children with severe handicaps were served by Head Start. Handicapped children were therefore defined by Congress as those who require special services because they are

- mentally retarded

- hard of hearing

- deaf

- speech impaired

- visually handicapped

- seriously emotionally disturbed

- crippled

- health impaired

The purpose of PL 92-924 is to insure integrated preschool classes. In such a setting, handicapped and nonhandicapped children learn and grow together. At the same time, the special needs of the disabled child are met.

In 1976, BEH (in collaboration with the Administration of Children, Youth, and Family Services) established a network of Resource Access Projects (RAP's). These are designed to assist Head Start in its efforts to provide services to young handicapped children. This network serves as a brokerage system. That is, they link Head Start agencies to various resources so that the special needs of the handicapped are met.

CHILD ABUSE

President Richard Nixon also signed an important piece of legislation on behalf of children. This was Public Law 93-247, The Child Abuse Prevention and Treatment Act. The act defines child abuse and neglect as "physical or mental injury, sexual abuse, negligent treatment or maltreatment of a child under the age of 18." There are no accurate figures on the number of abused children in the United States. Estimates range from 60,000 to a half million cases a year. Many of these abused and neglected children are most certain to become handicapped. The only way such damage can be prevented is through very early detection and correction of the abuse. The law states that all cases of suspected child abuse must be reported. Teachers are therefore legally responsible to report such cases to the proper authorities.

EDUCATION FOR ALL

Another law dealing with the integration of the handicapped is Public Law 94-142, the Education for All Handicapped Children Act. It was signed by President Gerald Ford on November 28, 1975. It, too, is hailed as landmark legislation. Many people refer to it as the Bill of Rights for Handicapped Children. Some of the main purposes of the act are as follows:

- to identify all children in need of services

- to ensure that all handicapped children have available to them a free, appropriate public education

- to assure special education and related services designed to meet the unique needs of the handicapped

- to ensure that the rights of handicapped children and their parents or guardians are protected

- to assist states and localities in providing for the education of all handicapped children

- to assess and assure the effectiveness of efforts to educate handicapped children

The purpose and design of the Education for All Handicapped Children Act is significant. It is to stop the unconstitutional exclusion of handicapped children from the public school system. This law states that handicapped children, to the maximum extent possible, be educated with children who are not handicapped, figure 4-5. Education in the "least restrictive" setting has become a popular way to describe this directive. President Ford summed it up this way:

Our school systems must be strengthened, so that they can provide the appropriate education which both the law and our conscience say may not be denied to retarded or otherwise handicapped children. By appropriate education I mean training in academic, vocational, and

Fig. 4-5 One purpose of PL 94-142 is to insure that both handicapped and nonhandicapped children are educated together.

social skills which will enable these children to live up to their highest potential.[1]

The Bill of Rights for Handicapped Children has many important parts. One that is often talked about is the due process component. Basically, due process means that parents and guardians are assured legal protection. The law protects their rights and the rights of their handicapped children. Such legislation is a major breakthrough for the handicapped.

PRESCHOOL INCENTIVE

Another important part of the law is a special preschool incentive grant. This incentive money is to be used to encourage states to provide education and related services to preschool handicapped children. Each handicapped child in the state (aged three to five) who is served, guarantees additional funding for the state. This money goes to the state education agency and must be used to provide preschool services.

President Carter's administration provided regulations governing privacy rights of parents and students (the Buckley Amendment). It has also laid out regulations on Section 504 of the Vocational Rehabilitation Act. These deal with architectural barriers as related to preschools. Regulations have also been published governing the implementation of PL 94-142. Furthermore, an increased budget allowed an expansion of effort within Head Start. President Carter and Congress approved several million dollars to increase Head Start services.

Other legislative acts on behalf of handicapped children have been enacted over the years. Many members of Congress and their constituents work for the handicapped,

[1] President Ford's 1974 meeting with Committee on Mental Retardation

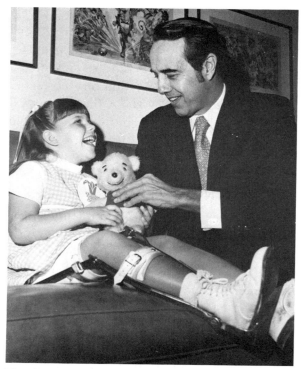

Fig. 4-6 Senator Dole has offered extensive legislation on behalf of the handicapped.

figure 4-6. These activities are too numerous to discuss specifically. However, the legislation discussed in this unit is some of the most significant in terms of mainstreaming.

SUMMARY

During the last fifteen years, the federal government has begun to pass important laws regarding handicapped children. The first and most important of these was Public Law 88-164, Facilities for the Mentally Retarded. This legislation was signed by President Kennedy. It marked a breakthrough in federal services for the handicapped and is an example of landmark legislation.

Other important laws that were passed during the next several years had to do with such things as developmental disabilities and child abuse. An amendment to Head Start funding was also put into effect. It called for 10 percent inclusion of seriously impaired children in all Head Start classes. At about the same time, federal funding for model preschool programs became available.

Another landmark law was signed by President Ford in November of 1975. This is PL 94-142, the significant Education for All Handicapped Children Act. It is often referred to as the Bill of Rights for Handicapped Children. This law requires that handicapped children be educated in the least restrictive educational environment. The main goal is that the majority of handicapped children be integrated into regular school settings. Of particular importance to early childhood is the preschool incentive clause. This clause is to encourage the states to locate and serve handicapped children under the age of five.

The Congress and President Carter have also acted on behalf of handicapped children. Of particular importance to preschool-age handicapped children is the multimillion dollar expansion of Head Start services.

STUDENT ACTIVITIES

- Find out what kind of laws your state has regarding assistance to the handicapped.
- Write to your senator and members of Congress. Ask where they stand regarding legislation for the handicapped.
- Inquire about the child abuse programs in your community. If there is a center, find out what they do and how they are funded. Find out where and how suspected child abuse is to be reported.
- Contact your state office of education and inquire about services for the preschool handicapped child.

REVIEW

A. Define each of the following terms.

1. landmark legislation
2. lobbying
3. "six-hour retarded child"
4. mandate
5. child abuse

B. Select the best answer from the choices offered to complete each statement.

1. Most of the legislation for the handicapped occurred
   a. immediately following the Civil War.
   b. during the "war on poverty."
   c. during and since President Kennedy's administration.
   d. before 1950.

2. Landmark legislation is
   a. any law affecting land grant colleges.
   b. a first time for passage of significant legislation.
   c. any law signed by President Kennedy.
   d. any legislation on behalf of the handicapped.

3. Public Law 88-164, Facilities for the Mentally Retarded, called for
    a. the building of more institutions for the retarded.
    b. better preschool and day care facilities for the retarded.
    c. service, training, and research activities in the field of mental retardation.
    d. aid to parents of mentally retarded children.

4. The passage of many important pieces of legislation can be attributed to
    a. lobbying.
    b. public speaking.
    c. writing articles.
    d. demonstrating and marching.

5. The Developmental Disabilities Act (PL 91-517) was designed to serve
    a. only the mentally retarded.
    b. primarily the physically handicapped.
    c. only the epileptic and the cerebral palsied.
    d. children with learning difficulties who showed no clear-cut neurological disorder.

6. The number of abused children in the United States is estimated at
    a. 60,000 to 1/2 million.
    b. 1/2 to 3/4 million.
    c. about 5,000 per state.
    d. too few to worry about.

7. The Education for All Handicapped Children Act (PL 94-142) was signed into law by
    a. President Nixon.
    b. President Ford.
    c. President Kennedy.
    d. President Johnson.

8. The main purpose of PL 94-142 is to
    a. provide special services for the handicapped.
    b. restrict the kinds of schools the handicapped can attend.
    c. make it illegal to put the handicapped in institutions.
    d. stop the unconstitutional exclusion of handicapped children from the public school system.

C. Briefly answer each of the following.

1. What was one reason that the Kennedy administration was seen as sympathetic to the handicapped?

2. Give four reasons why the handicapped section of PL 89-313 (Elementary and Secondary Education Act) was so difficult to administer.

3. Why was President Johnson said to be sympathetic to the learning disabled?

4. In 1972, an important Head Start amendment came into effect. What did it focus on?

5. What is the main purpose of the validated model preschools?

D. Match each item in Column I with the correct phrase in Column II.

Column I	Column II
1. least restrictive environment	a. legal means to protect one's rights
2. BEH	b. educating handicapped and non-handicapped together, to the maximum extent possible
3. child abuse law	c. inclusion of 10 percent handicapped
4. NARC	d. all are welcome
5. Bill of Rights for Handicapped Children	e. officially sanctioned model preschools
6. Preschool Incentive Grant	f. Bureau of Education for the Handicapped
7. due process	g. President Nixon
8. Head Start mainstreaming	h. National Association for Retarded Citizens
9. open door policy	i. $300 per preschool child
10. validated preschool model	j. Education for All Handicapped Children Act

Unit 5 MAINSTREAMING: WHAT IT MEANS

OBJECTIVES

After studying this unit, the student will be able to

- Trace changes in society's attitudes toward handicapped children.

- Discuss the importance of critical learning periods and teachable moments.

- Give five examples of integration of handicapped children.

Mainstreaming handicapped individuals is an important new concept. Basically it means giving handicapped individuals the opportunity to participate in every activity that is available to everyone else, figure 5-1. Thus, all handicapped children, youths, and adults should be integrated into all social, recreational, and educational activities of the regular community. *Integration* is another word that is often used in this connection. It, too, describes this process of including the handicapped in everyday activities. The two words, integration and mainstreaming, are used interchangeably throughout this book.

EARLY ATTITUDES

Making a place for the handicapped in the everyday affairs of the community is a fairly recent development. Ten years ago the idea of mainstreaming was almost unheard of. Integration applied only to efforts to include ethnic minorities in the regular activities of society. In fact, historically, handicapped individuals were kept almost completely segregated. "Out of sight and out of mind" seemed to be the motto.

It has been suggested that there are three stages that society has gone through in its treatment of the handicapped.[1] This is especially true of those who were labeled as mentally retarded.

Forget and Hide

In this first stage, it seemed that people tried to forget all about the handicapped, figure 5-2. These children were seldom seen.

Fig. 5-1 Handicapped children should have the opportunity to participate in all activities.

[1] Bettye M. Caldwell, "The Importance of Beginning Early," eds. June B. Jordan and Rebecca F. Dailey, *Not All Little Wagons Are Red,* CEC Information Center, 1974.

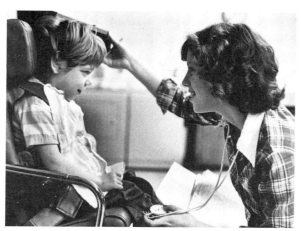

Fig. 5-2 **Handicapped children are no longer hidden away.**

Fig. 5-3 **The playground was often a dreary fenced-off corner.**

They were often kept in a back room or in the attic. During this stage, parents were almost always advised to put their "defective" child into an institution soon after the child was born. In fact, many times it was advised that parents, especially the mother, not even see the child.

Screen and Segregate

In this second stage, efforts were made to identify the handicapped and retarded children and to bring them out of the back rooms where they had been hidden. Parents were counseled to be less ashamed and more accepting of their deficient or atypical children.

It was during this time that Special Education came into the public schools. Unfortunately, this did not make much difference for handicapped children. They were tested; they were labeled as deaf, or hard of hearing, or blind, or mentally retarded; *then* they were segregated into special classes.

Usually, these classes were in the least desirable space in the school. Often it was a basement room, poorly ventilated and poorly lighted. The playground was often a dreary corner fenced off with a seven-foot cyclone fence, figure 5-3. It was as if people feared

that handicapped children might somehow contaminate the other children. The attitude seemed to be that handicapped children must be kept completely away from normally progressing children who might, for some unknown reason, be held back by coming into contact with the atypical children.

Identify and Help

After 20 or 25 years of the Screen and Segregate period, the current stage began. This is referred to as the Identify and Help period. Now there are widespread efforts to identify and provide integrated learning experiences for all handicapped or potentially handicapped children. Such efforts are particularly important for very young children. The screening and early identification aspects of this process are discussed in a later unit. In this unit, focus is on the importance of integration or mainstreaming for the very young child.

FOUNDATION LEARNINGS

The very early years (between birth and five or six) are crucial years in the development of all children, figure 5-4. These are the years when children acquire a broad range of basic skills or learnings in every area of development. These basic learnings include:

- *motor skills* - the use of all parts of the body in a coordinated fashion
- *intellectual* or *cognitive skills* (or mental functioning as it used to be called) - the ability to think, question, and solve problems
- *communication* or *language skills* - the ability to talk, listen, and understand
- *social skills* - the ability to manage one's own needs and to get along with others

During the first five years of life, most young children learn to move about independently. They learn to manipulate objects. They acquire a large speaking vocabulary. They think, get ideas, and solve problems. They respond when others speak to them. They are learning to take care of most of their own personal needs. They are finding out how to get along with others through sharing and taking turns, figure 5-5.

Fig. 5-4 The very early years are the crucial years.

CRITICAL LEARNING PERIODS

These early years are marked by what has been called critical or optimal learning periods. These are periods of development when a child may be most able to learn particular skills. These critical periods have also been thought to produce significant teachable moments. *Teachable moments* are times when the child is highly motivated, and eager and able to learn particular skills, such as how to tie shoelaces.

Even the most handicapped children have many such teachable moments. Unfortunately, these may go unrecognized. Much isolation is built into a handicapped child's environment simply because of the handicap. Blind or deaf children, for example, can respond to fewer of the incidental or unplanned learning opportunities occurring constantly in everyday life. Yet these are the experiences that are so readily available to nonhandicapped children who turn almost automatically, a hundred times a day, to look and listen and learn.

Physically handicapped children also may be denied the everyday, incidental learning experiences but for different reasons. They cannot move themselves about easily.

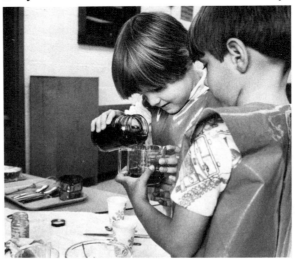

Fig. 5-5 Sharing and taking turns is an important early learning.

Fig. 5-6 Getting into this and that.

Fig. 5-7 Preschool experiences are an open door to learning.

They cannot explore their environment in the same ways. Often they cannot open doors and get into cupboards, or learn simply by getting into mischief. Contrast this with normal children who are on the move from morning to night. They are touching, reaching, running, jumping, climbing, getting into this and that, figure 5-6. They may try their parents' patience at times but they are learning, every moment, from these unplanned activities.

It must be recognized that such learning opportunities are crucial to early development. Therefore, for handicapped children, special care must be taken to provide an incidental learning environment. Care must be taken, too, to take advantage of every teachable moment. Often this means recognizing the handicapped child's teachable moments. These moments may take quite different forms than those of the nonhandicapped child. Example: When the blind baby begins to cruise from chair to coffee table to sofa, allow and encourage the child to do so. Make it safe and easy. Keep things off the floor that the baby might fall over. Keep the furniture in the same place. Play simple games to keep the child moving: "Find Daddy." Use words to describe to the baby what is happening.

The more the baby moves about, the more that baby will learn.

THE IMPORTANCE OF PRESCHOOL

A good preschool situation is important for young handicapped children. It is there that full advantage can be taken of critical learning periods. The preschool can provide many experiences and build upon many spontaneous learning opportunities. Furthermore, it can do so in a setting where there are other children to learn from. This is most important. Finally, the preschool places children with adults who understand the developing child and can take advantage of those precious teachable moments.

For children with any kind of developmental deficiency, disability, or handicapping condition, being in the mainstream of preschool education is an open door, figure 5-7. Often the integrated preschool is the only doorway to these very special early experiences, activities, and learnings.

THE INTEGRATED PRESCHOOL

It must be recognized, however, that there is much more to the idea of integration than just placing handicapped and nonhandicapped children together in the

Fig. 5-8 **Working with and learning from professionals in other fields.**

same preschool classroom. Integration means many things. It means a learning and growing environment in which handicapped children interact with nonhandicapped children in a variety of activities. These activities must be related to all areas of development: physical, social, verbal, and intellectual. It means individualizing programs to meet each child's specific needs and abilities. At the same time, however, it means arranging a balance of large and small group activities. All children, then, can be active and interactive participants in a wide variety of activities.

Integration means recognizing that there are no well-defined lines or boundaries between normal and atypical or handicapped children. As suggested in an earlier unit, the range of normalcy is wide. Many so-called normal children may have problems that are potentially handicapping.

Integration means avoiding the labeling of children. To call a child mentally retarded does not help anyone to help the child. It may even do the child harm. For example, children with unidentified hearing losses often behave in peculiar ways. To call such children emotionally disturbed or mentally retarded may lock them into programs totally unsuited to their needs.

Integration means working with and learning from professionals from many other fields, figure 5-8. This is often called the interdisciplinary approach. These professionals can help the preschool teacher provide sound individualized learning experiences for each child. The professions or disciplines most commonly associated with helping young handicapped children are the following:

nursing	nutrition
pediatrics	social work
speech therapy	occupational or physical
audiology	therapy
(hearing)	psychology
ophthalmology	dentistry
(vision)	

Integration means all of the things mentioned above and much more. Most important of all, it means an opportunity

Fig. 5-9 Significant learnings take place in the early years.

for the preschool staff - administrators, teachers, aides, and volunteers - to work together, to grow and benefit from helping children with special needs. By becoming more aware of the needs of special children, adults become more attuned to the needs of all children. Thus, they can provide for each child with a higher quality of early education and child care programs.

SUMMARY

Mainstreaming or integration means keeping handicapped persons involved in the regular social, recreational, and educational activities of the community. In the past, this was not the case. Handicapped children used to be hidden away. Next they were brought out of hiding but were segregated into special classes. Now, the focus is on identifying and helping handicapped children.

For young children, the very early years are the years when significant learning takes place, figure 5-9. One of the best ways to insure that these learnings occur is by providing a good preschool experience. To be most beneficial, the preschool must be integrated; it should include nonhandicapped as well as handicapped children. The program must be planned so that all children's needs are individually met. There must also be many group activities where all children are active and interactive participants.

Integration also has a number of other meanings which must be considered. One of the most important of these is recognizing how much a preschool or child care staff can learn about all children from having handicapped children in their programs.

STUDENT ACTIVITIES

- Talk with a Head Start teacher or a staff person in a day care center. Find out all you can about the handicapped children in their programs. If there are no handicapped children, try to find out why.

- Observe an integrated preschool or day care center. See if you can identify the children who might be handicapped in some way. Afterwards, check with the teacher to see if you are right.

- After you have talked with teachers who have handicapped children in their programs, briefly describe what you think their attitudes are toward these children.

REVIEW

A. Briefly answer each of the following.

1. What does mainstreaming mean?

2. What other word can be used to describe the mainstreaming process?

3. Name the three stages that our society has gone through in regard to the handicapped.

4. Give examples of four basic skills acquired during the very early years of childhood.

5. Define the term "teachable moments."

6. Give two reasons why the handicapped child should be in the mainstream of early education.

B. Select the one best answer from the choices offered to complete each statement.

1. Mainstreaming the handicapped means that they
   a. should have their own special activities.
   b. are often invited to special events.
   c. have the opportunity to participate in all community and educational activities.
   d. occupy special classrooms in the regular school.

2. Earliest attitudes toward the handicapped were characterized by
   a. taking them on frequent outings and field trips.
   b. keeping them "out of sight and out of mind."
   c. finding ways for them to function in the regular school.
   d. mixing handicapped and nonhandicapped children in the same class.

3. Teachable moments are those moments which
   a. arise from a child's special interests.
   b. are planned well in advance by the teacher.
   c. provide experiences that all children respond to alike.
   d. never happen for handicapped children.

4. An incidental learning opportunity is one in which
   a. the child is told exactly what to do.
   b. the teacher selects a book and reads to a child.
   c. a child finds something that is exciting and runs to show the teacher.
   d. children sit in a circle and sing the songs that the teacher has on a list.

5. Handicapped and nonhandicapped children
   a. are very different from each other.
   b. can be readily distinguished in the classroom.
   c. have many characteristics in common.
   d. should be kept separated.

6. Labeling a child as emotionally disturbed or mentally retarded
   a. is necessary at all times.
   b. helps the teacher to help the child.
   c. explains why a child may be behaving in a peculiar fashion.
   d. may lock the child into a program that is unsuitable.

C. From the following list select the several phrases that best define the word "integration" as used in this unit.

1. handicapped and nonhandicapped interacting in a variety of activities
2. individualized programs combined with large or small group activities
3. handicapped children sitting and watching, or playing by themselves
4. labeling children as handicapped
5. working with speech therapists, nutritionists, nurses, and other professionals
6. providing experiences for all children in all areas of development
7. certain times of day for normal children to have their own private activities
8. being sure to point out to visitors who the handicapped children are
9. special activities in which all children can participate in some way
10. handicapped and nonhandicapped children learning from each other

D. List at least eight professions that might be of help to a preschool teacher in planning integrated programs for handicapped children.

E. What reasons would you give if someone asked you why young handicapped children should go to a regular preschool?

Unit 6 EARLY IDENTIFICATION: SCREENING AND CHILD FIND

OBJECTIVES

After studying this unit, the student will be able to

- Discuss the need for comprehensive screening of children 0 to 6 years old.
- List five characteristics of a good screening device.
- Give specific examples of how the results from a screening test are *not* to be used.

EARLY DETECTION

During the last ten years an increasing amount of activity has been directed toward the identification of young handicapped

Fig. 6-1 Focus is now on the maintenance of healthy development.

children. There are several reasons for these efforts:

- The Early and Periodic Screening, Diagnosis, and Treatment (EPSDT) amendment to Title 19 of the Social Security Act passed in 1967. This bill calls for the screening of all Medicaid children under the age of 21.

- Increasing knowledge about the developmental importance of the first three years of life. To fail to identify errors or delays in development during these years may be very harmful.

- A shift in emphasis among professionals who work with young children. This shift focuses on prevention; it also stresses the maintenance of healthy development, figure 6-1. (In the past, emphasis was on the treatment of problems *after* they had developed.)

The Shift to Prevention

The shift to prevention (and maintenance of healthy development) is of great importance. It calls for the very early location of high-risk infants and children. High-risk children are those who are most likely to become handicapped or learning disabled. These children must be identified as early as possible, preferably in infancy. This calls for comprehensive community screening programs. *Screening*, as used here, refers to the testing of a large number of children. The testing is aimed at identifying children who are handicapped or most likely to become handicapped.

It is *not* the purpose of this procedure to set these infants and young children apart. In other words, the purpose is not to screen and segregate (unit 5). Instead, the purpose is to locate children who need special help very early. By doing this, problems can be prevented, or treatment begun, before a problem becomes unmanageable.

Easily Recognized Problems

Some handicapped or potentially handicapped children are easily identified. Their problems are usually quite visible and show

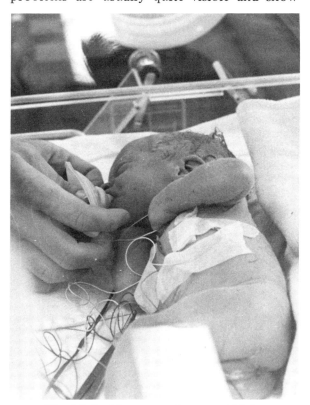

Fig. 6-2 **Problems may show up at birth**.

up at birth or shortly thereafter, figure 6-2. The following are a few examples of readily identified conditions:

> *hydrocephalus* — overabundance of fluid in the brain, accompanied by an enlarged head
> *microcephaly* — abnormally small head usually associated with mental retardation
> *cleft lip* — failure of the two sides of the upper lip to grow together
> *cleft palate* — a split or opening in the roof of the mouth causing severe feeding problems
> *Down's syndrome* — (described in unit 2)
> *"small-for-date" babies* — overly small for number of gestation months
> *low Apgar rating* — (The Apgar is a newborn scoring system developed by Virginia Apgar, M.D., administered at one minute and 5 minutes after birth.)

Phenylketonuria

Other potentially serious problems can be detected during the first few days of life. Although these problems may not be readily visible, routine screening procedures can detect them easily. One of the best known of such conditions is PKU (phenylketonuria). Untreated PKU individuals are among the most severely retarded residents in state institutions.

With the knowledge available, no child need be so afflicted. All that is required is a routine blood test. This should be done four or five days after the child is born. If PKU signs are present, the special diet necessary to prevent retardation can be started very early. This is in contrast to the once popular "diaper test" (urinalysis). The diaper test cannot be given until the baby is about one month of age. It takes that long for the damaging protein component (phenylalanine) to spill over into the baby's urine. By the time the child is one month of age, brain damage has already begun. In fact, research shows significant differences in intelligence between children who were put on the required diet during the first or second week of life. They are intellectually superior to children who were not diagnosed or treated until four weeks later.

Subtle Signs

Not all handicapping conditions are so easily identified. Many potential problems are very subtle. Often, they produce a wait-and-see attitude on the part of the physician or other professionals. Other potential problems do not show up until much later in early childhood. By this time, damage may have already occurred. The time period during which handicaps remain undetected must be greatly shortened. Formal screening of all young children, therefore, is necessary, figure 6-3. This need should be brought to the attention of all families of young children. A comprehensive public relations effort in every community is required. These activities are often referred to

as *Child Find* programs. They are part of the effort to meet the national goal of providing programs for all handicapped children by 1980.

CHILD FIND AND SCREENING

An effective Child Find program depends upon two things. One is a widespread publicity campaign to make all families aware of the program. The second is the selection of a suitable screening test, also called a screening instrument, figure 6-4. These two issues will be discussed separately.

Publicity

There are several inexpensive ways to help parents be aware of the opportunity to have their children screened. These include:

- articles in newspapers and community publications
- notices posted in religious institutions, libraries, laundromats, supermarkets, and other public gathering places

Fig. 6-3   Routine screening procedures protect all babies.

Fig. 6-4 Choice of a screening instrument is important.

- public service "spot" announcements on radio and television

- letters to, or other contacts with, all social and health service organizations that serve young children and their families

Publicity about the screening process should be carefully prepared. It should:

- be positive and nonthreatening in tone, figure 6-5

- stress the importance of early intervention (that research shows handicapped children can be helped by attending preschool)

- make it obvious to the parents that they are not the only ones with a handicapped child, and that there are always a number of such children in every community

- emphasize the fact that many handicapping conditions are very subtle (so that parents of apparently normal children will have them screened)

- be encouraging but accurate; the publicity should not, for example, imply that all children who receive help at an early age will be able to go to regular school

Rights of Parents

The publicity must also assure parents that their rights and those of their children will be protected. Before any testing takes place, parents must be given the opportunity to read and sign parent consent forms. Parents must be assured that all information about the child will be held in complete confidence. This means that no test information can be passed on to any other person or agency unless the parents sign a release form. These procedures are more than just courtesy measures. It is the law: the rights of all individuals must be carefully preserved.

Where to Screen

Where the screening takes place is also an important consideration, figure 6-6. It must be held in a location that is easy for people to get to. Space can usually be found in centrally located schools, religious institutions, or community centers. Some screening programs such as the HICOMP (Handicapped Infants and Children Comprehensive Outreach Model Program) in Pennsylvania use a mobile unit similar to a motor coach. The unit is driven

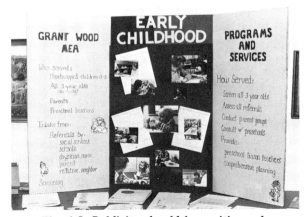

Fig. 6-5 Publicity should be positive and nonthreatening.

Fig. 6-6 Where the screening takes place is an important consideration.

from shopping center to shopping center. This has proven to be a most effective way to reach large numbers of families with young children.

Screening Instruments

The choice of a screening instrument is important. For community screening activities, it should usually be one that can be given by trained volunteers or paraprofessionals teamed with one or two professionals. This is in the interest of economy. Few screening programs are funded well enough to provide for an all professional team. Fortunately, an all professional team is not necessary for routine screening.

A comprehensive screening program should also test all major developmental areas such as speech and language development, concept development, gross and fine motor development, social development, and development of self-help skills.

In some instances, gross vision and hearing tests are included as a part of the comprehensive screening, figure 6-7. Great care must be taken in accepting the results of these tests, however. Screening for visual and hearing problems is very difficult in young children. Researchers do not agree on the most effective procedures. Many disorders, such as lazy eye (amblyopia), can be missed entirely. A recent government report recommended that *mass* screening of preschool children for hearing and vision problems be discontinued until such screening devices are better evaluated. This report recommends two things instead: one, that it be mandatory that high-risk infants be followed up at regular intervals; and second, that physicians, preschool teachers, and others who see young children over time be trained in the early detection of hearing and vision problems.

Involvement of Parents

The involvement of parents in the screening program is also an important consideration. Not all screening instruments include parents. Whenever possible, however, it is better to select one that does include parents. Parents know a great deal about their own children. They are a valuable source of information about what their child can do in a nontest situation. Furthermore, parents are often the first to suspect that something may be wrong, even though they cannot be specific about what it is. It has been estimated that 65 to 75 percent of the hearing problems in young children are identified first within the family. This is true even in cases where the child has had the regular services of a pediatrician. Many pediatricians have neither the time nor the techniques to pinpoint such developmental problems.

Cultural Implications

A note of caution is in order regarding the screening of minority or culturally different children. Instruments chosen to test these children must reflect the language or

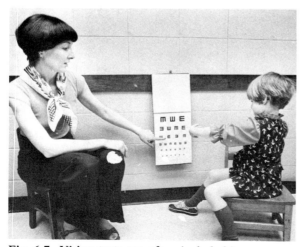

Fig. 6-7 Vision tests are often included in a comprehensive screening.

Fig. 6-8 Screening tests must employ the language the child is most familiar with.

dialect spoken by the children, figure 6-8. The tests also must reflect the experiences with which the children are familiar. Otherwise, many "false positives" may show up; that is, children will score as handicapped or retarded when actually they are not. Several ways of overcoming the problem have been suggested:

- Translate existing tests into the appropriate language or dialect.

- Adopt testing procedures that do not penalize a culturally different child for important (and healthy) cultural differences.

- Use more than one set of norms (averages). In this way, children can be scored in terms of the dominant culture and their own culture.

Examples of Screening Instruments

There are a number of screening programs available that help to avoid confusing a cultural trait with a handicapping condition. Several of these instruments are included in the list of screening programs which follows:

Ability Development Program
Division of Special Products
Southwest Educational Developmental Laboratory
221 East 7th
Austin, TX 78701

The manual comes in both Spanish and English. It is an excellent instrument to use with young Spanish-American children.

CIP - Comprehensive Identification Process
R. Reid Zehrbach
Scholastic Testing Services
480 Meyer Road
Bensenville, IL 60106

This instrument is useful for locating and screening young children who may need special help. It also ensures appropriate follow-up services to identified children. Parents are part of this screening process, figure 6-9. A special feature of the CIP is the identification of mildly handicapped children. These children are often overlooked by the traditional screening approaches.

DDST - Denver Developmental Screening Test
W.K. Frankenburg and J.B. Dodds
Lacoda Project and Publishing
  Foundation
East 51st and Lincoln
Denver, CO 80216

The DDST involves parents and covers four major areas of development up to 6 years of age.

DIAL - Developmental Indicators for Assessment of Learning
Carol Mardell and D.S. Goldenburg
Office of the Superintendent of Public
  Instruction
State of Illinois
Springfield, IL 62700

While this instrument was developed specifically for the State of Illinois, it has a high degree of general usefulness.

Developmental Profile
C.D. Alpern and T.J. Boll
Psychological Development Publications
Indianapolis, IN 46200

This is an excellent instrument although very long and detailed. It is sometimes seen as unsuitable for mass screening, especially by paraprofessionals.

Developmental Screening Questionnaire for Preschool Children
Program Development for Preschool
  Handicapped Indian Children
Department of Special Education
University of Arizona
Tucson, AZ 85721

This is a screening instrument to be used with Native American children. It has proven to be very useful when working with Native American preschoolers.

Head Start Screening: The Fork in the Road
OCD - BEH Outreach Program
Bill Wilkerson Hearing and Speech
  Center
Nashville, TN 37212

This is a booklet (one copy free) describing how 35,000 preschool children were

Fig. 6-9 The CIP involves parents.

screened for communication disorders within 5 months.

LAP - Learning Accomplishment Profile

Chapel Hill Training Outreach Project
Ann Sanford, Director
Chapel Hill, NC 27514

This test (or profile, as many such instruments are called), tests 6 major areas of development, figure 6-10. It also provides a coordinated curriculum guide.

The Way a Child Grows - Developmental Testing

Alaska Head Start Special Services Project
Easter Seal Society
726 E. Street
Anchorage, AK 99501

This material has been reported as very useful with Alaskan Indian children.

The list just given contains only a few of the many good screening instruments available. These examples do, however, represent quite different types of tests and were cited for that reason.

Warning Notes

Several warning notes must be given at this point. The results of a screening test *do not* make a diagnosis. A child must never be labeled on the basis of such a test. The results of a screening test should never be interpreted as indicating that a child has a specific problem. Special preschool activities for a given child must never be based on results from a screening test. The information gained from a screening test should be used for only one purpose: to locate and refer children who are in need of a more thorough assessment, figure 6-11.

It was mentioned earlier that parents can be helpful in identifying problems or potential problems in young children. Preschool teachers, too, are valuable sources of information.

Fig. 6-10 The Learning Accomplishment Profile tests major developmental areas.

Fig. 6-11 Comprehensive screening identifies children with special needs.

This discussion of early identification will be continued in unit 7 by focusing on the role of the teacher.

SUMMARY

The early identification of handicapping conditions is an important part of comprehensive services to young children and their families. Often, the handicap or potential handicap can be identified at the time of birth, or in the newborn nursery. Many other conditions are not as easy to recognize or do not show up until later in early childhood.

Comprehensive screening of all young children can identify large numbers of children with special needs and problems. This can best be accomplished through intensive public service publicity and the spotting of screening programs in easily accessible community gathering places.

The choice of a screening instrument is important. It must be inexpensive to administer. It must be applicable to large numbers of young children. It should be simple enough that it can be given by a paraprofessional or trained volunteer. It is most effective if it includes the parents' input. It must also allow for cultural differences. A large number of screening instruments have been devised during the past ten years. A few representative tests are listed in this unit. Included in the list are several tests that are suitable for use with the culturally different child.

The results of screening tests are never to be used to diagnose or to label a child. They are to be used for one purpose only: to locate those children who need more thorough assessment in one or more areas of development.

STUDENT ACTIVITIES

- Write to one of the addresses given in the list of screening instruments. Ask for a copy of the test or for information about it.

- Contact someone connected with your local hospital's newborn nursery. Find out what tests they use at the time of birth and during the first few days of life.

- Find out what kind of Child Find activities there are in your county or state. Attend a session if possible.

REVIEW

A. Which of the following statements do you agree with? Which do you disagree with? Write an A for those you agree with and a D for those you disagree with.

1. Prevention of developmental problems and maintenance of good health are as important as the treatment of problems.

2. There is a shift away from a primary focus on treatment and a shift toward prevention of problems in the professional care of young children.

3. The purpose of screening is to segregate handicapped children.

4. Three months of age is the ideal time to begin the special PKU diet.

5. Child Find activities cannot be carried out in large cities.

6. Screening activities are always carried out by an all professional team.

7. Mass vision and hearing tests should be a part of all early identification programs.

8. Screening instruments must be geared to cultural differences in children.

9. The Alpern-Boll Developmental Profile is sometimes considered unsuitable for mass screening.

10. The results of a screening test do not make a diagnosis.

B. Match each item in Column I with the correct description in Column II.

Column I	Column II
1. cleft palate	a. uses mobile unit screening program
2. CIP	b. newborn scoring system
3. Apgar	c. overabundance of fluid in the brain
4. amblyopia	d. Comprehensive Identification Process
5. small-for-date babies	e. PKU
6. DDST	f. a split or opening in the roof of the mouth
7. HICOMP	g. lazy eye
8. parents' rights	h. a law of the land
9. hydrocephalus	i. Denver Developmental Screening Test
10. phenylalanine	j. infants overly small for gestation period

C. Briefly answer each of the following.

1. Give three reasons for the increased interest in early identification of handicapping conditions.

2. What is the Apgar?

3. What is Child Find?

4. What issues should be considered in preparing Child Find publicity?

5. Gross vision and hearing tests may not be suitable for mass screening programs. Why?

6. Why should parents be included in screening programs?

7. What is meant by a "false positive" test result?

8. Why is the CIP considered a particularly useful screening instrument?

9. What is the major purpose of information gained from a screening test?

10. Why is it important that the PKU infant be identified within the first few days of birth?

Unit 7 EARLY IDENTIFICATION: THE ROLE OF THE TEACHER

OBJECTIVES

After studying this unit, the student will be able to

- Give several reasons why the preschool teacher is well qualified to help in the early identification of potential problems in young children.
- List three uses that must *not* be made of information gathered by preschool teachers.
- Describe and give examples of three types of recorded information.

The passage of Public Law 94-142, the Education for All Handicapped Children Act (described in unit 4), has made provisions for handicapped children as young as age three. A few states extend their services to even younger children. For children with developmental problems or delays, the sooner intervention is begun, the more effective it will be.

KEY CONTRIBUTOR

Today, the increasing importance of preschool teachers and day care personnel is being recognized. It is obvious that the early childhood educator's role will expand, broaden, and become more demanding over the next ten years. One part of the teacher's role that has already expanded is in the early identification

Fig. 7-1 The teacher can be a key contributor in the identification process.

of handicapping or potentially handicapping conditions. The preschool teacher can be a key contributor in this identification process, figure 7-1. It is also important, however, to understand that there are certain things teachers do *not* do.

Teachers do not diagnose. Diagnosis implies decision-making based upon recognizing a disease from its symptoms or signs. Symptoms, however, can be very misleading. Example: One child hit himself constantly about the mouth, cheeks, and jaws. This was usually accompanied by whining, crying, and even shrieking. He had been diagnosed clinically as emotionally disturbed. However, the teacher noted many times when there was no evidence of emotional disturbance. It was discovered that the child had severely abscessed back teeth. When the child was treated and relieved of his pain, the "emotionally disturbed" behaviors disappeared.

Teachers do not label. Labeling a child can have disastrous effects. If a child is labeled as retarded, brain-damaged, hyperactive, or anything else, a stigma (negative mark) is placed upon the child. Often the child's program is planned on the basis of the stigmatic label. Thus, the child may become what the label implies. This is called a *self-fulfilling prophecy*. The healthier individual that might have developed if the label had never been hung on the child is lost. Example:

A five-year-old was labeled as mentally retarded and placed in a day care center. Little was expected of her because of her "condition." One aide, assigned to gather behavioral data on the child, was most uncomfortable with the label. The aide's records indicated that the child had many good problem-solving behaviors. The child also engaged frequently in unique and creative ways of using materials. On the basis of the aide's data, the head teacher also made several

systematic observations. These showed the same types of high-level behaviors. The child was referred to the appropriate clinician for further assessment. Eventually she was removed to a preschool center for normal children. Within a year, she could not be distinguished from any other child on the basis of mental functioning.

Teachers do not tell parents that there is a particular thing wrong with their child. Parents of handicapped children or children with severe behavioral problems know they have a problem. They do not need a teacher to tell them what they already know. A teacher, therefore, should be as positive as possible without setting up false hope. The teacher can report what the child can do, as well as what the child cannot do. Thus, teachers can help parents to be more hopeful, yet direct them toward seeking additional professional help in order to build upon the child's strengths. This topic is further discussed in unit 20.

WHAT TEACHERS DO

What do teachers do in the identification process if they are not to diagnose (figure 7-2), label, or serve as informants to parents?

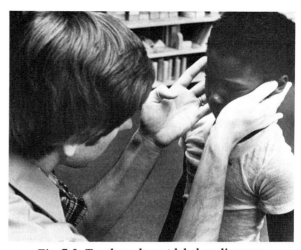

Fig. 7-2 Teachers do not label or diagnose.

Fig. 7-3 Throughout the day there are many opportunities to note strengths and needs.

They pinpoint their concerns about particular behaviors of a child in specific areas of development. This, as previously mentioned, can lead to referral to the appropriate professional for a thorough assessment. In accomplishing this, the preschool teacher needs to be a systematic observer. This means that teachers observe children and write down at regular intervals what they see and hear the child doing or saying.

Systematic Observations

Few adults are better qualified to make systematic observations of children than preschool teachers or day care workers. They understand child development. They have been trained to work with young children. They see each child in a natural kind of environment. In such an environment, there are a number of other children of similar age and interests by which to judge the range of normalcy. Teachers see each child for longer periods of time and in more varied situations. This is usually in contrast to the physician, psychologist, hearing specialist, or other clinicians. These professionals usually do not see the child as much as the teacher does, and visits are often brief, in a setting that is not natural to the child. There the child may be

ill at ease and behave quite differently than at school or at home. The clinical person is usually focusing on one special problem or problem area. This also gives a different picture than that of the "whole" child, the one that the preschool teacher is familiar with.

Throughout the day, there are many opportunities for teachers to note strengths and spot problems in the children they teach and care for, figure 7-3. In most preschools, children are routinely presented with pre-academic tasks. They also have opportunities for social and verbal interactions and many large and small motor activities. All of these give teachers a chance to systematically monitor children's development. Monitoring is not as difficult a task as it may seem to a teacher who has never consciously done it before. It is simply writing down, in some organized way, what behaviors each child engages in. Such information is often referred to as behavioral data.

Checklists

All teachers (and aides, volunteers, and parents) can learn to take systematic behavioral data. A simple checklist and some easy-to-follow guidelines can provide valuable information. (See the chart on pages 61 to 63.)

Teacher Observation Form and Checklist
For Identifying Children Who
May Require Additional Services

Child's Name: _____ Birth Date: _____

Date: _____ Recording Teacher's Name: _____

LANGUAGE	YES	NO	SOMETIMES
Does the child:			
1. use two- and three-word phrases to ask for what he wants?			
2. use complete sentences to tell you what happened?			
*3. when asked to describe something, use at least two or more sentences to talk about it?			
4. ask questions?			
5. seem to have difficulty following directions?			
6. respond to questions with appropriate answers?			
7. seem to talk too softly or too loudly?			
8. Are you able to understand the child?			

PREACADEMICS	YES	NO	SOMETIMES
Does the child:			
9. seem to take at least twice as long as the other children to learn pre-academic concepts?			
10. seem to take the time needed by other children to learn preacademic concepts?			
11. have difficulty attending to group activities for more than five minutes at a time?			
12. appear extremely shy in group activities; for instance, not volunteering answers or answering questions when asked, even though you think the child knows the answers?			

MOTOR	YES	NO	SOMETIMES
Does the child:			
13. continuously switch a crayon back and forth from one hand to the other when coloring?			
14. appear clumsy or shaky when using one or both hands?			
15. when coloring with a crayon, appear to tense the hand not being used (for instance, clench it into a fist)?			
16. when walking or running, appear to move one side of the body differently from the other side? For instance, does the child seem to have better control of the leg and arm on one side than on the other?			
17. lean or tilt to one side when walking or running?			
18. seem to fear or not be able to use stairs, climbing equipment or tricycles?			
19. stumble often or appear awkward when moving about?			
*20. appear capable of dressing self except for tying shoes?			

*Question applies if child is four years or older.

SOCIAL	YES	NO	SOMETIMES
Does the child:			
21. engage in more than two disruptive behaviors a day (tantrums, fighting, screaming, etc.)?			
22. appear withdrawn from the outside world (fiddling with pieces of string, staring into space, rocking)?			
23. play alone and seldom talk to the other children?			
24. spend most of the time trying to get attention from adults?			
25. have toileting problems (wet or soiled) once a week or more often?			

VISUAL OR HEARING	YES	NO	SOMETIMES
Does the child:			
26. appear to have eye movements that are jerky or uncoordinated?			
27. seem to have difficulty seeing objects? For instance, does the child: tilt head to look at things? hold objects close to eyes? squint? show sensitivity to bright lights? have uncontrolled eye-rolling? complain that eyes hurt?			
28. appear awkward in tasks requiring eye-hand coordination such as pegs, puzzles, coloring, etc.?			
29. seem to have difficulty hearing? For instance, does the child: consistently favor one ear by turning the same side of the head in the direction of the sound? ignore, confuse, or not follow directions? pull on ears or rub ears frequently, or complain of earaches? complain of head noises or dizziness? have a very high, very low, or monotonous tone of voice?			

GENERAL HEALTH	YES	NO	SOMETIMES
Does the child:			
30. seem to have an excessive number of colds?			
31. have frequent absenses because of illness?			
32. have eyes that water?			
33. have frequent discharge from: eyes? ears? nose?			
34. have sores on body or head?			
35. have periods of unusual movements (such as eye blinking) or "blank spells" which seem to appear and disappear without relationship to the social situation?			

GENERAL HEALTH (continued)	YES	NO	SOMETIMES
36. have hives or rashes? wheeze?			
37. have a persistent cough?			
38. seem to be excessively thirsty? seem to be ravenously hungry?			
39. Have you noticed any of the following conditions: constant fatigue? irritability? restlessness? tenseness? feverish cheeks or forehead?			
40. Is the child overweight?			
41. Is the child physically or mentally lethargic?			
42. Has the child lost noticeable weight without being on a diet?			

By taking such simple checks of what the child can and cannot do at regular intervals, the teacher becomes a systematic observer. These checkmarks provide important clues to the teacher and parents. The checks can be an early warning that further help may be needed. Such measures are sure to lead to better identification of potentially handicapping conditions in young children at a time when intervention is likely to be most effective.

Exercising Caution

Although teachers' observations can be of great value, certain cautions must be kept in mind. Failure to observe these cautions may cause unnecessary anxiety and hardship for the child and the child's family. The competent teacher is in a sensitive and advantageous position for making judgments that carry weight. The preschool teacher is not, however, qualified to make a definitive diagnosis of any disorder. It may be damaging to a child to attach too much importance to a developmentally "normal" irregularity (for example, the child who lisps). Sometimes

this can be as damaging as failing to recognize a problem. It must be remembered, too, that some behaviors are not what they appear to be, figure 7-4. For example, a child may appear to be hyperactive, constantly jumping out of the chair or leaving his place in the circle. This may, however, be the child's attempt to bring things into closer eye or ear range because of a vision or hearing problem.

Fig. 7-4 A child may exhibit a developmentally "normal" irregularity.

KINDS OF RECORDED OBSERVATIONS

It can be seen that teachers need the help of other professionals in interpreting behavioral signs. Teachers' recorded observations and behavioral data are, however, of key importance in assuring that appropriate referrals are made. These data are also important in planning intervention programs for the child once the clinical evaluation is made. Several types of observation systems are described here in addition to the checklist mentioned earlier.

Simple Counts

Recorded observations can often be simple counts (measures) such as how often a child flits from activity to activity, tantrums when frustrated, or shies away when an adult approaches. Recorded observations can also take the form of duration measures, that is, how long at a time a child is sucking fingers or thumb, remaining isolated from the group, or wandering aimlessly about the room.

One of the most important rules in recording observations on children is that

teachers be objective. To be objective means that teachers describe only what they actually see the child do, or hear the child say. This is in contrast to being subjective (teachers putting their own interpretation on a child's behavior). Note the difference in the following examples:

> Subjective: Susie was happy today.
> Objective: Susie laughed and smiled frequently when playing with Jeri and Beth.
> Subjective: Mark does not like Ms. Clark.
> Objective: Mark stamped his feet and shouted "No" several times when Ms. Clark told him, with no advance warning, to put his blocks away.

Running Record

Recorded observations can be much more detailed, of course. The running record is a very nice way to get a feel for the "whole" child and the impact of the total environment (teachers, children, space, and equipment). This form of behavioral data is obtained by writing down everything the child does for certain periods of time or during certain

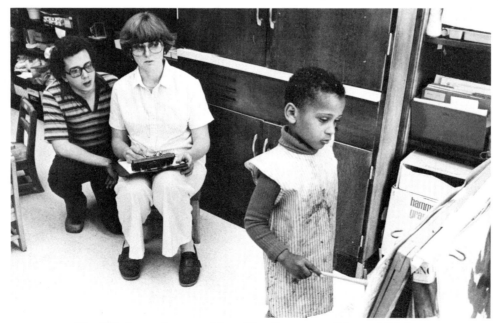

Fig. 7-5 A running record is writing down everything a child does.

activities, figure 7-5. As a general rule, the teacher cannot be supervising at the same time. Example:

Running Record
Child's name: Steve R   March 10, 19_
Setting: Free play, indoors   9:13 a.m. to
                                9:23 a.m.

Steve ran to the dough table which was unoccupied. He hammered a rolling pin on the table and looked toward the teacher who was talking with Linda. The teacher did not look in Steve's direction. He hammered the rolling pin a few more times and then began to roll out the dough. "Gonna make a donut," said Steve over and over, seven times. Again he looked toward the teacher who still did not look up. He rolled and patted the dough for about five minutes and then formed it into a large, thick circle. "Hey, teacher, looky at my giant donut!" shouted Steve. The teacher gave no evidence of hearing him. "Gonna bake it now!" yelled Steve, as he put the donut on a cookie sheet and then into a pretend oven. Again he looked toward the teacher who was busy writing children's names on their drawings. Steve slammed the cookie sheet down on the table loudly and began sweeping flour off the table and onto the floor.

Language Samples

Language samples are another useful way to get information about children, figure 7-6. This calls for writing down verbatim (word for word, or sound for sound) exactly what the child says or what sound the child makes.

Example 1:
  Bret R   March 22, 19_
  Snack time
      Gimme mo'
      'top that
      All gone

Fig. 7-6 **Language samples tell the teacher exactly how a child talks.**

      Uh huh
      Eeeee
      'top at

Example 2:
  Amy S   January 26, 19_
  Preacademics
      Teacher, give me a blue one, too.
      Hey Jimmy, you got way more pegs than
          I got and that's not fair.
      Keep quiet.
      I want to do some more, lots more.
      Those are my horses and cows and you
          can't have them.

Discrete Notes

Taking anecdotal developmental notes on 3" x 5" cards is another form of taking behavioral data. Very brief notes are recorded on each child in each area of development at regular intervals, figure 7-7. These brief anecdotes (short accounts) can be recorded while the teacher is supervising. The reason for using small cards is to ensure brevity.

Example:

Child: John A. May 5, 19_
Outdoors a.m. MOTOR DEVELOPMENT
J. climbed up 5 rungs on the jungle gym.
Each time he started with his left foot and
brought his right foot up beside it before
attempting the next rung. He grasped the
bar directly above with both hands each
time he moved up a rung. He came down
in an exact reverse pattern.

The choice of an observation system usually depends upon two things. One is how much staff time is available; the other is the ratio or number of adults there are in relationship to the number of children. Volunteers can be useful for taking data. They can also relieve teachers for a few minutes at a time. This gives teachers free time for collecting written information. Where there is a low ratio of adults to children, behavioral data may have to be limited to the simple counts or duration measures. The point is that some kind of data must be collected on each child. All teachers and aides should be trained and expected to collect information on children. This ensures that each teacher or aide will learn about the unique and special qualities of each child. It will also ensure assessment of the developmental appropriateness or inappropriateness of each child's behavior.

MAKING JUDGMENTS

In making judgments, that is, deciding whether a behavior is appropriate or not, teachers must exercise care. They must realize that whether a behavior is a healthy and necessary one may depend upon various factors. The most important factors are the ways or customs of the family or community in which the child lives. This may be different from those with which the teacher is accustomed. Certain questions should be asked:

Fig. 7-7 Anecdotal note: "Today John climbed to the top of the jungle gym."

Does the behavior interfere with the child's ability to engage in a variety of learning experiences?
Does it interfere with the child's willingness to engage in activities that will promote good social, intellectual, and physical development?

If the answers are "No," then it is not likely that the teacher needs to be overly concerned.

Children are Different

It must be remembered, too, that no two children develop exactly alike. To expect such uniformity is contrary to all basic child development principles. On the other hand, a nonintervention policy that looks for some mysterious process of "growing-out-of-it" to cure the child is not acceptable either. This condemns some children to unnecessary deficiencies and delays. These accumulate into problems that may become almost impossible to remedy.

This is still another reason for insisting on the collection of behavioral data at regular intervals. Teachers can monitor the questionable behaviors or a child's delay in acquiring certain behaviors. They can check to see if natural processes are moving the child along a healthy developmental path. If not, they can recommend that help be sought.

Excessive Occurrence

There is still another consideration which must be kept in mind. This has to do with the degree rather than the kind of potentially disabling condition. Most inappropriate behaviors are seen in every child (and even in many adults) at one time or other. They are seldom considered harmful or unusual in the average individual. For example, every young child cries, whines, sulks, withdraws, clings, disobeys, and talks back at times. These are normal, even desirable, behaviors

in a healthy growth process, figure 7-8. They are not signals for alarm unless they:

- occur excessively
- are used almost exclusively instead of more appropriate responses (whining and crying instead of asking)
- interfere with the child's participation in various learning experiences

Some behaviors that concern teachers may occur under certain conditions and not others. This indicates that the problem probably lies somewhere in the environment instead of within the child. For example, lack of sharing in a preschool child is often caused by a shortage of materials or equipment rather than selfishness.

Because of the complexity of children's behavior and the environment in which it occurs, the use of more than one recording system is often advisable. This provides a cross-check so that errors in judgment do not occur. Rarely should judgments be made on the basis of a single measure. A child who performs a certain task poorly one day may do well on that same task the following week. Everyone has "off" days. Children may enjoy helping to keep their own data, figure 7-9.

Fig. 7-8 A behavior is not cause for alarm unless it occurs excessively.

Fig. 7-9 Children often can help keep their own data.

The information gained from systematic observations often serves a dual purpose. It can identify possible problems and can also serve as a basis for educational programming. Example: Four-year-old Sally is observed to never button her own coat, take off her own boots, or put on her own mittens. Sally is thus identified as lacking certain self-help skills. Teachers have pinpointed exactly which self-help skills are needed to help Sally learn. It is this kind of direct observation that allows for individualized programming for each child.

SUMMARY

The identification of handicapping or potentially handicapping conditions in young children is an important part of the preschool teacher's job. The identification procedure can be a set of simple checklists and counts, or more detailed reports. The type of information collected depends upon the amount of staff time available. The important issue is that behavioral data be collected on every child.

Teachers must exercise care in using their behavioral data. They are not to use it to make a formal diagnosis. They are not to use it to label children. They are not to stir up parental anxiety by reporting that there is something wrong with a child. Teachers' data is especially valuable when used to seek additional help for a child.

Behavioral data gathered by the teaching staff should come from more than one instrument. Such double checking reduces error and provides for better programming for each child.

STUDENT ACTIVITIES

- Talk with a preschool or day care staff in your community to find out what types of information they collect on each child.

- Locate a preschool child and ask the parents' consent and help in administering the Teacher Observation Form. (See pages 61 to 63.)

- Observe a child in a play situation or day care setting and write down everything that the child says and does for four separate five-minute periods. Remember to be objective.

REVIEW

A. Define the following terms.

1. objective reporting
2. subjective reporting
3. duration measure
4. language sample

5. anecdote
6. diagnosis
7. symptom

B. Select the three best answers from the choices offered to complete each statement.

1. Teachers do not
   a. diagnose a child's condition.
   b. talk to parents.
   c. label a child.
   d. inform parents of a child's disability.

2. Systematic observation means
   a. watching children.
   b. writing down what is seen and heard.
   c. watching and writing at regular intervals.
   d. making educated guesses about why a child behaves in a certain way.

3. Preschool teachers are well qualified to make systematic observations of young children because
   a. most of them have children of their own.
   b. they see the children for longer periods of time than do the other professionals.
   c. they understand child development and the "whole child" concept.
   d. children in the preschool are in a comfortable environment.

4. The least time-consuming kinds of data to record are
   a. duration measures (how long a behavior lasts).
   b. counts of how often a behavior occurs.
   c. running records.
   d. checklists.

5. Teachers should collect data on each child in order to
   a. appropriately program for each individual.
   b. segregate the delayed children from the normal children.
   c. evaluate the effectiveness of each child's progress.
   d. monitor each child to see that the child is moving steadily along a sound developmental path.

6. Teachers should not be concerned about particular behaviors in children unless the behaviors
   a. are an imitation of a younger brother or sister.
   b. occur excessively.
   c. always take the place of more appropriate behaviors.
   d. prevent the child from participating in desirable learning experiences.

7. Children should not be labeled as having one condition or another because
   a. it places a stigma on the child.
   b. the child's program may be based on the label rather than on what the child can do.
   c. a child labeled as mentally retarded may become mentally retarded without just cause.
   d. preschool and day care directors do not like to have children labeled.

8. An objectively recorded observation is confined to
   a. what the teacher saw the child do.
   b. what the teacher heard the child say.
   c. what the reasons were for what the child did.
   d. where, when, and with whom the child was interacting.

C. Briefly answer each of the following.

1. Give an example of a misleading kind of symptom (either from the text or your own experience).

2. How can teachers use their observational data to help parents?

3. In what ways can volunteers assist teachers in early identification efforts?

4. What are two important ways that teachers should use their records?

5. Why are 3″ x 5″ cards best for recording anecdotal notes?

Unit 8 INDIVIDUALIZED EDUCATION PROGRAMS

OBJECTIVES

After studying this unit, the student will be able to

- Give at least five characteristics of a good assessment tool to use with a preschool handicapped child.
- Describe the Preschool Profile and explain why it is an example of a good assessment tool.
- List and briefly explain the seven components of an acceptable IEP.

Of increasing importance in providing for handicapped children is the Individualized Education Program (IEP). The IEP is a statutory (by law) requirement of PL 94-142 (the Education for All Handicapped Children Act of 1975). The IEP must be in written form, figure 8-1. It should be planned by the teacher and child-study team. Planning should also include the child's parents (or guardian) and even the child, on some occasions.

PL 94-142 is directed mainly toward school-age children. There is also a preschool incentive plan. States that use the special preschool funding will do well to adhere to an IEP plan also. For one thing, it provides the best possible overall scheme for planning sound programs for all children. It also helps to ensure educational and developmental continuity for handicapped or developmentally disabled children. This can all too easily be lost as children move from one program to another in the mainstreaming format.

The teacher is responsible for much of the writing and implementing of the IEP. Teachers (educators) are the only professionals required by law to provide services to children and youth. All other professions can provide for handicapped children at their own discretion — that is, they may do so if they wish. Hopefully, however, in carrying out this legal responsibility, the classroom teacher will have access to the services of these other professionals. Teachers must learn to call upon and draw from developmental therapists in other fields, figure 8-2. Such interaction leads to appropriate IEPs in the specialized areas. IEPs are likely to be developmentally sound and more easily carried out if this is done. For example, it may be quite difficult for a teacher

Fig. 8-1 The IEP must be in written form.

to know how to teach a child in a wheel-chair to get onto the toilet independently. A little help from a physical therapist or nurse is usually all that is needed. Teachers can readily learn this teaching skill and how to adapt it to individual wheelchair children.

In order to begin writing an IEP, teachers must first identify each child's problems. This was discussed in some detail in unit 7. A variety of identification tools were listed. Many identification tools are also assessment instruments. They tell a teacher what a child can and cannot do at a particular point in time. Assessment is not a one-time, or once-a-year, event. It needs to be an ongoing procedure. In other words, the child is assessed to pinpoint existing or entering skills in several performance areas. Then an IEP is written.

THE EFFECTIVE IEP

How can it be determined if the IEP is effective? This is done by checking period-ically (in some instances, even daily) to see if the child is learning. In other words, teachers must collect behavioral data points over time. This is the only way to evaluate how each child is responding to the IEP.

It can be seen that good assessment procedures and writing a sound IEP are importantly related. Therefore, before describing how to write the IEP, the main points in the assessment procedure will be reviewed.

- Assessment is the careful pinpointing of a child's skills and deficiencies.

- It should be required for all children and especially those who may be handicapped.

Fig. 8-2 Teachers must learn from developmental therapists.

Fig. 8-3 **Assessment needs to be a team effort.**

- It should include taking multiple behavioral data (perhaps language, motor, and social data) in the natural setting (for example, the preschool).

- It should include the search for a possible secondary handicap. (Is the child non-attentive because of a hearing loss, perhaps?)

- The results of assessment (just as in screening) should not be used to label children. Instead, the results should be used to prepare appropriate IEPs.

- Assessment procedures must be matched to the individual child. A deaf child cannot be adequately assessed for concept development on a standard intelligence test.

- Assessment (like screening) should be based on objective data; that is, information about what the child actually does and says.

- Assessment needs to be a team effort, calling on the cooperation of several professionals, figure 8-3. This is the interdisciplinary concept so important in providing for handicapped children.

Once a child has been identified as handicapped and an assessment made of what the child can and cannot do, writing the IEP is the next step. There are seven requirements in this process:

1. A statement of the child's present levels of educational functioning.
2. A statement of annual goals.
3. A statement of short-term instructional objectives.
4. A statement of specific educational services to be provided for the child.
5. A statement of how much of the time the child will be mainstreamed.
6. A date for the beginning of services and the length of time services will be available to the child.
7. An outline of accountability: evaluation procedures and time points for determining if instructional objectives are being met.

Each of these seven requirements will be discussed separately in this unit.

STATEMENT OF THE CHILD'S PRESENT LEVELS OF PERFORMANCE

This is what the preceding discussion on assessment was all about. One important thing here is to get the assessment information put together in a form which is easy to use. One such form is the Preschool Profile, figure 8-4, pages 74 and 75. This profile is an excellent

	Gross Motor Skills	Fine Motor Skills	Preacademic Skills	Self-help Skills	Music/Art/Story Skills	Social Skills and Play Skills	Understanding Language	Oral Language
0–12 months	Sits without support. Crawls. Pulls self to standing and stands unaided. Walks with aid. Rolls a ball in imitation of adult.	Reaches, grasps, puts object in mouth. Picks things up with thumb and one finger (pincer grasp). Transfers object from one hand to other hand. Drops and picks up toy.	Looks directly at adult's face. Tracks objects (follows them smoothly with eyes). Imitates gestures: e.g., pat-a-cake, peek-a-boo, bye-bye. Puts block in, takes block out of container. Finds block hidden under cup.	Feeds self cracker: munching, not sucking. Holds cup with two hands, drinks with assistance. Holds out arms and legs while being dressed.	Fixes gaze on pictures in book.	Smiles spontaneously. Responds differentially to strangers and familiar persons. Pays attention to own name. Responds to 'no.' Copies simple actions of others.	Looks at people who talk to him. Responds differentially to variety of sounds: e.g., phone, vacuum, closing doors, etc. Responds to simple directions accompanied by gestures: e.g., *come, give, get*.	Makes different vowel sounds. Makes different consonant-vowel combinations. Vocalizes to the person who has talked to him. Uses intonation patterns that sound like phrases: e.g., intonations that sound like scolding, asking, telling.
12–24 months	Walks alone. Walks backward. Picks up object without falling. Pulls toy. Seats self in child's chair. Walks up and down stairs with aid.	Builds tower of 3 cubes. Puts 4 rings on stick. Places 5 pegs in pegboard. Turns pages 2 or 3 at a time. Scribbles.	Follows one direction involving familiar actions and objects: e.g., *Show me (toy). Give me (toy). Get a (familiar object).* Completes 3 piece formboard. Matches similar objects.	Uses spoon, spilling little. Drinks from cup, one hand, unassisted. Chews food. Removes garment. Zips, unzips large zipper. Indicates toilet needs.	Moves to music. Looks at pictures in book, pointing to, or naming objects or people. Paints with whole arm movement, shifts hands, makes strokes.	Recognizes self in mirror or picture. Refers to self by name. Plays by self; initiates own play activities. Imitates adult behaviors in play. Plays with water and sand. Loads, carries, dumps. Helps put things away.	Responds to specific words by showing what was named: e.g., toys, family members, clothing, body parts. Responds to simple directions given without gestures: e.g., *go, sit, find, run, walk*.	Asks for items by name. Answers *What's that?* with name of object. Tells about objects or experiences with words used together (2–3 words): e.g., *more juice*.
24–36 months	Runs forward well. Jumps in place, two feet together. Stands on one foot, with aid. Walks on tiptoe. Kicks ball forward. Throws ball, without direction.	Strings 4 large beads. Turns pages singly. Snips with scissors. Holds crayon with thumb and fingers, not fist. Uses one hand consistently in most activities. Imitates circular, vertical, horizontal strokes.	Matches shapes. Stacks 5 rings on peg, in order. Demonstrates number concepts to 2, (i.e., selects set of 1 or 2; can tell how many, 1 or 2).	Uses spoon, no spilling. Gets drink unassisted. Uses straw. Opens door by turning handle. Puts on/takes off coat. Washes/dries hands with assistance.	Participates in simple group activity: e.g., sings, claps, dances. Chooses picture books, points to fine detail, enjoys repetition. Paints with some wrist action, makes dots, lines, circular strokes. Rolls, pounds, squeezes, pulls clay material.	Plays near other children. Watches other children, joins briefly in their play. Defends own possessions. Engages in domestic play. Symbolically uses objects, self in play. Builds with blocks in simple lines.	Responds to *put it in* and *put it on*. Responds by selecting correct item: big vs. little objects; one vs. one more object. Identifies objects by their use: e.g., *Show me what mother cooks on* by showing stove, or *Show me what you wear on your feet* by showing shoe.	Asks questions. Answers *Where is it?* with prepositional phrases: e.g., *in the box, on the table.* Answers *What do you do with a ball?* e.g., throw, catch. Tells about something with functional sentences which carry meaning: e.g., *me go store* or *me hungry now.*

Fig. 8-4 Preschool Profile

	Gross Motor Skills	Fine Motor Skills	Preacademic Skills	Self-help Skills	Music/Art/Story Skills	Social Skills and Play Skills	Understanding Language	Oral Language
36–48 months	Runs around obstacles. Walks on a line. Balances on one foot 5 seconds. Hops on one foot. Pushes, pulls, steers wheeled toys. Rides (i.e., steers and pedals) trike. Uses slide without assistance. Jumps over 15 cm. (6'') high object, landing on both feet together. Throws ball with direction. Catches ball bounced to him.	Builds tower of 9 cubes. Drives nails and pegs. Copies circle. Imitates cross.	Matches 6 colors. Makes tower of 5 blocks, graduated in size. Does 7 piece puzzle. Counts to 5, in imitation of adults. Demonstrates number concept to 3.	Pours well from pitcher. Spreads substances with knife. Buttons/unbuttons large buttons. Washes hands unassisted. Cleans nose when reminded. Uses toilet independently. Follows classroom routine with minimum teacher assistance. Knows own sex. Knows own age. Knows own last name.	Knows phrases of songs. Listens to short simple stories (5 minutes). Painting: names own picture, not always recognizable; demands variety of color. Draws head of person and one other part. Manipulates clay materials: e.g., rolls balls, snakes, cookies, etc.	Joins in play with other children; begins to interact. Shares toys, takes turns with assistance. Begins dramatic play, acting out whole scenes; e.g., traveling, playing house, pretending to be animals.	Responds to *put it beside* and *put it under.* Responds to commands involving 2 objects: e.g., *Give me the ball and the shoe.* Responds to commands involving 2 actions: e.g., *Give me the cup and put the shoe on the floor.* Responds by selecting correct item: e.g., hard vs. soft objects. Responds to *walk fast* and to *walk slowly* by decreased pace.	Answers *Which one do you want?* by naming it. Answers *if . . . what what & when* questions: e.g., *If you had a penny, what would you do? What do you do when you're hungry?* Answers questions about function: e.g., *What are books for?* Asks for or tells about with grammatically correct sentences: e.g., *Can I go to the store? I want a big cookie.*
48–60 months	Walks backward heel-toe. Jumps forward 10 times, without falling. Walks up/down stairs alone, alternating feet. Turns somersault.	Cuts on a line continuously. Copies cross. Copies square. Prints a few capital letters.	Points to, names 6 basic colors. Points to, names 3 shapes. Matches related common objects: e.g., shoe, foot; apple, banana. Demonstrates number concept to 4 or 5.	Cuts food with a knife; e.g., sandwich, celery. Laces shoes. Knows own city/street. Follows instructions given to group.	Sings entire songs. Recites nursery rhyme. "Reads" from pictures (i.e., tells story). Recognizes story and retells simple facts. Painting: makes and names recognizable pictures. Draws a person with 2–6 parts.	Plays and interacts with other children. Dramatic play: closer to reality; attention to detail, time and space. Plays dress-up. Builds complex structures with blocks.	Responds by showing penny-nickel-dime. Responds to command involving 3 actions: e.g., *Give me the cup, put the shoe on the floor, and hold the pencil in your hand.*	Asks how questions. Answers verbally to *Hi* and *How are you?* Tells about something using past tense and future tense. Tells about something using conjunctions to string words and phrases together. e.g., *I have a cat and a dog and a fish.*
							Above items are selected from *The Sequenced Inventory of Communication Development,* University Press, University of Washington, 1975	
60–72 months	Runs lightly on toes. Walks a balance beam. Can cover 2 meters (6'6''), hopping. Skips. Jumps rope. Skates.	Cuts out simple shapes. Copies triangle. Traces diamond. Copies first name. Prints numerals 1-5. Colors within lines. Has adult grasp of pencil. Has handedness well established. (i.e., child is left or right handed).	Sorts objects on one dimension: i.e., by size or by color or by shape. Does 15 piece puzzle. Copies block design. Names some letters. Names some numerals. Names penny, nickel, dime, quarter. Counts by rote to 10. Can tell what number comes next.	Dresses self completely. Learns to distinguish left from right. Ties bow. Brushes teeth unassisted. Crosses street safely. Relates clock time to daily schedule.	Recognizes rhyme. Acts out stories. Draws a person with head, trunk, legs, arms, and features. Pastes and glues objects appropriately. Models objects with clay.	Chooses own friend(s). Plays simple table games. Plays competitive games. Engages in cooperative play with other children involving group decisions, role assignments, fair play. Uses construction toys to make things; e.g., house of legos, car of rig-a-jig.	See preacademic skills.	Child will have acquired basic grammatical structures including plurals, verb tenses and conjunctions. Following this developmental ability, the child practices with increasingly complex descriptions and conversations.

This profile is a working draft only and was prepared by the Communication Disorders Specialists Linda Lynch, Jane Rieke, Sue Soltman, and Teachers Donna Hardman and Mary O'Conor. The authors would appreciate feedback on the usefulness of this profile which is in the process of revision. The Communication Program was funded primarily as a part of the Model Preschool Center for Handicapped Children by Grant No. OEG-072-5371

U.S. Office of Education, Program Development Branch, BEH., Washington, D.C. Dr. Alice H. Hayden is Project Director. Experimental Education Unit (WJ-10) of the College of Education and Child Development and Mental Retardation Center, University of Washington, Seattle, WA

Fig. 8-4 Preschool Profile (continued)

tool for preschool use. It lends itself readily to ongoing assessment.

Preschool Profile

What exactly is the Preschool Profile? It is a chart which can be used as an individualized record of a child's performance in the following areas:

- Gross motor skills
- Fine motor skills
- Preacademic skills
- Self-help skills (figure 8-5)
- Music, art, and story skills
- Social and play skills
- Understanding language (receptive language skills)
- Oral language (expressive language skills)

It is important to note that the behaviors included in each square in figure 8-4 represent broad behavior patterns. They should be used only as guidelines. A child may show proficiency (ability) in a skill in a variety of ways. For example, in the 0 to 12 months preacademic skills square, there is the response, "puts blocks in, takes blocks out of container." The underlying skill is the ability to pick up and release an object within a defined area. An infant who can put a cookie in a cup and take it out obviously has that ability and would be passed on that item. The authors of the profile suggest a color-coded reporting system. Highlighting pens are good for this purpose. Initial assessment items passed by the child are lined through in one color. Subsequent assessment items are marked with different colors. Items that the child can do sometimes (once in a while) are especially important. These are marked with some sort of an alert signal such as an asterisk. For example, when a child enters the program, assessment items that the child can do are lined through in yellow. Behaviors that the child cannot perform are left unmarked. Items of inconsistent success, those "sometimes" responses, are marked with an asterisk. The "sometimes" responses are most important, figure 8-6. They often indicate where to start programming for the child.

At the end of three months, the profile is updated. At this time it is often found that several asterisked items are now consistently within the child's ability. These are lined through in a new color, perhaps green. Usually several previously unmarked items (items of no success at the time of entry) can now be performed sometimes. These are now marked with an asterisk. This system provides an

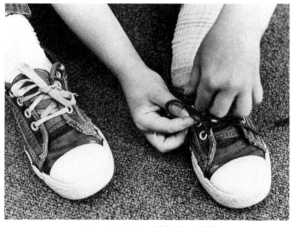

Fig. 8-5 A self-help skill.

Fig. 8-6 The "sometimes" responses are important.

easily updated visual picture of a child's functioning. It is useful because it includes a view of:

- general overall level of functioning related to normal development

- areas of strength and areas of weakness

- specific patterns of learning

- areas of progress

- areas requiring further programming

There are other advantages of the Preschool Profile. It serves as a reminder of the range of needs within the young child. It also makes clear the interrelationships between developmental areas. This means that when writing an IEP, the teaching staff takes into account a child's functioning across all areas. Thus, it is important to note that there is much overlapping of items across the skill areas. For example, several levels of the ability to follow directions are included under Preacademic Skills, Self-help Skills, and Understanding Language.

Successful performance of an item in one area may be a prerequisite to behaviors in another area. A *prerequisite skill* is one that must be learned before another skill can be expected to be accomplished. For instance, a child cannot be expected to button and unbutton clothes unless the pincer grasp (thumb and forefinger used in opposition) has been established, figure 8-7. Deficiencies in one area may then explain delays in another. A child with language disabilities usually has trouble interacting with peers. It can be seen that the use of a tool such as the Preschool Profile can be most helpful in planning and writing IEPs.

STATEMENT OF ANNUAL GOALS

There are general, long-range targets to be worked toward throughout each school year. Long-range goals are usually stated in

Fig. 8-7 The pincer grasp is a prerequisite to other skills.

Fig. 8-8 Long-range goal: Doug will learn to get along with other children.

Fig. 8-9 Short-term objective: Johnny will be able to hop 5 times on each foot.

broad and rather vague terms. The following is an example:

The child will:
  become more independent and self-sufficient;
  develop an improved self-image;
  become better coordinated;
  learn to get along with children, figure 8-8.

All of these are admirable statements of purpose. They would vary, of course, from child to child. As they are, however, these goals do not tell teachers what they must do in order to help children reach the goals. The third item in the IEP procedures gives this information.

STATEMENT OF SHORT-TERM INSTRUCTIONAL OBJECTIVES

An objective is the statement of a specific achievement that can be measured and is to be accomplished within the framework of the program goals. These objectives state the in-between steps to be taken or behaviors to be learned to reach the annual goals.

Short-term instructional objectives refer to behaviors or skills that a child can acquire in a few days or a few weeks. Usually a series of short-term objectives are arranged in sequence, one after the other, in order to reach the long-range goals. It has been suggested[1] that a good behavioral objective for instructional purposes has four parts:

1. WHO is going to be engaging in the behavior

2. WHAT the behavior is

3. WHEN and/or WHERE the behavior is to occur

4. HOW WELL the behavior is to be perfected

Following are two examples of instructional objectives which the authors have written in this behavioral format:

WHO	Johnny
WHAT	will be able to hop on one foot

[1]Dave Evans and John Kiely, *Educational Training,* Head Start Personnel. Sequencing tasks to meet objectives.

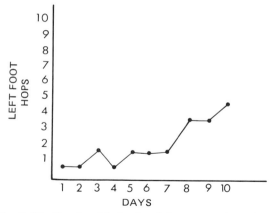

Fig. 8-10 Graph of behavioral data: number of left-foot hops per day.

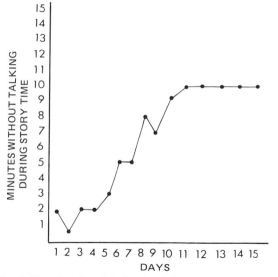

Fig. 8-11 Graph of behavioral data: minutes without talking per day during story time.

Fig. 8-12 Learning to stay at story time.

WHEN/WHERE   during physical education

HOW WELL   five hops on each foot within 30 seconds (see figure 8-9)

The behavioral data here is a frequency count (see unit 7); it states how many times a hop must occur in a given length of time. Another example:

WHO   Becky

WHAT   will be able to sit quietly without talking

WHEN/WHERE   during story time

HOW WELL   for ten of the fifteen minutes of story for five days in a row.

The behavioral data here includes a measure of duration or how long (ten minutes), and a measure of frequency (five times in five days). Many teachers find that by graphing the behavioral data points they bring the child's progress into sharp focus. Using the example of Johnny, suppose it takes him 10 days to reach the objective as stated. If teachers were plotting (marking down data points each day), they might have a graph like the one in figure 8-10.

It can be seen that it was difficult for the child to learn to hop on the left foot. If he had not been able to master the left-foot part of the task this might have been a warning sign. The teacher might suspect a possible secondary handicap in need of further exploration by appropriate professionals.

Figure 8-11 is a chart of Becky's progress plotted with behavioral data points.

It can be seen that Becky was staying at story time without talking only one or two minutes per day at first. Then certain instructional procedures were introduced. On day 11, she reached the object of staying at story time for 10 minutes without talking. She continued to do so for the next 5 days, thus meeting the requirements, figure 8-12.

Fig. 8-13 Specifying particular foods that ease self-feeding might be part of an IEP.

Fig. 8-14 Bussing to and from the integrated pre-school will be provided.

Graphs such as the ones shown in figures 8-10 and 8-11 require very little teacher time. In fact, they are time-savers. They give teachers quick and easy feedback on the effectiveness of their teaching programs.

STATEMENT OF SPECIFIC EDUCATIONAL SERVICES TO BE PROVIDED FOR THE CHILD

This part of the requirement for the IEP includes providing such things as

- the service of a speech therapist or a physical therapist (or both)
- special tutoring in preacademic skills
- a behavior management program to reduce aggressive behaviors
- particular foods to facilitate self-feeding, figure 8-13
- bus service three days each week for special services at a communications preschool, figure 8-14

Also included would be a description of self-help devices to be used. A self-help device is any kind of special equipment designed to help a child develop more easily. Glasses, hearing aides, and wheelchairs are common examples. Some less common ones are the following: a device for a paralyzed child to hold in the mouth in order to use a typewriter; bells hung in strategic places to help young blind children learn to get around; plates and bowls anchored to the table with suction pads to facilitate self-feeding; and specially designed work chairs for the cerebral palsied child.

THE EXTENT TO WHICH EACH CHILD WILL BE ABLE TO PARTICIPATE IN REGULAR EDUCATIONAL PROGRAMS

Within the mainstreaming concept, every child must be moved toward regular school services as soon as possible. This does not mean that special education classes are to be abandoned. It simply means that every effort must be made to give children as many opportunities as possible to learn with nonhandicapped children.

THE PROMISED DATE FOR BEGINNING OF SERVICES: LENGTH OF TIME SERVICES WILL BE AVAILABLE

These are fairly straightforward requirements. The first is aimed at insuring that no child is left waiting indefinitely for services. The second part of this requirement is to insure that services are available for a reasonable length of time to accomplish instructional objectives.

Child's Name: Billie L.   Age: 4 yrs 2 mo
Maple Leaf Preschool for the Deaf
September 17, 19 _

Present Level of Functioning

Social development: Billie does not play with other children. He runs away every time a child approaches.

Annual Goals

Billie will learn to play cooperatively with other children.

Short-Term Objectives

Billie will play next to other children in the sandbox, at the water table, or in other side-by-side activities, for two 10 minute periods each day.

Special Services

Bussing each afternoon to the integrated preschool
Behavior management program

Amount of Time Mainstreamed

Billie will go each afternoon, Monday through Thursday, from 1:30 to 3:30 p.m., to the Community Preschool.

Beginning and Duration of Services

Billie will begin attending the Community Preschool on October 5. The behavior management program will be put into effect in both preschools on October 12. The joint placement will continue until December 20.

Evaluation

Billie will be reassessed on the Preschool Profile in mid-December. A graph will be kept showing the amount of time Billie spent playing next to children each day.

Fig. 8-15 Example of an individualized program.

A STATEMENT OF ACCOUNTABILITY

This is one of the most important requirements of an IEP. It means that appropriate objective criteria (standards) be stated. It also means that there is a statement of specific evaluation procedures. Finally, it means that there are schedules for determining, at least once a year, if instructional objectives are being achieved.

The Preschool Profile described earlier in this unit is one example of sound and objective accountability reporting. All items are stated in terms of child behaviors that can be changed with appropriate instruction. Add to this the data gathered on specific instructional objectives such as the two examples given earlier (hopping and listening to stories). The two, together, provide convincing evidence of the effectiveness of an IEP. Figure 8-15 is an example of an acceptable IEP.

SUMMARY

The Individualized Education Program (IEP) is an important part of PL 94-142. It begins with a thorough assessment of the child in order to determine what the child can and cannot do.

The Preschool Profile is a useful assessment tool. It indicates the child's entering skills in several areas of development. It also allows for ongoing assessment and gives a picture of how developmental areas are related.

The requirements for writing an IEP are discussed. The IEP should be written by a child-study team which includes the teacher, the parents or guardian, and in some instances, the child. It must spell out specific long- and short-range goals for the child, how these will be accomplished, and under what circumstances. The IEP must also state specifically how the effectiveness of the program will be evaluated.

STUDENT ACTIVITIES

- Contact your local school and ask to see an IEP on a kindergarten or primary grade handicapped child.

- Plot the following data on graph paper (you can draw your own graph paper):

  Leslie spoke to teachers 3 times on September 27, 11 times on September 28, not at all on September 29, 30, and October 1. On October 4 she spoke to teachers 7 times and for the next four days alternated between 8 and 7 times per day.

- Show a copy of the Preschool Profile to a preschool or day care teacher. Ask the teacher to comment on its strong and weak points.

REVIEW

A. Briefly answer each of the following.

1. Give two reasons for writing an IEP for a preschool handicapped child.

2. Why should preschool teachers learn to work with other disciplines?

3. List five (or more) main points to be considered in an assessment procedure.

4. What is the Preschool Profile?

5. List five reasons why the Preschool Profile is cited as an exceptionally useful tool.

6. What is the difference between long-range goals and short-term objectives?

7. What are the four parts of a good instructional objective?

8. Describe a self-help device.

9. What are the most important features of the statement of accountability in an IEP?

10. Why is it helpful for teachers to graph behavioral data?

B. Select the three best answers from the choices offered to complete each statement.

1. An IEP for each handicapped child
   a. is required by law.
   b. is part of PL 94-142.
   c. may be written down if the teacher wishes.
   d. should include parent participation in the planning.

2. Some of the professions not required by law to provide services to handicapped children are
   a. nursing.
   b. teaching.
   c. medicine.
   d. audiology.

3. Self-help devices are things designed especially to help a handicapped child, such as
   a. spoons with large rubber handle grips.
   b. hearing aids.
   c. blackboards and chalk.
   d. artificial arm.

4. Among the things that an IEP must specify are the following:
   a. the special services required.
   b. how much the special services will cost.
   c. when the special services will start.
   d. what portion of the time the child will be in a regular classroom.

5. Examples of long-term goals are:
   a. the child will learn to read.
   b. the child will learn self-help skills such as dressing.
   c. the child will learn to button three buttons on the button board in 2 minutes.
   d. the child will make friends during kindergarten.

C. Match each item in Column I with the correct item in Column II.

Column I	Column II
1. preschool incentive plan	a. assessment instruments
2. a profession required by law to provide services to handicapped children	b. wheelchair
	c. record of what a child actually does and says
3. sometimes the same as identification tools	d. a good tool for ongoing assessment
4. standard IQ test	e. part of PL 94-142
5. objective data	f. there was 7 minutes of thumb-sucking
6. Preschool Profile	
7. quick visual feedback on a child's progress	g. skills a child can acquire in a few days or weeks
8. a duration measure	h. teaching
9. self-help device	i. behavioral data graphs
10. short-term objectives	j. an unsuitable test for a deaf child

SECTION 3
TEACHING THE HANDICAPPED AND NONHANDICAPPED

Unit 9 TEACHER SKILLS AND ATTITUDES

OBJECTIVES

After studying this unit, the student will be able to

- Explain why preschool teachers do not need extensive retraining in order to include handicapped children in their group.
- Explain this statement: A thorough knowledge of normal growth and development is of great importance in planning effectively for handicapped children in the preschool.
- List five major considerations in planning a daily schedule for the integrated preschool.

The most important part of effective preschool and day care programs is the teaching staff. This is true regardless of the kind of program or types of children being served. In every sound early education program there are a number of basic skills and attitudes which all successful preschool teachers seem to exhibit. These are apparent whether the teachers are working with handicapped children, nonhandicapped children, or a combination of both, figure 9-1.

MINIMAL RETRAINING

Learning to teach and to work well with handicapped children does not require extensive retraining. Many teachers who thought they might have to get a degree in Special Education found that they do not need to do this.

Fig. 9-1 The teaching staff is a most important part of the integrated preschool.

Fig. 9-2 **Teachers who truly understand young children can teach the handicapped.**

Lectures and workshops sponsored by such agencies as United Cerebral Palsy Association, the National Easter Seal Society, or the local Association for Retarded Citizens have provided excellent learning experiences. These agencies and many others have local contact offices in almost every community. They are eager to help teachers work more effectively with handicapped children.

Agencies can also recommend or provide films, articles, books, and other helpful information. Such materials describe specific handicaps, detail problems that confront the child, and offer suggestions for managing specific situations. If there is a blind child in the class, for example, it is important for the teacher to find out about blindness and the needs of young blind children. This information can be found in books and pamphlets from The American Foundation for the Blind. Such information is often more useful to the classroom teacher than formal courses in Special Education.

Understanding Normalcy

Young children are more alike than they are different. The best way to acquire skill in managing a program which includes young handicapped children is to learn about and work with all young children.[1] Including handicapped children in a preschool program may not be easy all of the time. However, any teacher who really understands young children can work with the handicapped. One essential ingredient is to get to know each child well. Another is to develop an awareness of the likes, dislikes, joys, and anxieties of each child. Teachers who do these things can teach *all* young children effectively, figure 9-2.

It is important to view each child as a child, rather than as a stutterer or an epileptic. This helps teachers realize that much of the child's behavior is not necessarily related to the disability. It is too easy to attribute a child's shyness or tantrums to the child's handicap. It is better to view these maladaptive behaviors as normal developmental problems often found in all types of young children.

Understanding the "normalcy" of some developmental problems, as well as the need

[1] Jenny W. Klein, "Headstart Services to Handicapped: Mainstreaming the Preschooler," *Head Start Newsletter,* 9 (1977), pp. 2-15.

88

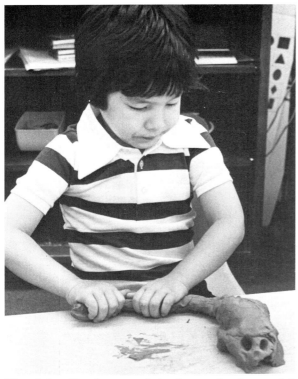

Fig. 9-3   Teachers need to know developmental sequences.

for concern over others, is a special skill needed by all early childhood teachers. Fortunately, it is one that is easily acquired. As pointed out in earlier units, an understanding of developmental irregularities requires a thorough understanding of normal growth and development. Particularly, it calls for a practical knowledge of developmental milestones and developmental sequences, figure 9-3.

Identifying Developmental Lags

When normal development and growth are thoroughly understood, it is easier to recognize developmental irregularities or lags. A *developmental lag* exists when a child is long past the age at which certain developmental skills should have been achieved. In the area of feeding, for example, a two-year-old who is eating only pureed baby foods is seldom cause for concern. However, the

four-year-old with similar eating habits may be cause for great concern, in some instances. If the child continues to eat only soft, slushy foods, this may lead to other developmental lags. These are in addition to the ones directly associated with the inappropriate food preferences. Poor articulation is one example of what might result.

A thorough understanding of child development also helps teachers to be sensitive to individual differences. For example, in a day care situation, some three-year-olds fall asleep instantly at nap time. For others it is almost impossible to fall asleep. Each type of child should be managed on a different plan. Serious problems may develop from trying to force sleep on a child who does not require it. Disruptiveness at nap time is one such behavior problem that can arise.

Children often show individual differences as a result of the differing environments in which they are reared. Some five-year-olds never cry or stamp their feet when frustrated. Others do it every once in awhile. A few five-year-olds use this behavior as their sole means of getting what they want. Each of these five-year-olds is quite different in the way that they have learned to handle frustration in their home environment. Each requires a different kind of responding from their teachers.

Recognizing Readiness

Readiness and teachable moments are important developmental concepts, too. Readiness is a combination of maturation, motivation, and opportunity. When these three come together a teachable moment, or critical period, is at hand, figure 9-4. Example: at some point most infants reach for the spoon while being fed. This is usually a cue that the babies are ready to begin to learn to feed themselves. They should be assisted in

Fig. 9-4 Building on a teachable moment is an important teacher skill.

learning to self-feed when this occurs. Other examples are toddlers who hold their diapers, fuss and cry when wet, or step out of their diapers by themselves. These children, who may range in age from 12 to 36 months, are giving clear cues that they are ready for toilet training.

There are many ways in which the concepts of readiness and teachable moments can be translated into classroom practices. The most effective of these is the principle of incidental teaching. An incidental teaching episode is usually started by the child. The child approaches the teacher, asking for help, materials, or information. White has conducted significant research on mother-child interactions along these lines[2]. He reports that the most effective mothers of very young children rarely spent 5, 10, or 20 minutes teaching their children. Nevertheless, they got a great amount of teaching in "on the fly," figure 9-5. This occurred mainly at those moments when the children contacted their mothers.

Fig. 9-5 Mothers teach their young children "on the fly."

Incidental Teaching

When used systematically, incidental teaching has led to dramatic increases in children's language skills.[3] The essential feature in incidental teaching is having the

[2]Burton L. White. *The First Three Years of Life.* (Englewood Cliffs, New Jersey: Prentice-Hall, Inc. 1975).

[3]Betty Hart and Todd R. Risley. "Community-based Language Training." In *Intervention Strategies for High Risk Infants and Young Children,* ed. Theodore Tjossem (Baltimore: University Park Press, 1976).

Fig. 9-6 The contact should be fun for teacher and child.

child initiate it. The more often the child contacts the teacher, the more opportunities there are for teaching. Thus it is important that children make frequent contacts. To insure this, the teacher should:

- be readily available

- be interested

- be positive

- have attractive materials and activities at hand

- have a strong desire to help each child to learn

- keep the contact brief and focused on the child

- be sure that the contact is fun for child and teacher, figure 9-6.

Example: Teaching color words may be a curriculum item being worked on during preacademics. During free play, a child approaches the teacher and asks for a truck. The teacher asks which color truck. If the child does not say red (or blue or yellow), the teacher asks if the child can say, "I want the red truck." When the

child says, "I want the red truck" (or similar statement), the teacher hands over the truck. The teacher also confirms the child's response: "That's right. It is a red truck."

PLANNING THE ENVIRONMENT

It is important for teachers to be able to plan an environment in which all kinds of learning (both incidental and teacher-structured) can occur. This skill also comes from knowledge about child development.

Equipment

Equipment needs to be simple yet versatile. Outside, teachers should be sure that there are such things as ladders, planks, jumping boards, and simple climbing frames. These can be combined and recombined in various ways. Such versatility accommodates the skill level of every child from the severely delayed to the more developmentally advanced. Indoors, the unit blocks, water play activities, and housekeeping area are examples of activities that accommodate developmental differences. This concept of planning activities and choosing equipment that accommodates

Fig. 9-7   Young children need periods of vigorous activity.

children's differences is important when planning an integrated program. Handicapped children can learn through observing and imitating their more able playmates. Non-handicapped children can learn to be caring and considerate of others less skilled than themselves.

Teachers also need to plan several well-defined centers of interest. Crowding and conflict are prevented if children have more than one attractive area to choose from. Five or six children of various capabilities, playing store at one time, can have a satisfying learning/play experience. It is difficult for a child to learn anything of significance, either socially or cognitively, when 10 or 12 children are crowding into an area at one time.

Daily Schedule

The daily schedule is also very important. Activities need to follow an orderly and predictable sequence. Many young children, including the handicapped, cannot accept changes and departures from routine. There is great security in knowing "what comes next." Another feature that teachers must include in good scheduling is a balance and alternation between quiet and more active periods, figure 9-7. There must be plenty of time allowed for children to finish each

Fig. 9-8 Plan transitions so children can move at their own pace.

activity and to accomplish each routine. All children must be allowed the satisfaction gained from task completion. Those who move very slowly and with great difficulty need it most of all. It is an insult to carry a child who, given enough time, can walk. Activities and transitions must be scheduled in such a way that children can move at their own individual paces, figure 9-8, whether fast or slow. In this way, children's efforts are not demeaned.

Time must also be planned for teacher-structured activities and for child-directed activities. The more severely handicapped the child, the greater the need to help the child take part in activities of both kinds. Too often, only teacher-structured activities are allowed for.

The two main characteristics of a good preschool schedule are large blocks of time and as few transitions (moving from one activity place to another) as possible. This results in a more relaxed and pleasant preschool day for children and teachers. Following is an example of a highly functional daily schedule.[4]

DAILY SCHEDULE

8:45 to 9:15 - Arrival

Individual health inspection, figure 9-9.

Greetings and brief conversation with each child and the parent (if the parent brings the child to school).

Practice in self-help skills needed upon arrival (dressing, toileting, getting drink of water, using nose tissues, etc.).

Getting started on large motor activities, preferably out of doors if weather and facilities permit.

9:15 to 9:45 - Large Motor and Social Skills Activities

Child-initiated and teacher-prompted (tricycles, kiddie cars, wagons, large hollow blocks, climbing equipment, walking boards and sliding boards, rocking boat, large ball play).

Severely impaired children can usually make good use of only very brief periods of "free" play; therefore, the teacher must take the initiative and structure many interesting large-motor play experiences so that handicapped children can learn to manage their bodies in space and get physical control of their environment. Mazes and obstacle courses, which can be made simple or complex and set up to accommodate wheelchairs and children on "tummy boards" or crutches, are examples of good teacher-structured large-motor activities, figure 9-10.

[4]K. Eileen Allen. "Early Intervention," *Hey, Don't Forget About Me!* ed. M. Angele Thomas (Reston, Virginia: The Council for Exceptional Children, 1976).

Fig. 9-9 Individual health inspection.

Fig. 9-10 Large motor activity on a tummy board.

9:45 to 10:00 - Transition

Rehabilitation of play area by children with teacher's help. (All children can help, at least minimally, in rehabilitating the environment - this is an important way of contributing to and participating in the group.)

Self-help activities (removal of wraps, toileting, nose care, handwashing).

10:00 to 10:20 - Snack and Small Group Language and Social Interaction

Self-feeding skills - drinking, finger feeding, pouring, learning to use utensils.

Social skills - passing, sharing, inviting.

Conversation - children, depending upon their developmental levels, joining in with gestural, vocal, or verbal responses; also specific "casual" language experiences introduced by the teacher.

10:20 to 10:50 - Preacademics (Cognitive, Perceptual-Motor and Language Development Activities)

In small groups, at work tables for most children, with a carefully selected balance of the following activities: sorting, matching, object naming activities; size and form recognition; spatial orientation; number and counting experiences; stories; pencil and scissor tasks.

Learning experiences aimed at task orientation. Learning to attend to auditory and visual stimuli (the teacher and the materials) must be built in as prerequisites, figure 9-11.

10:50 to 11:05 - Transition

Rehabilitation of academic area by children, with teacher's help.

Toileting for those who need it and for those who are being toilet trained. (Children who are being toilet trained may need to be taken to the toilet more frequently.)

11:05 to 11:35 - Creative Activities

Work with creative materials and craft activities: easel paint, fingerpaint, clay, crayons, chalk, paste, scissors, water, wood, glue, stitchery.

> Much teacher prompting and guidance is required for most of these activities, especially in the beginning. Art experience and craft work is an important part of the daily program, however. "Multiply handicapped children *can* learn to work with purpose, with an end product in view. They discover that hands are tools for

Fig. 9-11 Attending to visual stimuli.

> making objects . . . The sense of achievement is a giant step toward some forms of independence."[5]

11:35 to 11:50 - Music and Rhythmic Activities (large group)

Songs and finger plays

Calls, chants, and jingles to promote auditory responses and tone discrimination.

Rhythm instruments.

Patterned rhythmic activities (for example, Looby Lou, Hop Old Squirrel) and free rhythmic movements.

> Severely handicapped children often are not able to improvise movement to music as freely as do normal children, yet there is much they can do even with minimal locomotive skills. Joining in movement and music-making is a tremendously satisfying group experience for all children, but especially for the severely impaired who have little opportunity for communal activities of any kind.

[5] Regina Schattner, *An Early Childhood Curriculum for Multiply Handicapped Children.* The John Day Co., New York, 1971.

Fig. 9-12 Getting ready to go home.

Fig. 9-13 **Teachers must have unlimited enthusiasm for progress.**

11:50 to 12:00 - Departure

Self-help: getting outdoor clothes on, collecting possessions to take home, figure 9-12.

Exchange of farewells - a brief recall of the day's events and a quick preview of what tomorrow holds in store.

TEACHER ATTITUDES

There are a number of other skills that teachers of young handicapped children must have. Many of these, such as observing, recording, setting goals, and determining instructional objectives, have been discussed in earlier units. Others, such as work with parents and application of behavioral principles, will be discussed in later units.

Flexibility

In concluding this unit a few important teacher attitudes regarding handicapped children will be mentioned.[6] Teachers of

[6]J. Weiss. "The Teacher as Actualizer," *Early Intervention: A Team Approach,* eds. K. E. Allen, V. A. Holm, and R. L. Schiefelbush (Baltimore: University Park Press, 1978).

handicapped children must be flexible and able to improvise. They must be able to change the program at short notice in order to match a child's immediate interest or problem. They must be able to accept and cope with children's biological functions and disfunctions. Many handicapped children lack control in crucial areas such as toileting and feeding. Teachers of the handicapped must also maintain an almost unlimited enthusiasm for progress, figure 9-13. They must be able to rejoice for a child regardless of how slow progress may be. An apathetic, indifferent child can "catch" enthusiasm from a patient, skillful, enthusiastic teacher.

Teachers of young handicapped children need to be able to carefully monitor their own responses in order to respond to the most important goals for each child. For example, a goal for one child might be to get that child to talk to other children instead of hitting them. This child may suddenly yell "Mine" while refusing to share a toy. The teacher does *not* try to teach the child how to share at this moment of language success.

Interdisciplinary Interests

One final attitude necessary for the successful teacher of young children (especially the handicapped) will be mentioned. This has to do with working with a variety of other disciplines. It requires keeping an open mind toward the suggestions of other professionals. It requires a willingness to try to create a bridge between the treatment or therapy setting and the classroom. It is in the classroom that the child has many opportunities to practice what has been worked on in speech therapy, physical therapy, or in nutrition sessions. Most children are willing and eager to practice a skill until they master it, if the practice is fun. Through specific planning by the preschool staff such practice can occur naturally and spontaneously, figure 9-14. For example, the speech therapist may want a language-disabled child to practice the "L" sound. Many simple games, songs, and chants can be devised that are fun for all of the children to engage in. The disabled child is not singled out or made to feel different.

SUMMARY

A teacher involved in preschool and day care programs that integrate handicapped children needs the same skills that all preschool teachers need. Of major importance is getting to know the special child as well as possible, and remembering that regardless of the handicap, a child is a child. Thus, teachers must constantly be aware of developmental patterns and learn about the likes, dislikes, and anxieties of each child.

Recognizing teachable moments is important when teaching handicapped and nonhandicapped children. Making use of incidental

Fig. 9-14 Practice of a skill should occur naturally.

teaching opportunities is another skill that allows for effective teaching of all children in the preschool. Another skill that a successful preschool teacher needs is the ability to plan and arrange the environment and the daily schedule appropriately. This allows all children, regardless of skill level, to have satisfying learning experiences.

Teachers with handicapped children in their class need to be flexible and able to improvise. They also need to be able to accept and be pleased with much smaller steps in the learning patterns of many handicapped children. One other special attitude is the willingness to work with other professionals and to incorporate their suggestions into classroom practices.

STUDENT ACTIVITIES

- Locate and list several agencies which serve the handicapped in your community. Select one and find out what kind of training activities or materials they have available for teachers.

- Talk with the teachers in an integrated preschool or day care situation about their handicapped children. Report on their comments, reactions, and special concerns, if any.

- Observe a preschool class. Count the number of children-to-teacher contacts and make a special note if any were used as incidental teaching episodes.

REVIEW

A. Short essay (75 to 125 words)

If extensive retraining is not necessary, what is required to successfully teach young handicapped children?

B. Match each statement in Column I with the correct ending in Column II.

Column I

1. Learning to teach young handicapped children does not require
2. Teachers can obtain assistance in working with handicapped children through such agencies as
3. An essential ingredient in working with handicapped preschoolers is
4. Knowledge of developmental sequences helps in identifying
5. Readiness is a combination of
6. An essential feature of incidental teaching is
7. It appears that mothers do a tremendous amount of teaching
8. Having several attractive centers of interest in the classroom allows for
9. Two important characteristics of successful preschool teachers in integrated settings are
10. Preschool teachers must try to create a bridge between

Column II

a. "on the fly"
b. the treatment (therapy) setting and the preschool classroom
c. extensive retraining
d. avoidance of crowding and conflicts
e. flexibility and an ability to improvise
f. maturation, motivation and opportunity
g. Easter Seal Society, United Cerebral Palsy Association, American Foundation for the Blind
h. child initiation to teacher
i. developmental lags
j. getting to know each child well

C. List seven areas of activities in a preschool daily schedule in addition to the transition periods between activities.

Unit 10 BEHAVIORAL PRINCIPLES AND THE PRESCHOOL TEACHER

OBJECTIVES

After studying this unit, the student will be able to:

- Build a strong case for the use of behavioral principles in teaching all young children and especially young handicapped children.

- Define adult social reinforcement, give reasons for its importance when working with young children, and give examples of five different types.

- Give a detailed summary of what the teacher must do in order to shape (that is, help young children to acquire) new behaviors that are developmentally appropriate.

The preschool and day care teacher who has basic knowledge of child development and early childhood education can readily learn to teach young handicapped children successfully. There is, however, one additional approach to early education that will make the job easier and more enjoyable. This approach is to use the teaching tactics that come from the principles of behavior analysis. Developmental theory provides the basic framework within which behavior changes are planned and implemented. This can lead to an effective learning environment.

BEHAVIOR CHANGE AND LEARNING

All teachers need such training. Effective teaching involves changing children's behavior in certain, specifiable ways. Behavior change is what learning is all about, figure 10-1. Every time a child learns a new response, that child's behavior has been changed. Example:

Fig. 10-1 Behavior change is what learning is all about.

Yesterday Joy could not count to 10; today she can.

Last month Susie could not ride a tricycle; yesterday she learned.

This morning Bart built a block town for the first time.

In these examples, children's behavior has been changed. The children can now behave in ways which they could not have earlier.

The use of behavioral procedures to ease learning is especially important for teachers of young handicapped children for several reasons:

- Handicapped children have so much more to learn because of their deficits and delays.

- Handicapped children often learn more slowly.

- Handicapped children may have much difficulty in learning.

- Even simple tasks that are learned easily by most children may require great effort on the part of the handicapped child.

Valuable developmental time can be saved when a teacher knows how to sequence preschool tasks in different ways and in different-sized steps for different children, figure 10-2. Additional developmental time can be saved when a teacher knows how to intervene so that undesirable responses are not learned. This is a very important behavioral principle where handicapped children are concerned. Their learning must not be disturbed further by acquiring inappropriate responses that interfere with the learning of basic developmental tasks.

All Children Are Teachable

A knowledge of behavioral principles also prevents a teaching staff from taking the "easy way out." In one article, it has been stated: "Traditionally, an individual who did not learn what was presented was considered

Fig. 10-2 Teachers must know how to sequence tasks.

incapable, indifferent, unmotivated, or lacking. The behavioral view, on the other hand, is that if the student does not learn, something is lacking in the teaching situation."[1]   The behavioral approach never blames the child for not learning. Every child, even the most severely handicapped, is considered teachable. This is a very important concept for teachers to understand when working with all young children.

OVERVIEW OF REINFORCEMENT TECHNIQUES

Much has been written about behavioral management with young children, both handicapped and nonhandicapped. Several useful books are listed at the end of this unit. An in-depth treatment of the subject is not,

[1]S. W. Bijou and B. W. Cole. "The Feasibility of Providing Effective Educational Programs for the Severely and Profoundly Retarded," *Educating the 24-hour Retarded Child* (Papers presented at the Conference on Education of Severely and Profoundly Retarded Students, National Association for Retarded Citizens, New Orleans, LA, March, 1975) Arlington, TX: NARC, 1975.

however, within the scope of this text. Therefore, a practical and nontechnical overview is presented. These principles, referred to as reinforcement procedures, have proven to be useful in working with young children. The same principles are often labeled in other ways, such as:

- applied behavior analysis
- behavior management
- behavior modification
- contingency management
- operant conditioning

A well-organized preschool curriculum usually sets specific child skills and behaviors as goals. These are taught through guidance procedures and techniques based on reinforcement principles. Such procedures apply to both group and individual behaviors.

Adult Social Reinforcement

These principles are taken from research in behavior analysis, more commonly called

behavior modification. This research demonstrates that behavior responds to its immediate consequences. A common readily controlled consequence of the behavior of all young children is adult attention. Studies have shown that adult attention is a powerful reinforcer (consequence). Attention tends to increase those behaviors which it consistently and immediately follows. The opposite is also true. When attention is consistently and immediately withdrawn or withheld, the behaviors are decreased.

Adult attention, or adult social reinforcement, includes the following kinds of attention directed towards a child or a group of children:

- Verbal responses and comments directed to the child and appropriate to the situation: approval, praise, and appreciation.

- Standing or sitting close to a child and looking at, watching, nodding at, smiling at, listening to, or showing genuine interest in the child, figure 10-3.

Fig. 10-3 Positive reinforcement: a teacher's smiling, watching, listening, and caring.

- Physical contact with a child such as a pat, a hug, or holding a child's hand.

- Giving support on equipment, pushing a swing, or joining in a child-initiated activity.

- Bringing the child special supplementary materials, or providing a special activity or short excursion (trip to the preschool kitchen, ride in the elevator) with an adult.

The practical application of reinforcement principles to guidance and teaching in the preschool or day care setting involves carrying out two basic procedures:

- Teachers should immediately attend to (reinforce) the child's desirable behaviors.

- Teachers should immediately withdraw their attention (withhold reinforcement) every time an undesirable behavior is observed. Attention should be withheld for as long as the undesirable behavior lasts, figure 10-4.

These procedures can be used to teach the specific skills outlined in any curriculum. They are carried out through the techniques which follow.

Fig. 10-4 Withholding teacher attention.

Shaping, or Reinforcement of Successive Approximations

This involves programming an ordered sequence of learning tasks. It is often referred to as task analysis, which is breaking a task down into small, orderly, logical steps. This also calls for selective reinforcement of each progressively better step toward successful accomplishment of a task.

With this format, a learning task sequence is adapted for each child. It starts with what the child can do - what approximation to the desired end behavior the child can do right now. The process progresses from the known, simple, and easy to the more difficult and complex. This order provides opportunities to reinforce the child's present successes. It also allows the teacher to watch carefully in order to give reinforcement for responses which come closer to achieving the desired end behavior (terminal behavior).

An example of such a programmed sequence, used to teach ladder climbing, follows:

a. The ladder is set up safely in an interesting arrangement with other equipment.

b. The child is first reinforced for approaching and touching the ladder.

c. The child is then reinforced for putting a foot on the lowest rung of the ladder. Both verbal and physical help may be offered to aid the child in learning the specific movements needed to climb the ladder.

d. Reinforcement is given for all ladder-climbing that represents progress in independent climbing.

e. The ladder can then be moved to other locations, and reinforcement for climbing continued.

f. A longer ladder or other ladders may then be introduced for use in different climbing situations.

g. When climbing behavior is well established, social reinforcement for climbing

Fig. 10-5 **When climbing behavior is well established, teacher attention is gradually reduced.**

Fig. 10-6 **"You got your coat down all by yourself!"**

is gradually reduced, figure 10-5. The activity itself has become fun for the child and is therefore self-reinforcing.

Some techniques call for giving and then reducing physical assistance, verbal directions, and cues in the teaching of a new skill. In the beginning phases of teaching a new skill, the teacher helps the child perform the necessary movements involved in the skill. This is often called *prompting*. Prompting can also take the form of simple and easily understood verbal directions to the child. As the child gains competence in learning the task, the teacher's help and directions are gradually withdrawn. Instead, independent performance is reinforced.

For example, in teaching a child to hang up a coat, the following prompts (help and directions) can be offered:

1. The child is led to the locker with the verbal cue, "This is your locker; here is the hook for your coat."
2. The teacher demonstrates and explains, "Use this loop to hang your coat on this hook."

3. "Find the loop on your coat. That's right."
4. "Hold the coat by the loop. Good."
5. "Slip the loop over the hook. Fine. You did it all by yourself!" figure 10-6.

Physical assistance is gradually reduced (faded) while verbal directions are continued. As the child learns the sequence of actions necessary to hang up the coat, the teacher reduces the verbal directions. The teacher uses only those directions required to cue the child to make the next step. Cues and help should be given often and long enough that the child succeeds while learning.

Some children may require more steps, smaller and more precise. Some might need more teacher assistance. In many cases, the teacher can place a hand around the child's hand, and guide the child's hand through the required motions. Once the child has the "feel" of the required movements, the teacher gradually reduces that particular kind of physical prompting. Such assistance is often referred to as manual prompting.

Before going on to the other basic reinforcement concepts, the crucial processes of shaping (prompting and fading) will be reviewed.

Summary of Shaping Procedures

1. Observe the child. Find out what the child can do.
2. Decide upon an objective - what the child should be able to do as an end product.
3. Begin the task analysis process. Break the objective down into smaller tasks or units.
4. Sequence these units or subtasks in an orderly fashion from least to most difficult.
5. Begin to teach the first step, reinforcing the child immediately after each appropriate attempt. Each step may take quite a while. Prompts may be needed often.
6. Reduce (fade) prompts as a response is learned and begin to move toward the next step.
7. Give reinforcement only for behaviors that are closer and closer to the desired end behavior goal.
8. Move through the steps gradually. Never hurry the child, figure 10-7. Be sure the child has mastered each step before moving on.
9. Do not nag or scold. When teachers find it necessary to do that, the steps are probably too large. The steps should be made smaller so that the child can succeed and the teacher can reinforce that success.

The key to successful shaping is to "think small." The smaller the steps the better. This gives the child more chances to succeed and thus move more rapidly through the steps.[2]

[2]Adapted from Head Start manual, Dave Evans and John Keily

Fig. 10-7 Never hurry the child.

Scheduling

Scheduling refers to the amount and frequency of reinforcement given for the behavior being learned. A schedule of continuous reinforcement is the most effective type in the beginning stages of learning a new behavior. On a continuous reinforcement schedule, the teacher gives positive attention every time the behavior occurs. As the skill is learned, the success achieved by the child seems to take over as a reinforcer for the behavior. This is often referred to as intrinsic reinforcement. The amount and frequency of teacher reinforcement can then be reduced gradually.

A five-step reinforcement schedule for the ladder-climbing sequence can be planned as follows:

1. Every incident of the use of the ladder is reinforced while the behavior lasts.
2. Reinforcement is given for all ladder-climbing that represents any slight improved skill in climbing.
3. The first few minutes of each incident of ladder-climbing is reinforced.
4. Every second or third incident of ladder-climbing is approved and attended to.
5. Occasional reinforcement for ladder-climbing, similar to that given to any child engaged in a constructive activity, is maintained, figure 10-8.

Chaining[3]

All behaviors in everyday life are actually complex chains composed of many smaller behaviors. For example, a young child who has learned to eat soup by herself has learned many other behaviors. These behaviors, when linked together, lead to the neat and tidy eating of soup. Behaviors in the chain of successful soup-eating include mastering a number of behaviors along a developmental sequence:

1. grasping the spoon
2. dipping with it
3. keeping a liquid on the spoon while carrying it to the mouth (this was preceded

[3]Robert P. Hawkins, "Behavior Analysis and Early Childhood Education: Engineering Children's Learning," *Psychological Processes in Early Education* (NY: Academic Press, Inc., 1977).

Fig. 10-8 Occasional reinforcement for ladder climbing is maintained.

Fig. 10-9 The child tightens the bow.

by a developmentally simpler task, that of getting and keeping solids on the spoon)

4. getting the spoon and the soup into the mouth instead of down the chin
5. getting the soup off the spoon and into the mouth without choking

Chaining can be used as a teaching device in two different ways: backward chaining and forward chaining. In backward chaining, the last link in the chain is taught first. Next, the second-to-last link is taught, and so on, in reverse order, throughout the entire response chain. For example, teaching children to tie their shoes can best be done through backward chaining. The teacher (or parent) does the whole job except for the final tightening of the bow, figure 10-9. The child is taught to do this through manual and verbal prompting. Once the child can tie the bow, the next-to-the-last step is taught: pulling one half of the bow through the loop. Now the child can do the last two links in the chain. This process is continued until the child can do the entire shoe-tying job alone.

Forward chaining is exactly the reverse. It begins by teaching the first link in the chain. Certain response chains can only be taught in this way. The soup-eating task is one example. The child who has not learned to grasp a spoon cannot be taught to get a spoonful of liquid into the mouth. Soup-eating must be taught by forward chaining according to this example.

There are certain chains of behavior which may be taught either way. For these behaviors there is no one right way. In each instance, teachers should select the way that is fastest and requires the least effort on the part of child and teacher. The choice should also rest on which process, backward or forward, is likely to produce the fewest errors. It is very important to keep errors from developing in the chain. Once errors

Fig. 10-10 Chaining can be used to establish bathroom routines in the preschool.

have been practiced a few times they become very difficult to eliminate.

There are a number of chains that children need to learn in preschool and day care settings. These include such things as:

- getting out materials and putting them away
- going through the bathroom routine, figure 10-10
- preparing for nap time
- leaving for home

Certain teaching procedures are advisable when teaching the above chains (routines) or any other chains common to a preschool program. Teachers should arrange orderly practice sessions. These practice sessions should include many prompts. Only a small group of children practice at one time. In this way, teachers can easily spot errors and prevent them from becoming set in the chain.

Prompts can gradually be reduced and the groups increased in size. Eventually, all children will perform the chain without error and with a minimum of teacher intervention.

Reinforcing Behaviors

The reinforcement of skills and behaviors which are incompatible with (that is, compete with) undesirable behaviors is another important and basic reinforcement principle. It can be understood more readily by giving an example:

Often there is a child who lacks skills in block-building; some children actually do not know how to play with blocks. Such children are often disruptive in the block area, causing frustration for other children and teachers. In other words, their behavior in the block area is most undesirable. All such children may be helped to develop block-building skills if the teacher gives attention to their most basic attempts to structure the blocks. Such a structure may be a tower only 3 blocks high or a road only three blocks long which the teacher has helped the child to build. At the same time, the teacher ignores all incompatible

Fig. 10-11 Focusing teacher attention on one child's positive block activity.

behaviors — aimless and disruptive block manipulation. Improved skills tend to increase the child's interest and participation in constructive block play. The undesirable manipulation of blocks is "crowded out." This technique focuses the teacher's attention on the positive aspects of the child's behavior, figure 10-11, rather than on the negative aspects.

Withdrawing or Withholding Reinforcement

Teachers may withhold reinforcement from a child who is engaging in inappropriate behavior by:

- busying themselves with something else and thus not giving the child attention

- removing the equipment or material from the child who is misusing it

- removing the child from the play situation

For example, the child who is playing aimlessly or disruptively with the blocks might first be ignored while the teacher watches for some improvement in block play that could be attended to. If the undesirable play continues, the child might be told, "We will put the blocks away if you are not going to build with them." If the child becomes more disruptive, kicking or throwing the blocks, the teacher then removes the child with the statement, "You cannot play with blocks when you kick them."

In some extreme instances, a teacher may have to use "time-out." Time-out is removing a child from the activity. The child may be directed to an area of the room where no attention of any kind, from either teacher or children, is given to the child. The time-out procedure should be used only as a last resort. It should be used only for very serious behaviors that teachers have not been able to eliminate through ignoring inappropriate behavior and reinforcing the desirable behaviors.

In those rare cases where time-out has to be used, the time-out period should be kept short. A good rule of thumb is that time-out should last no longer than 1 to 3 minutes after the child is quiet in the time-out area. It must be remembered that in time-out, children only learn what *not* to do. In order to learn what *to do* they must be free to operate in the preschool setting, figure 10-12, where teachers can attend to the children's appropriate behaviors.

Fig. 10-12 Learning "what to do" requires that children have opportunities to engage in the activity.

Consistency

A necessary part of an effective reinforcement schedule is to maintain consistent consequences (contingencies) for children's behaviors. All guidance procedures should be formed and analyzed in frequent staff conferences. All decisions should be based on ongoing observations made by teachers and consultants. This leads to consistent contingency management. Teachers agree on expectations for the behavior of each child. They also agree on uniform procedures for guiding and teaching the group, figure 10-13. No teacher, for example, would let any child leave a coat tossed carelessly on the floor of the cubby if the staff agreement was that all children should be learning to hang up their coats.

In maintaining consistency in managing the children it is also important to keep school rules to a minimum. Rules in a preschool should establish limits essential to the health and safety of all the children. These would include such things as:

- No pushing in high places.
- No hitting with hard objects in the hands.

Fig. 10-13 Teachers must agree on uniform procedures for guiding the group.

- No throwing of blocks, rocks, or other similar objects.
- No throwing of sand.
- No leaving the play yard unless a teacher goes along.

Once a rule has been stated it must be followed by all the children. "No sand throwing" means just that for every child in the group, even the most severely retarded. There must not be a double standard. Skillful use of reinforcement procedures allows all children to learn what to do and what not to do.

In addition to keeping rules at a minimum, teacher directions should also be kept to a minimum. Directions should be given only if the teacher can make sure the directions are carried out. This may require giving additional prompts and cues to many children. When giving directions or instructions, remember that it is more helpful to say, "Hold tight with both hands" than it is to say, "Be careful." The same is true when verbally reinforcing or praising children. Use descriptive praise. If the teacher says, "Good for you. You put all the red pegs in the red holes." instead of, "Good boy" or "Good job" the child knows exactly what has been done correctly. The teacher has praised that child descriptively, figure 10-14.

The procedures described are the basic behavioral procedures used for teaching all young children, both handicapped and nonhandicapped. The use of reinforcement procedures allows teachers to truly respect all individual differences. Each child's program is based on the developmental level of that particular child. It is also based upon how fast or slowly the child can learn and how large or small the steps need to be for that child. Such considerations are essential when carrying out all kinds of preschool programs for all kinds of children. These principles are further described in Section 4 of this text. The reader will learn about the practical application of these procedures in helping children to acquire the various developmental skills.

SUMMARY

Teachers of young children need a thorough understanding of behavioral principles. These are often referred to as reinforcement procedures. Reinforcement procedures combined with a sound developmental approach provides a positive learning environment for all young children.

Adult attention is a powerful reinforcer for young children. It can be used effectively to help a child learn new or more complex behaviors. Such procedures are often referred to as shaping, or reinforcing successive approximations to the desired behavior. Task analysis is one of the skills a teacher uses with this part of the process. Task analysis requires breaking the task down into small, logical steps.

Other procedures in a behavior approach to early education include the appropriate

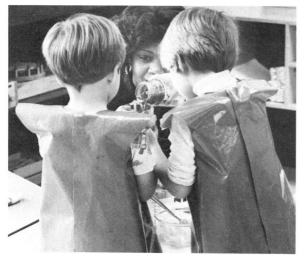

Fig. 10-14 Descriptive praise: "Good! You are pouring the honey so carefully."

scheduling of reinforcers, the reinforcement of behaviors that are incompatible with undesired behaviors, and forward and backward chaining. The withholding or withdrawing of reinforcement and the use of time-out are other important procedures. Time-out should be used as little as possible and then only briefly, not more than three minutes after the child is quiet.

Consistency is one of the most important parts of an effective child development-behavioral approach to early education. Rules should be few but held to firmly for all children. A good behavioral procedure to use with all children is to tell them what to do, instead of what not to do. Descriptive praise is another effective procedure in helping children learn what to do.

STUDENT ACTIVITIES

- With several members of your class, write to the author of this text. Request case studies which the author has published regarding the use of reinforcement procedures in early childhood education. Read these case studies in small groups and report back on each to the class as a whole.

- Observe in a preschool or day care setting. Write down every instance of adult reinforcement that you see or hear directed toward a child.

- Write a backward chaining sequence for teaching normally developing children to make their own beds.

REVIEW

A. Briefly answer each of the following.

1. List three skills that show that behavior change demonstrates learning.

2. Give three reasons why handicapped children may need more extra help than normally developing children.

3. There are a number of terms which mean nearly the same as reinforcement procedures. One of these is applied behavior analysis. Give four more.

4. List five types of adult social reinforcement.

5. What are two basic procedures for teachers to remember in the practical application of reinforcement procedures?

6. Briefly summarize the five main steps in the shaping procedure.

7. Name the two types of chaining.

8. Specify three examples of routines, or chains of behavior, that young children in a preschool need to learn.

9. What are two ways that teachers can withhold adult social reinforcement from a child who is behaving inappropriately?

10. What is the most important reason for avoiding the use of time-out for a misbehaving child?

B. Match each item in Column I with the correct item in Column II.

Column I	Column II

Column I

1. behavior management
2. adult social reinforcement
3. reinforcing successive approximations
4. prompting
5. schedule
6. chaining
7. incompatible behavior
8. consistent consequences
9. descriptive praise
10. task analysis

Column II

a. behaviors linked together
b. contingencies
c. shaping
d. approval, praise, appreciation
e. specifying what the child has done right
f. physically helping a child to perform necessary actions
g. breaking a task into small, logical steps
h. operant conditioning
i. frequency of reinforcement
j. competing behavior

BOOK LIST

Evans, Ellis D. "Behavior Analysis Procedures." *Contemporary Influences in Early Childhood Education,* NY: Holt, Rinehart, and Winston, 1975, pp 87–171.

Gelfand, Donna M. *Social Learning in Childhood: Readings in Theory and Application,* 2nd ed., Monterey, CA: Brooks/Cole Publishing Company, 1975.

Haring, Norris G. *Behavior of Exceptional Children: An Introduction to Special Education.* Columbus, OH: Charles E. Merrill Publishing Company, 1974.

Krumboltz, John D. and Helen. *Changing Children's Behavior.* Englewood Cliffs, NJ: Prentice-Hall, Inc., 1972.

Patterson, Gerald R., and Gullion, M. Elizabeth. *Living With Children: New Methods for Parents and Teachers,* rev. ed., Champaign, IL: Research Press Company, 1971.

Sheppard, William C. *Teaching Social Behavior to Young Children,* Champaign, IL: Research Press Company, 1973.

Vance, Barbara. *Teaching the Prekindergarten Child: Instructional Design and Curriculum.* Monterey, CA: Brooks/Cole Publishing Company, 1973.

Watson, Luke S. Jr. *Child Behavior Modification: A Manual for Teachers, Nurses, and Parents.* Elmsford, NY: Pergamon Press, Inc., 1973.

SECTION 4
THE DEVELOPMENTAL CURRICULUM

Unit 11 CURRICULUM APPROACHES

OBJECTIVES

After studying this unit, the student will be able to

- Name and briefly describe five approaches to curriculum design.
- Describe curriculum from two actual preschool programs in some detail.
- Discuss the advantages of a developmental approach for the integrated preschool.

The aim of every early childhood education curriculum is to help each child grow and develop more completely and more happily. This means that each child must have the opportunity to learn and use a wide range of skills and behaviors, figure 11-1. These skills and behaviors range from simple motor skills to very complex behavioral patterns. An example of this range might be from simply standing on one foot to a complicated game of hopscotch.

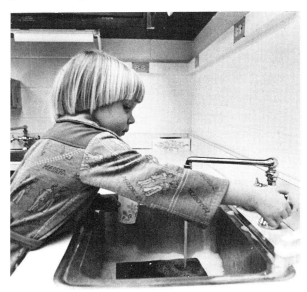

Fig. 11-1 Each child has the opportunity to use a wide range of behaviors.

CURRICULUM RATIONALE

Every curriculum model should represent a point of view. In other words, the model is based upon a particular rationale, theory, or philosophy. Statements should be made regarding:

- purpose of the curriculum
- content areas (learning activities to be included)
- methods of implementation
- long- and short-range goals
- age and type of children for which curriculum is intended.

There are many approaches to designing curriculum for young children, both handicapped and nonhandicapped. A review of design procedures was made by examining information from twenty First Chance programs.[1] The First Chance Network began in 1968 as a part of the Handicapped Children's Early Education Program. An analysis of twenty of these programs led to

[1] Mary M. Wood and Oliver L. Hurley. "Curriculum and Instruction," *Early Childhood Education for Exceptional Children: A Handbook of Ideas and Exemplary Practices,* eds. June B. Jordon, et. al., (Reston, VA: Council for Exceptional Children, 1977).

the conclusion that First Chance curricula were organized in five basic ways. These are described below and can be considered representative of most preschool intervention programs.

Amelioration of Deficits Approach

Amelioration means to improve. A curriculum based on this rationale starts with the specific problems of the children. The content of the curriculum, that is, the "what to teach" part, comes directly from the assessment of each child. Teaching is directed toward the correcting of specific deficits or delays.

Basic Skills Approach

Curriculum planning in this approach begins with the skills children use in the process of learning. Curriculum content and activities are organized around such skills as

- language
- paying attention
- sensory motor processes
- social skills

Fig. 11-2 When children are asked to line up for recess, do they show they heard what was said?

- perception (awareness of objects and events)
- auditory processes (acting appropriately upon what is heard), figure 11-2
- gross and fine motor skill
- self-help skills
- memory

The Developmental Approach

Curriculum models patterned upon this approach use sequences of normal development as a base. Tasks for skill development are arranged in a hierarchy or specific order. The order comes from sequencing from the least difficult to the most difficult skills. The sequencing may also come from the order found in normal growth and development. This is often referred to as the maturation process. For example, one would not try to teach a young child to run if that child was not yet walking. In this curriculum approach, content tends to be based upon broad areas of child development. These are usually classified as physical, social, affective (emotional), and intellectual.

The Psychological Constructs Approach

This approach is based upon concepts from psychological theories. A curriculum organized around this rationale may include one or more of the following:

- improving self-concept
- establishing self-control and self-management
- creativity, figure 11-3
- motivation
- sex role identification
- gratification of needs
- cognition

Fig. 11-3 Fostering creativity is one curriculum goal.

Fig. 11-4 Music and rhythm in early education.

These items represent psychological processes thought to explain human behavior. Curriculum activities are directed toward improving the chosen process.

Educational Content Approach

This curriculum model begins with areas of academic content. Curriculum content is built upon the preacademic skills that are to be learned. The areas most often focused upon are

- prereading
- prearithmetic
- language
- early forms of social studies
- music, art, and dance, figure 11-4
- nature

Curriculum models do not usually represent a pure form of any one major theoretical approach. Most models are constructed around a combination of these basic approaches. A number of curriculum models combine the first and second types. Thus, the deficits amelioration and the basic skills approaches seem to work out well when used together. The second and third types (basic skills sequenced developmentally) have also been combined effectively. Seldom is a curriculum developed entirely around a psychological concept. However, almost every curriculum approach includes some psychological constructs, such as self-concept, cognition, or motivation.

REPRESENTATIVE MODELS

Four curriculum models are described briefly. These represent the various approaches which were just described. (The psychological model is not described because it is not usually used alone.) The similarities and differences among the models are noted.

The Detroit Preschool[2]

This curriculum model is one that has a deficits amelioration focus. It is built upon three major objectives:

[2]The Detroit Michigan Preschool Technical Assistance Resource and Training Center.

Fig. 11-5 Motor functioning is an important curriculum area.

Fig. 11-6 Motor-social development is another item in the preschool curriculum.

- to identify strengths and weaknesses in each child

- to improve the weaknesses

- to conduct systematic and periodic reevaluations of the children

The curriculum covers five areas:

- gross motor functioning, figure 11-5

- fine motor functioning

- visual perception and discrimination

- auditory discrimination

- language functioning

The children are taught individually and in groups. The project uses its own Preschool Developmental Assessment Scale to obtain a periodic progress report on each child. The information is then analyzed to plan group and individual learning activities aimed at improving deficiencies.

Schaumburg Early Education Center (SEEC)[3]

The SEEC curriculum focuses on primary basic skills and developmental tasks. It begins with a checklist of developmental milestones. Directions for aiding a child's development are targeted. Developmental goals are worked out. Activity planning comes next. Finally, guidelines for carrying out ongoing evaluation are specified. The curriculum is thus individualized for each child.

The basic curriculum materials are entitled Development Milestones - Miniwheel and Maxiwheel and Action Experiences. The curriculum content is organized around the child. The teachers react to the child and use five developmental milestones as a frame of reference. These milestones are

- intellectual development

- language development

- motor-social development, figure 11-6

[3]Schaumburg Early Education Center (SEEC), Community Consolidated School District 54, 804 W. Bode Road, Schaumburg, IL 60172.

- social-emotional development
- self-help skills

The curriculum is intended for children 3 to 6 years of age.

Developmental Tasks Approach

The Chapel Hill Project[4] is a good example of a developmental tasks orientation. This First Chance Project is known for its LAP curriculum materials. These come in three volumes:

The Learning Accomplishment Profile
The Infant LAP
A Planning Guide to the Preschool Curriculum: The Child, The Process, The Day

The LAP itself has three sections:

An evaluation checklist. This is developmental from 0 to 6 years of age. It is used to identify a child's abilities and deficits. Curriculum objectives for each child are found from this. The LAP covers basically the same areas as the SEEC:

- gross and fine motor development
- language development
- cognitive development
- social skills
- self-help skills, figure 11-7

A task level profile of skills. This describes different activities in terms of levels of functioning. It serves as a checklist and as a guide for what to teach and the sequence in which to teach it. The items on the checklist are easily translated into behavioral objectives.

Concepts units. This consists of 44 units divided into discrete concepts. These are arranged from simple to complex.

Fig. 11-7 Self-help skills are necessary learnings.

Educational Content Approach

The curriculum for the Early Learning Center[5] is titled *Curriculum Guide: Early Learning Center for Exceptional Children.* It is an example of an educational content orientation with some of the basic skills approach blended in. The curriculum contains the following sections:

- the role of the social worker
- language program
- speech therapy at home
- story telling and finger play
- holidays and field trips

[4]Chapel Hill Training Outreach Project, Chapel Hill, Carrboro City School System, Lincoln Center, Merritt Mill Road, Chapel Hill, NC 27514

[5]Early Childhood Learning Center, Patricia G. Adkins, Director, 1 Zuni, P. O. Box 10716, El Paso, Texas 79905

Fig. 11-8 Playground activities are a part of each day.

- art activities

- cooking

- self-help and socialization

- music

- physical activities and playground activities, figure 11-8

- conceptual skills

Various units and activities are presented within each section. The program is intended for multihandicapped children 3 to 5 years of age.

There is also a follow-up curriculum for kindergarten and first grade children. This is entitled *Structured Experiences for Developmental Learning.* It is useful in providing educational continuity for handicapped children as they are mainstreamed into public school settings.

DEVELOPMENTAL AND BEHAVIORAL COMPONENTS

As can be seen from these four samples of so-called different approaches to curriculum design, there are many similarities. Looking at early childhood curricula as a whole, there

is no evidence that one approach is better than another. This is true for curriculum models intended for handicapped children, for nonhandicapped children, and for integrated groups of children. For all children, and especially handicapped, there appears to be two parts that are crucial, however, to truly effective programming.

Fig. 11-9   Teachers must understand the "whole child."

The first is a systematic behavior management approach used in implementation of the chosen curriculum. Research studies suggest that a behavior management approach is the most effective way of helping handicapped children to learn. This concept will be explored in detail in the following unit. The other part of an effective curriculum is a firm, theoretical anchoring in normal growth and development. This means a good grasp of developmental milestones and sequences. It also means recognizing how all areas of development are related. This has been labeled the "whole child" concept, figure 11-9. This concept has many implications for sound developmental learning experiences for all children in the integrated preschool. It is this part of a good integrated early childhood curriculum which will be discussed here.

Developmental Considerations

As mentioned before, young children, whether handicapped or not, are more alike than they are different. Their needs are very much alike. All need

- opportunities to learn through exploring, experimenting, and discovering

Fig. 11-10 Opportunities to learn by imitation from other children and responsive adults.

- activities designed to provide stimulation of all of the senses - vision, hearing, touch, taste, and smell

- well-arranged play experiences balanced by carefully sequenced, teacher-structured learning activities

- opportunities to learn by imitation from other children and responsive adults, figure 11-10

Handicapped and nonhandicapped children need to be cherished and respected. They need opportunities to try and to succeed. Thus they can receive recognition and praise for their efforts, as well as for their achievements. A developmental program format is suitable for all types of children. For handicapped and nonhandicapped children it can be adapted to a wide range of developmental differences among children. It can

- accommodate group as well as individualized programming

- allow children to move at their own paces, yet ensure they do keep moving, with some gentle insistence, if needed

- provide planned and integrated learning experiences in all areas of development (these will be the focus of future units)

- operate in the least restrictive social and physical setting possible so that no child is unnecessarily constrained

Learning Through Play

Many of the learnings in a developmental curriculum are acquired through a variety of play experiences. Nonhandicapped children seem to move through a play-oriented program on their own, self-propelled. They learn new skills and practice them in the course of self-initiated play activities. They are quick to participate in group play activities. They give eager attention to teacher-suggested play activities.

This may not be the case with many of the more severely handicapped children in an integrated preschool. These children often have very few, if any, play skills. Nevertheless, a developmental curriculum that relies on play as the major avenue for learning is usually suitable for these children, too. It is suitable, that is, if teachers actually teach these children how to play. This can be done, even though it may sound contrary to traditional child development principles. It requires

- getting the child oriented in the direction of an activity
- helping the child to make visual and physical contact with the material or piece of equipment, figure 11-11
- rejoicing with the child when the first contact with the material is accomplished (even if the child is involved with the material only because the teacher has a hand around the child's hand, physically shaping the grasping response)
- arranging for the child to be near other children in a given activity in order to promote imitation of play behaviors
- gradually helping other children to include the handicapped child in play activities (this will not be effective until the child has acquired responses)

Gentle Insistence

Sometimes a gentle type of pressure may be necessary to get a child to even try a play

Fig. 11-11 Helping the child to make visual and physical contact with materials.

Fig. 11-12 Using basic principles of child development in planning curriculum.

activity. For example, the physical therapist may suggest tricycle riding for a particular 3 1/2 year old girl. It becomes an instructional objective for this child even though, for most children, it is play. This particular child, however, never rode a tricycle and appears to be fearful of it. She resists even getting on one.

Efforts to get such a child on a tricycle often result in the child's resistance and crying. This is where gentle, helpful insistence may be what is needed. The teacher may have to put the child on the tricycle in spite of the child's resistance. If this is necessary, the teacher is careful to provide the child with constant physical support. Physical support is continued until the child begins to enjoy the fun of riding the tricycle. This usually occurs very soon, especially if the tricycle has been adapted for the particular child with various devices such as trunk support bar and stirrups. As the child's skill develops, other children are gradually introduced into the activity. Thus, another curriculum area, the development of social skills, can be worked on in the context of a play experience.

Using basic principles of child development in planning curriculum for the integrated preschool works well for all children, figure 11-12. These principles can be used in combination with most approaches. They provide an underlying structure with which most teachers are comfortable.

SUMMARY

Curriculum models for early education programs should have a rationale, representing a philosophical point of view. There are five common rationales, although most are used in combination. The developmental approach is the one often combined with some other approach.

There is no evidence to suggest that one approach is better than any other. One strong similarity, however, that runs through many integrated preschool curricula is the developmental approach. There are a number of reasons for this. It can accommodate all types of children. It shows that handicapped and nonhandicapped children are more alike than they are different. It is an approach with which most preschool teachers are comfortable.

STUDENT ACTIVITIES

- Observe a preschool or day care classroom. Make notes that will help you decide if the program is like any of the curriculum models described in this unit.

- Talk with some members of an early childhood staff regarding the rationale for the curriculum model used in their classroom.

- Write to one of the preschool programs mentioned in this unit and ask for more information about their program.

REVIEW

A. List the five basic ways in which the First Chance curriculum models were grouped. Give the major principles for each.

B. Select the three best answers from the choices offered to complete each statement.

1. The Detroit Preschool curriculum covers
   a. gross and fine motor skills.
   b. reading, writing, and arithmetic.
   c. visual and auditory discrimination.
   d. language functioning.

2. The three sections of the LAP are
   a. the TAP (Teacher Attribute Project).
   b. the evaluation checklist.
   c. the task level profile.
   d. 44 concept units.

3. The Early Learning Center has
   a. a curriculum guide for exceptional children.
   b. a follow-up curriculum for kindergarten and first-grade children.
   c. an extend curriculum for 4th, 5th, and 6th grades.
   d. a curriculum which is a combination of educational content and a basic skills approach.

4. The SEEC curriculum
   a. focuses on primary basic skills and developmental tasks.
   b. has a checklist of developmental milestones.
   c. has materials entitled Action Experiences for Miniwheel Activities.
   d. is for children 3 to 6 years of age.

5. None of the four preschool models described
   a. focus primarily on reading, writing, and arithmetic.
   b. are for all children aged 0 to 8 years.
   c. are strictly home-based.
   d. include parts of one or more of the other models.

6. In an integrated classroom where a developmental approach is used, handicapped children can be provided with learning experiences
   a. unsuitable for nonhandicapped children.
   b. that can be obtained through play.
   c. designed to stimulate the various senses.
   d. that allow opportunities to imitate.

7. Handicapped children
   a. can learn through play.
   b. can seldom learn through play.
   c. may not know how to play.
   d. sometimes need to be taught to play.

8. Gentle insistence does not mean
   a. forcing a child to ride a tricycle no matter how frightened the child may be.
   b. making a child stay after school if that child refuses to wear the prescribed hearing aid.
   c. being sensitive to children's fears but finding ways to help them overcome their anxieties about engaging in healthful prescribed activities.
   d. removing a child from the class who will not cooperate in various healthful preschool activities.

9. Use of basic principles of child development in planning a curriculum for the integrated preschool
   a. works only for older preschoolers.
   b. is good for both handicapped and nonhandicapped children.
   c. does not need to take the place of other approaches.
   d. provides a curriculum foundation with which most preschool teachers are comfortable.

10. The aims of all good early childhood curriculum models for integrated classrooms should be
    a. to help each child grow and develop as completely and happily as possible.
    b. to provide each child with specific lessons in reading, writing, arithmetic, social studies, and physical education.
    c. to provide many opportunities for each child to learn and use a wide range of skills.
    d. to move children along a developmental path starting with very simple skills and moving toward more complex skills.

C. Briefly answer each of the following.
   1. What is the origin of the First Chance Network?
   2. How are concept units arranged?
   3. With what can the maturation process be compared?
   4. What two parts seem to be necessary additions to a curriculum approach if the approach is to be effective?
   5. State four ways in which a curriculum format based on developmental processes serves an integrated preschool group.

Unit 12 SOCIAL SKILLS

OBJECTIVES

After studying this unit, the student will be able to

- Define social skills in general terms including how these skills relate to other areas of development.
- Describe the stages of social development and social play from birth through the preschool years.
- List and describe five main strategies for helping delayed or handicapped children be a part of the social activities in the preschool.

Learning appropriate social behaviors is one of the major developmental efforts of all young children. Many authorities believe that this may be the child's single most important accomplishment. Every type of child, from the severely impaired to the most gifted, needs these skills. A good life for all children depends on having satisfying interactions with others, figure 12-1. Satisfying interactions

Fig. 12-1 A good life depends upon satisfying interactions with others.

cannot take place unless the child has learned the appropriate social skills.

APPROPRIATE SOCIAL SKILLS

What are appropriate social skills? These vary from society to society. They vary from community to community. They even vary from neighborhood to neighborhood. In fact, they can vary from home to preschool to neighborhood.

Example 1:

Doug was a small boy who had learned that he could get his own way with his parents and teenage brothers by crying every time he was crossed. The same behavior with the children in the neighborhood did not work out. They simply went off and left him or they taunted him by chanting "Cry baby." This made him cry all the more and thus be the target for further taunting.

Example 2:

Sherry was a little girl who spent much of her time playing in the street. Her playmates were very aggressive children. She

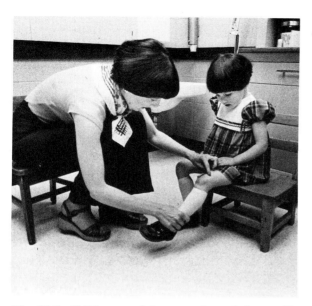

Fig. 12-2 **Children need to respond to adults outside their families.**

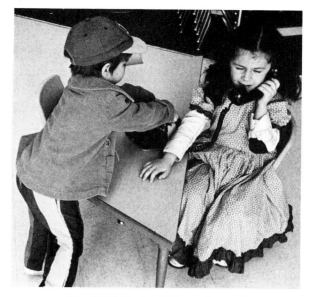

Fig. 12-3 **Social skills are learned.**

had learned to do a great deal of hitting, grabbing, running, and ducking. These were the "social" skills necessary for survival in the street setting. These same behaviors, when used at preschool, were considered inappropriate and maladaptive. This little girl had to learn to restrain the aggressive behaviors in the school setting, but to keep them readily available for use in the street setting.

Generally, social skills enable a child to respond appropriately to children and adults at home and away from home. The preschool curriculum must include many opportunities for this kind of learning. Children must learn to respond with enjoyment to adults other than their parents and close family members, figure 12-2. They must learn acceptable ways to approach and interact with other children. They must learn to work alone, even when others are nearby. They must also learn to be independent in a variety of other ways. Finally, children must learn to understand the difference between the expectations of home,

school, and other settings. Once children have learned this they must also learn to modify their behaviors to go with these expectations. The example just given of Sherry is a good illustration of this kind of learning.

SOCIAL SKILLS ARE LEARNED

One clear feature of all social skills is the fact that they are learned behaviors, figure 12-3. They are observable behaviors; that is, they are behaviors which can be seen. This is true even of those behaviors or responses that are often labeled "emotional." How can one tell when children are feeling good about themselves? Sympathetic? Hostile? Generous? Fearful? This is obvious by the social behaviors which the children engage in: laughing as they jump on the jumping board, sharing their cookies, running away from a large dog, or walking with their arms around each other. All of these, and many other emotional behaviors, are learned through the socialization process. Through observing behaviors such as facial expressions, bodily gestures, and verbalizations, children's emotions can be recognized and dealt with. It is necessary, too, to observe how others respond to a child. The responses of others often prompt emotional behaviors in a child.

Developmental Interrelatedness

Before discussing social skills, one other issue must be mentioned. This has to do with separating social development from other areas of development. Such separation is only for the purposes of discussion. Within the child it can never be viewed as developmentally separate. Social development, cognitive development, language development, and physical development are tightly interwoven. One influences the other. The following is an example of this interrelatedness, although the episode appears to be a simple social exchange.

Jane ran over to Ann, who was sitting in the sandbox filling cake tins with sand.

Jane: "Let's decorate cakes! Here's some decorations."

(Jane poured a number of blue and yellow plastic discs out of a container into Ann's cupped hands.)

Ann: "Hey, you gave me too many. (returned a few to Jane) Now we both got lots."

Jane smiled at Ann and began placing the discs around the edge of her cake. She alternated blue and yellow while singing to herself, "Now a blue one, now a yellow one."

Ann began to stick twigs in her cake. Then she put a disc over the top of each twig while singing "Happy Birthday" over and over.

Many separate developmental skills can be identified in this brief interaction. Such

motor skills as running, pouring, catching, picking, and placing were seen. A number of cognitive skills were also evident. For example, these four-year-old girls had the arithmetic concepts of "too many" and "lots." They also had the concept of "decorate." They knew color names, and they showed several problem-solving skills. The girls also had communication skills in the form of verbal exchanges, smiling, and handing materials back and forth.

All of these developmental skills contributed to the social skills that are so well developed in these two four-year-olds. These skills include the ability to

- initiate ideas
- follow suggestions
- share ideas and materials
- role play (for example, cake decorator)

The point of this analysis is not to put the various developmental skills into tight compartments. Instead, it is to reemphasize a point made in the beginning: Even though social skills are singled out for discussion in this unit, this does not mean that social skills can stand developmentally separate.

Social Reinforcement

The example just given points out another issue regarding social development. It depends upon interactions between people. Social skills cannot be developed unless they are reciprocal relationships (a child must get feedback and give feedback).

The socializing process begins shortly after birth. The most important element is to have adults in the environment who respond to the infant's waking hours, figure 12-4. It is during this period that parents (or major caregivers) become powerful social reinforcers. From the moment the child is born, the adults are constantly concerned with the

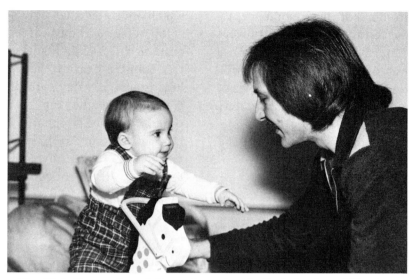

Fig. 12-4 Responsive adults are important in the infant's socialization.

infant's basic needs, such as food and warmth. While feeding the child and giving routine physical care, most parents talk to the baby. They usually pat, smile at, or sing to the baby at these times, too. Thus, while the adults meet the child's basic needs, the child learns to respond to all kinds of social reinforcement.

One government pamphlet for parents deals with this area of social reinforcement. It states:

When your baby first smiles, you pay attention to him and smile back. When he smiles again, you smile back and pay attention to him again, and you may talk to him and cuddle him. He soon learns that when he smiles good things happen to him, and he learns to do a lot of smiling when you are around. In just the same way, when you pay attention to his first cooing and gurgling sounds, your smile, your voice, and your fondling reward him. He coos and gurgles more and more frequently. When he is five or six months old, he begins to notice that you "reward" him more when he repeats sounds you make than when he makes just any old sound. Pretty soon he imitates everything you say, and

begins to learn to talk. If his smile is constantly ignored, he will stop smiling. And if his cooing and gurgling and making sounds is constantly ignored, he will soon stop making sounds. You actually teach your child to smile by rewarding him when he smiles, and you actually teach him to talk by rewarding him when he talks! You teach him by responding to what he does in a consistent way. If you want him to smile, you respond to the smile. If you don't want him to smile, you ignore it.

The same things hold true for almost all other kinds of behavior. When you respond to something your child does by giving your attention, a smile, a kind word, or by fondling or joy, your baby will do that thing more and more frequently. If you ignore it, it will be done less and less frequently. With these two methods, rewarding and ignoring, you will teach your child almost everything he learns.[1]

[1]*Infant Care* (Washington, D.C.: U.S. Department of Health, Education and Welfare Office of Child Development Children's Bureau, HEW Publication No. (OCD) 73-115, Children's Bureau Publication 8-1973).

Babies who do not have someone responding warmly tend to be less responsive socially. They are slower to acquire social skills and do not develop these skills well. Young children in institutions are examples of this. Often they are kept clean and adequately fed but receive little fondling and are seldom talked to. These children are usually behind in social development.

Children in Day Care

From infancy on, many children spend much of their time in day care. Delayed social development does not have to occur just because parents are not the primary caregivers. This is an issue to be looked at very closely for two reasons. There has been a great increase in our society in the number of working mothers with very young children. Also, there has been a rapid increase in one-parent families. Both of these situations have led to a doubling of the number of children aged 3 months to 3 years in full-day day care. These children can develop socially as well as any other children. It depends upon the caregivers and their understanding of the developmental importance of the socialization process, figure 12-5.

This issue has been studied by several other countries. They have collected evidence which indicates that children can and do develop socially in day care situations. Studies done in a few high-quality day care settings in this country provide the same evidence. The key to a sound day care program is the caregiver, just as the key to a sound preschool program is the teacher. It is necessary to have warm, nurturing, caring adults — adults who sing to the children, laugh with them, and respond to their antics and their efforts. The program needs adults who provide space, time, materials, and equipment for children's play activities. This requires adults who understand developmental processes and the development needs of infants and young children. With this kind of caregiving, it appears that children can develop well in a group-rearing situation. In fact, they seem to do as well as youngsters reared in a family situation.

Impaired Children

Unfortunately, some children are deprived of social stimulation through no fault of parents or caregivers. A potentially sound social environment cannot guarantee normal, happy development for severely impaired infants. Example:

A deaf infant cannot hear the crooning, loving sounds that mother makes during bathing, dressing, and feeding routines. Thus the baby does not respond to the mother as would an infant with normal hearing. This, in turn, may reduce the mother's efforts to interact with the infant. It may also cause her to respond negatively to the infant, because she, the mother, feels rejected. Unintentionally this sets up a reciprocal social situation that can seriously damage the child's social development.

This example is not meant to suggest that impaired children cannot acquire sound social skills. It simply shows how important

Fig. 12-5 Good day care provides many opportunities to interact socially.

it is to have early identification of a handi-capping condition. It points out, too, that many parents may need special help and training to foster social development in their handicapped child.

Most children follow a fairly regular progression in acquiring social skills. The social smile is one of the most important signs that an infant is well and thriving. The social smile usually appears between 2 and 4 months, figure 12-6. If the social smile has not appeared by the end of 4 months, it should be taken as a warning signal. Such a delay could suggest a potential developmental problem of one kind or another.

SEQUENCES IN SOCIAL DEVELOPMENT

During the first year of life social responsiveness is focused on persons close to the child, such as parents, siblings (brothers and sisters), grandparents, and other people familiar to the child. These are the ones whom the infant sees most often. They are the ones with whom the infant is most likely to interact. Games like peek-a-boo with daddy or big sister produce much social responsiveness during midinfancy. However, there are times of responsiveness to outsiders during this period, also. From the safety of the grocery cart in the supermarket or the pack on father's back, the child may smile at a smiling adult. From the security of the high chair in a restaurant infants may follow each other with their eyes. They may also laugh at each other's antics. Hammering on the high chair tray or throwing spoons to the floor can be very amusing to babies.

Play Activities

As young children begin to move about on their own, play activities become increasingly important avenues of social learning, figure 12-7. Through their play, children become interested in each other. At first, they do not see each other as personalities or playmates. Instead, a fellow toddler is something to be examined, touched, pushed, or pulled. For example, when pushing a doll carriage, a very young child may push it

Fig. 12-6 The infant's smile is an important social milestone.

Fig. 12-7 Play activities are major avenues of social learning.

directly into another small child. Children appear to do this with total unconcern. It is as if the first child regards the second child as just one more obstacle to be pushed down or shoved aside. When the second child falls down and cries, the first child may appear surprised.

The next step in very early social interaction with other children comes about through interest in the same play materials. Often, this leads to loud shrieking of "mine" as each child tries to hang on to the same toy. The following is an example of social interaction between two children aged two years old.

Two little boys, not quite two years old, were playing in the housekeeping corner in a day care center. One child was busily taking cups, plates, and silverware from the cupboard and putting them on the table. The other child was just as busy taking these objects off the table and returning them to the cupboard. It was a long time before either child noticed that they were at cross purposes. When they did, both became upset. Each began crying and shrieking "Mine!"

Fig. 12-8 Focus on materials is one step in the socialization process.

At the next stage of social skills, the child still seems to focus more on materials than on other people, figure 12-8. The start of cooperative play is just beginning to emerge. At this stage, young children can be seen interacting on the same block projects or sand activities. They also begin to run, jump, climb, and ride tricycles in small packs. Usually this occurs not so much because of friendship, but rather on the basis of common activity goals. These behaviors are, however, necessary first steps to later cooperative play interactions. They allow children to move more smoothly into the next period. In this stage, other children are valued as people and as playmates. A friend is chosen as someone to play with and to invite to your birthday party. Friends are also there to quarrel with and to make up with.

TEACHING STRATEGIES

These sequences in the development of social skills have been referred to as solitary, parallel, and cooperative interactions. By 5 or 6 years of age most children have begun to respond cooperatively to other children much of the time. However, learning suitable social skills depends in large part upon the child's environment. Children need to have access to a wide variety of good play materials and activities. Teachers of young children in preschool and day care settings must provide rich and varied play experiences.

In the integrated preschool it is the teacher's responsibility to draw handicapped and developmentally delayed children into social play activities. Research indicates that unless teachers consciously make this effort the handicapped children are not spontaneously included in the play of the nonhandicapped children.

It must be pointed out again, however, that many handicapped children do not know

Fig. 12-9 Many handicapped children must be taught to play.

Fig. 12-10 Children can be encouraged to double up on wheel toys.

how to play, figure 12-9. As discussed earlier, they must be taught. The question is where to start. As always, systematic observation of each child provides the answers. The teacher can then pinpoint what kind of play skills (if any) the child has. This enables the teacher to note where the child is in the social development sequence. Individualized planning can then begin.

There are many strategies for helping young handicapped children enter social play activities in the preschool. Success of these strategies depends upon the teacher's skill and creativity. Several of these strategies are described here.

Encouraging Imitation and Modeling

Handicapped children can learn a great deal about socializing from other children. They can learn how to play and how to interact socially. This learning occurs through the observation of nonhandicapped children. It comes about, too, through imitation and modeling of nonhandicapped children's social play behavior. To make sure that this happens, teachers should have children play in small groups of 2, 3, or 4 children. This means that teachers should plan several play activities and play centers. (It should be remembered that this is good planning for all children.) Very often, nonhandicapped children can serve as "teachers" of handicapped children. Thus both kinds of children benefit. The normal models can practice their own developing social skills while sharing those same skills with a more delayed child.

Presenting Materials

The kinds of materials which teachers provide for children to use will greatly influence social interaction. Examples of materials and activities which add to good social interaction are

- housekeeping
- water play
- painting together on a long sheet of paper
- toy trucks and cars
- simple lotto games
- musical instruments

Teachers must always see that enough materials are available. This ensures that each child in the small group can participate. Duplicate materials should also be available. This increases the opportunities for the handicapped child to imitate or model another child using the same material in an appropriate way.

There can be too much or too many kinds of materials and equipment available, however. When this occurs, children tend to play alone, to engage in solo activities. When there are only a few tricycles, for example, children can be encouraged to double up, figure 12-10, or take turns. One wheel toy for every three children is a good ratio. If a wheel toy is provided for each child, this defeats one of the major goals of most preschools - the teaching of cooperative social skills.

It is important, however, that teachers help the delayed children learn how to use these materials. Otherwise, the handicapped children may be viewed as poor playmates or as disrupters. This leads to the handicapped child being disliked unnecessarily.

Promoting Incidental Social Learning

Teachers need to be alert to any kind of social interaction that is going on naturally among children. These interactions need to be reinforced without being interrupted. If the teacher is too obvious with praise and attention, the children may turn to the teacher. This distracts them from their play. There are ways, however, of providing social reinforcement without distracting the children. The teacher can

- Move in close and watch with interest.
- Smile and nod if one of the children turns in the teacher's direction.
- Continue to focus on the activity and not on the child.

- Bring additional materials that will extend the play. (Additional drinking straws cut-up for candles on the birthday cakes will keep that activity going for a long time.)
- Make comments that reinforce the joint effort: "Missy and Sarah, you two are building the longest road I have ever seen."

Reinforcing Social Approximations

Teachers need to remember to reinforce any efforts a child makes toward social interaction. The child who stands and watches may be nearly ready to interact. The teacher can stand and watch with the child a few times while commenting favorably on the ongoing play activity. Later the teacher can actually help the child to get into play. One way is by helping the child to assume a role that provides entry to the play: "Here are two more passengers. Jimmy and I need to go to New York, too;" or "Jimmy is bringing another sack full of pinecones for all of you to use together;" or indirectly prompt the other children to include the child: "It sounds like you need one more drummer in your band. Ask Jimmy. He has an Indian drum."

Helping All Children Learn the Rules

All children must be helped to learn a few basic things about playing together. These rules may not be easy for many young children. Often the handicapped or delayed child may need even more help. The delayed child may also need many more opportunities to observe good models. Sharing is not always easy for young children, figure 12-11. Eventually, however, most children come to understand, "Two more turns around the driveway and then it's Sally's turn." A teacher can repeat this more than once when a child is just learning to take turns. "Watch,

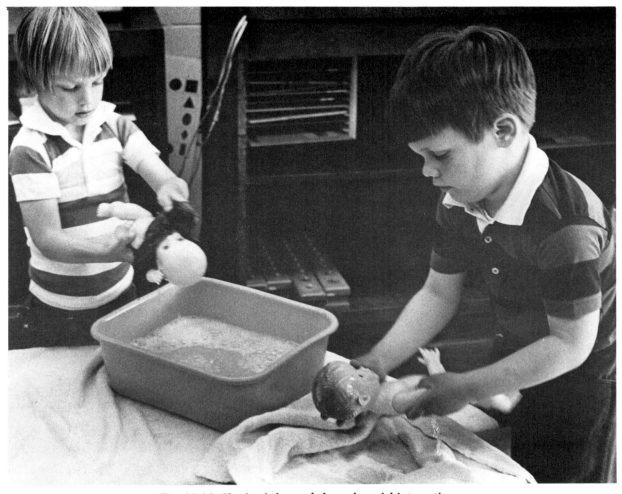

Fig. 12-11 Sharing is learned through social interactions.

Sally. Mary is going around the driveway two more times. It will then be your turn. Let's count."

Delayed and handicapped children may give in too easily. Like all children, they must learn to stand up for their rights. Children should learn to treat each other fairly. A teacher should never use the child's handicap as a reason for other children to treat that child any differently from the others.

Example:

Lisa, a four-year-old blind child, is playing with the interlocking floor train. Bart takes one of her pieces. Lisa, touching her train, realizes one piece is missing. She begins to whine. Teacher: "Bart has your car. Tell him 'Mine.'" The teacher says to Bart, "That is Lisa's caboose. She is telling you to give it back."

It cannot be overemphasized that the rules apply to all children, figure 12-12, handicapped and nonhandicapped. As noted in an earlier unit, there must be no double standards. A rule such as "no sand throwing" applies to all children regardless of age, kind of handicap, or degree of retardation. To allow any child to distress or disturb other children is to do that child a great injustice.

Fig. 12-12 The rules apply to all children.

Careful planning and program implementation assures that young handicapped children will become socially acceptable in the preschool. These children cannot usually learn social skills without special help from teachers. This is no different, however, from other young children. Almost every preschooler needs special help at one time or other in the area of social development.

SUMMARY

A young child's socialization is an important developmental process. It consists of learning a variety of social skills that enable the child to get along well with a variety of people in a variety of settings. These skills never stand alone and are never acquired in isolation. They are a part of the entire developmental skills network. Social development starts shortly after birth. It follows a fairly regular kind of pattern in most children.

All social behaviors are learned. This is true even of those referred to as emotional states. As learned behaviors they can be changed or modified. Even the most impaired or retarded child can "unlearn" inappropriate social responses and learn appropriate ones in their place. This requires skillful and patient guidance on the part of significant adults, figure 12-13.

The integrated preschool is an especially good place for handicapped children to learn basic social skills. Rarely can these children acquire the skills on their own. Special planning and programming is required. This includes a number of strategies. One is to provide many opportunities for a

Fig. 12-13 **Early socialization depends upon skillful and patient guidance from adults.**

handicapped child to observe and to imitate. A second is to make available materials and activities that increase social interaction. Promoting learning in incidental social exchanges is a third way. A fourth is to attend to (reinforce) all approximations to social interactions between handicapped and nonhandicapped children. Fifth, teachers must be sure that all children learn and follow the rules. Handicapped children should never be excused from learning appropriate social behavior on the basis of their handicaps. Though the learning may take longer and be more difficult for handicapped children, each must learn accepted social behavior. Unless they learn such behaviors, they will be rejected by the other children.

STUDENT ACTIVITIES

- Observe in a day care center, preferably one where there is a wide age range from toddlers to kindergartners. Record a social behavior for each of three different ages.

- Locate a preschool or day care center that has handicapped children. Talk with the teachers about concerns they may have about the social development of one of their children.

- While observing at a preschool, list the outdoor materials that seem to prompt cooperative play. Do the same indoors.

- Assume that you are the teacher of a developmentally delayed four-year-old boy who never plays with other children. Write out a set of plans for things that you might try in order to get that child into the social mainstream of the preschool.

REVIEW

A. Match each phrase in Column I with the correct term in Column II.

Column I   Column II

1. learning this kind of behavior is a major develop-   a. birth
    mental task for young children   b. learned
2. a child needs appropriate social skills in order to   c. first
    have satisfying ones with other people   d. emotions
3. a social skill is this kind of behavior   e. social
4. these are recognized through observing children's   f. ignored
    social responses   g. feedback
5. social, cognitive, language, and physical   h. interrelated
    development   i. interactions
6. a reciprocal relationship means that the individual   j. play
    gets and gives this   k. four months
7. the socializing process begins shortly after this   l. eight months
8. if an infant's smile gets this reaction, the infant   m. imitation
    may stop smiling   n. teacher
9. if the social smile has not appeared by this age,   o. modified
    it may be a warning signal   p. cooperatively
10. during this year of life, an infant's social respon-
    siveness is focused mainly on family members
    or principal caregivers
11. children become interested in each other through
    this
12. by five or six years of age, most normally develop-
    ing children have begun to play in this manner
    with other children
13. in an integrated preschool it is the responsibility
    of this person to draw handicapped children
    into social activities
14. a way for handicapped children to learn social
    skills from nonhandicapped children
15. social behaviors are learned behaviors and there-
    fore can be

B. Briefly answer each of the following.

1. How does a teacher know how a child is feeling emotionally?

2. How are parents (or principal caregivers) powerful as social reinforcers?

3. How can parents help their baby be a smiling, cooing infant?

4. Give one example of how a toddler might interact with another toddler.

5. Why is it a good idea to have a duplicate set of some materials?

6. Why is it important to help disabled children learn to play?

7. To which children in the preschool do the rules not apply?

8. How can nonhandicapped children help handicapped children learn appropriate social skills?

9. What does research indicate regarding the social interaction of handicapped and nonhandicapped children in the preschool?

10. In day care centers, what adult characteristics are most likely to create a good social climate for young children?

C. List at least three responses to each of the following.

1. Give examples of behaviors that might provide clues to a child's emotional state.

2. What can five-year-olds with good social skills usually do?

3. What are other names for the stages of social development?

4. How can teachers help children acquire good social skills?

5. In what ways can teachers help a child enter an ongoing play situation?

Unit 13 LANGUAGE SKILLS

OBJECTIVES

After studying this unit, the student will be able to

- Describe the major milestones in normal language development from birth through five years of age.
- Define articulation errors, lisping, and stuttering and suggest three do's and three don'ts for helping teachers and parents to handle these problems.
- List ten ways that preschool or day care staff can facilitate language learning in a child with a communications disorder.

Learning the native language (that is, the language of the home community), is an important developmental task. In fact, it is one of the most important and most complex of the developmental tasks that children must master. Such learning begins shortly after birth. Most normally developing children have full control of the basic aspects of their natural language by age five, figure 13-1.

There are some guidelines of what to expect in language development during the preschool years. These are very general. Variations in language development occur among children just as in every other area of

Fig. 13-1 Most young children have control of their native language by age 5.

development. It is the sequence that is important, not the exact age at which a specific language behavior occurs. A child may skip a certain step in the sequence. This does not necessarily harm the overall developmental pattern.

Preverbal Language

Very early language is preverbal. This means that no words are involved. It consists mainly of body movements, facial grimaces, and vocalizations. During this preverbal period the foundations for communication are established.

Newborn infants spend most of their time sleeping. When they are awake, their major form of communication is crying. Crying is the only way they have of making their needs known. By two months of age, however, most infants are doing something other than just crying. They laugh, coo, and squeal. These vocalizations are much different from crying.

By four to six months of age the baby is babbling. The infant is also doing a great deal of self-initiated play with sounds. Infants of this age turn to the sound of another's voice. They respond vocally to social stimulation.

Between six and eight months the first "words" begin to appear. These are usually syllable series such as "dadada" sounds strung together. During this period there are beginning efforts to imitate speech sounds.

Three main stages can be said to represent the rest of the language acquisition process.

Holophrastic Speech

This phase occurs during the eight-to-eighteen-month period. It is called holophrastic by a number of psycholinguists. (Psycholinguists are individuals who study the psychology of language.) Holophrastic speech is the child's use of a single word to express a

Fig. 13-2 One-word utterances are typical of very young children's speech.

complex idea, figure 13-2. These one-word utterances are never simple efforts to name something, however. When a word occurs it is always in relation to something else. The word seems to have sentence meaning. Thus the word "doggie," depending upon the inflection (change in pitch or tone of voice), can mean

- See the dog.
- Where is the dog?
- There is a dog.
- I'm afraid of the dog.

During this period there tends to be a great deal of overgeneralization. Thus, for awhile, doggie may mean all four-legged creatures. Hat may mean anything at all that is put on the head. Bye-bye means the absence or leaving of practically anything.

Telegraphic Speech

Between eighteen and twenty-seven months, children's language is often referred to as *telegraphic*. It consists mostly of two-word utterances:

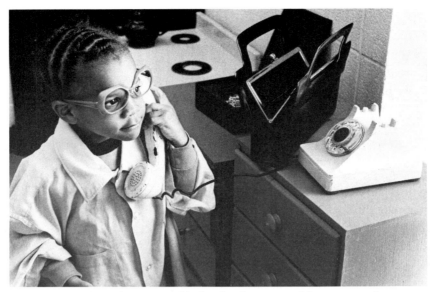

Fig. 13-3 Three-year-olds develop language with great speed.

- Where go?
- Baby cry.
- Daddy bye-bye.
- Momma purse?
- All gone!

There are no other parts of speech evident during this period. The child simply talks about who did what or who has what. These two-word sentences give the full meaning of the idea.

Such telegraphic phrases are important developmental milestones. They indicate that children are learning the grammar or word order of their language. It is word order that gives meaning to everything that is said.

Rapid Language Development

During the next period, twenty-eight to thirty-six months, the child begins three-word sentences. Omissions, or the telegraphic aspects of speech, continue for some time, however. During this period language develops very fast, figure 13-3. Children learn to use all of the "wh" questions: Where? When? Why? When? Who? They learn to transform positives to negatives: can/can't, do/don't. They learn to transform singulars to plurals: boy/boys, kitty/kitties. They also learn to use possessives: my, mine, daddy's, baby's.

So-called errors come into most children's language during this period of rapid language development. These are not really errors, however. They are faulty generalizations of some of the grammatical rules which the child is acquiring. For example, at first, many children say digged instead of dug. But when they learn dug as the past tense of dig they often add "ed" to it. Thus they say dugged for awhile. They may also mix up or overgeneralize the use of the plural. Many children say feet as feets. Others say mice as mouses, and then mices, before they settle upon the proper plural form. Children should not be corrected for these irregularities in their language. They should not be made to feel self-conscious or cute. Such normal developmental errors will self-correct spontaneously. This occurs as the child interacts with persons who speak the language correctly.

By the age of four or five, a child's syntactic development is almost complete. That is, most children will use every grammatical structure which adults use. This includes even the most complicated kinds of clauses and combinations of sentence structures. Vocabulary continues to develop, however. Most children who come to kindergarten can be expected to

- talk in full sentences

- ask questions

- express negatives, plurals, and possessives

- talk about relations: where and how, before, inside, because, and instead of

Teachers can expect normally developing children to understand most of what is said to them, figure 13-4. This is true only if the child possesses the vocabulary, however.

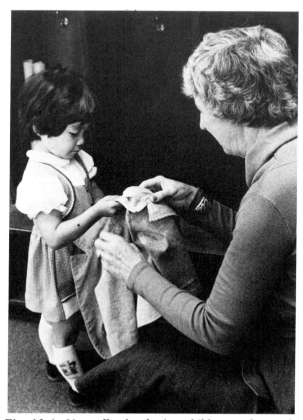

Fig. 13-4 Normally developing children understand most of what is said to them.

Thus if a teacher wants a child to "match the colors," the teacher must be sure the child understands the word "match." It must be in the child's vocabulary. If it is not, the teacher must teach it.

Language Assessment

The way to judge a child's language development is by observing the child and asking questions while observing. Does the child

- understand what is said?

- follow verbal directions?

- respond when spoken to?

- ask for things?

- tell about things that happen?

- assert self verbally with other children?

The naturalistic environment of the preschool gives an observant teacher the best information possible. Each child's developmental level can be assessed individually. Collecting language samples as described in unit 7 helps teachers be systematic about their observations.

For children whose language is developing normally there is not much extra that a preschool teacher needs to do. This assumes that the preschool or day care program is a sound program. Such a program includes:

- many opportunities for each child to use social language throughout the day

- frequent experiences in telling about things that are of interest to the child

- a curriculum rich in stories, music, and poetry

- opportunities to "play" with language: rhyming games, simple phonics games, and sound-imitating activities

- varied experiences (science, cooking, excursions) that motivate the child to

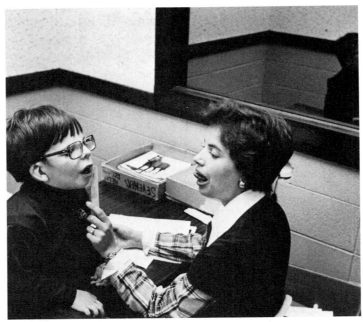

Fig. 13-5 **Specific speech interaction is sometimes necessary.**

learn the words which describe the experience

- a teacher who does not do all of the talking, but instead listens and responds to children

LANGUAGE DISORDERS

Specific intervention is needed for children who are not developing language normally, figure 13-5. Children with language disorders make up about 45 percent of the handicapped children in integrated programs such as Head Start. Preschool and day care teachers must learn to work with language-disordered children. First, however, it is necessary to mention the speech differences in a young child's speech that should not cause undue adult concern.

Articulation Errors

There are many errors in *articulation* (the making of speech sounds) which are

normal in young children. The two most common are

- omission - the child leaves out a sound: "tuck" for truck, "bo" for boat
- substitution - the child uses a different sound for the correct one: "vack" for back, "lello" for yellow

Lisping

Lisping is not considered a problem at the preschool level. If it continues in the primary school years, intervention may be indicated. This particular speech difference rarely persists, however.

Stuttering

What many people call stuttering is instead normal, nonfluent repetitions in speech. Many young children, at some time, will repeat sounds, syllables, and even whole words. The amount and kinds of repetitions vary from child to child. Even within the same child, repetitions may vary from situation to situation. Repetitive speech may last a short or long time. It may also disappear for awhile, only to reappear later.

Significant adults (teacher, parents, grandparents) must try to avoid giving attention to any kind of speech nonfluency. Eventually this disappears if the child is not nagged. Preschool and day care teachers can be helpful in two ways. One way is through carrying out the suggestions which follow. The second way is to counsel parents to do the same. Here are the suggestions:

- Do not call attention to a child's repetitions or misarticulations either by verbal correction, facial expression, or gestures.

- Do not tell a child: "Slow down," "Take it easy," or "Think before you speak."

- Do not interrupt a child; allow plenty of time for the child to talk, figure 13-6.

- Never attempt to change a child's handedness, for example, from left to right.

- Never compare the child's speech unfavorably with another child's speech.

Teachers and other adults can help by doing the following:

- Make sure the child is getting adequate rest, good diet, and lots of active play.

- Relieve as many tensions as possible.

- Discipline with calmness, firmness, and consistency.

- Remember that hesitations, repetitions, and misarticulations are natural in the speech of many young children. Remember, too, that they may continue for some time. Usually they disappear if the child is *not* made to feel too self-conscious about them.

- Enjoy the children; help them feel good about themselves.

All of these suggestions might be summarized by what one group of authors called "benevolent neglect." In helping children with any kind of articulation problem these authors suggest:

Begin by accepting errors in speech that *do not interfere with intelligibility*. To "correct" a child unnecessarily undermines his confidence as a speaker. For the child to improve he must keep talking. If he

Fig. 13-6 Allow plenty of time for children to say what they want to say.

Fig. 13-7 Children need receptive language skills.

Fig. 13-8 An infant turns to the sound of bells.

believes he will be criticized each time he speaks he begins to speak less and less. As a general rule, *never force a child to repeat a remark that you have understood.*[1]

Referral

There are young children who do need to be referred to a speech therapist, figure 13-7. One example is when articulation is so poor that the child is nearly unintelligible. Remember that speech deficiencies or deviations are often related to hearing loss. Therefore, it may be appropriate to refer a child to an audiologist. An audiologist is a specialist who can detect hearing loss.

The child who is speaking very little should never be subjected to any kind of articulation correction. Help in prespeech areas of language development is needed. Such help leads to increased verbal output. To help children increase their verbal output teachers need to understand the underlying communication process. This process is based upon the exchange of ideas. It involves a give-and-take, both verbal and nonverbal, between individuals. For this give-and-take to

occur, a child must have two kinds of language skills. These are often referred to as receptive and expressive skills.

BASIC LANGUAGE SKILLS

Receptive Language Skills

These are the behaviors necessary for children to process what they hear. Children do not have to be able to talk in order to indicate that they are aware of what is going on. They do not have to talk in order to indicate they understand what is being said. However, they do have to do something to show awareness or understanding. Examples:

An infant turns to the sound of a bell or rattle or mother's voice, figure 13-8. Understanding is demonstrated when a little girl runs toward her Daddy when she hears him call "Where's Jennifer?" An older child demonstrates understanding when carrying out instructions. Mother says, "Jonathan, will you go upstairs and get my pink sweater out of the bottom drawer of the tall chest?" Four and one-half year old Jonathan does it. He is

[1]Jane A. Rieke, Linda L. Lynch, and Susan F. Soltman, *Teaching Strategies for Language Development.* New York: Grune & Stratton, 1977, p. 43.

Does the child respond:	No	Yes	Some-times
to your voice by looking?			
to "What do you want?" by pointing?			
to "Give me the _____;" or "Find the _____" when there are no gestural cues?			
when there are gestural cues?			
to "Do you want it?" by nodding?			
with words?			
to "What do you want?" with words?			
to "Tell me about" with sentences?			
to "What is it for?" with phrases or sentences?			
to commands to get two different objects?			
to directions for two different actions?			
to questions with four- to five-word sentences?			

Fig. 13-9 Child's expressive response behaviors.

Does the child initiate by:	No	Yes	Some-times
making sounds in combinations?			
making "talking sounds" to get attention?			
using inflectional patterns to ask questions?			
pointing to items he wants?			
asking for items by name?			
talking in phrases that sound like words?			
telling you what he sees in two- and three-word phrases?			
telling you what happened?			
telling you where something is?			
"telling about," using adjectives?			
asking why?			
"telling about," combining sentences with *and*?			
asking how?			

Fig. 13-10 Child's expressive initiating behaviors.

showing good understanding, and well-developed receptive language skills in general.

A child must have receptive language skills in order to communicate with others. Almost every child can be helped to develop some receptive skills. This is true even of the child who may never develop adequate expressive language.

Expressive Language

Expressive language includes all of the ways that individuals express themselves. This is usually in the form of speech but it can include gestures and facial expressions.

Expressive language takes two forms. One form is when the child is the initiator, that is, the child starts a communicative interaction with another. The other form is when the child is the responder. Here the child answers or responds to another's initiation. The child must learn to do both. Both skills are equally important in the communication process.

As with growth of all kinds, responding and initiating behaviors occur in developmental sequence. Figures 13-9 and 13-10 give sequential examples of these behaviors.[2]

[2]K. Eileen Allen, Jane Rieke, Valentine Dimitriev, and Alice H. Hayden, "Early Warning: Observation as a Tool for Recognizing Potential Handicaps in Young Children." In *Educational Horizons*, 1972, 50: 2, 4.

Simple checklists such as these are helpful. They are aids in identifying where a child's problem may be. The items can be thought of as probes; that is, they are examples of communication behaviors along a developmental sequence. When the answer to a question is "no," it may indicate a problem. The teacher needs to follow up on it, figure 13-11. When the answer is "sometimes" the teacher can design a program around this emerging skill to strengthen it.

Nonverbal Communication

In working with children with language delays or deficiencies it is necessary to understand the nonverbal aspects of communication. Teachers must be alert to what children do as well as what they say, figure 13-12. Teachers need to respond when a child shrugs, scowls, smiles, flinches, or looks puzzled. For many delayed children these are their first approximations (first efforts) at communication. Failure to recognize and respond to these first nonverbal efforts may delay the child's verbal development even more. In other words, adults must try to respond to every effort a child may make to communicate. This is crucial if that child is to develop language. Just saying "Hi" for the first time may be a real breakthrough for a nonverbal child. It

Fig. 13-11 Simple checklists are helpful in language assessment.

Fig. 13-12 Teachers must be alert to what children do as well as what they say.

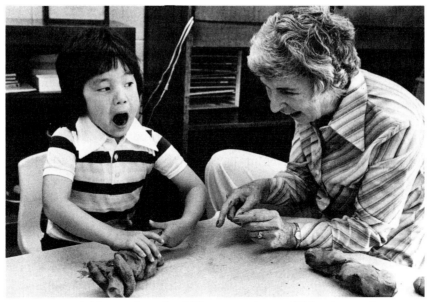

Fig. 13-13 Teachers should be responsive to children's speech.

should be responded to with praise and delight by teachers.

Example:

Teachers should greet the children by name each morning even though some might not respond. After many months there may be a dramatic breakthrough. For example, for months a teacher would stand near the lockers at school and greet Billy each morning as he came to kindergarten. Billy had cerebral palsy, little vision, and no speech. He never responded in any fashion. Together they hung up his coat and then would go into the classroom. One morning the teacher was busy in the classroom when Billy arrived. Suddenly she heard, "Hi—Hi—Hi." The sound came from the hall. When she went outside, there stood Billy in front of his locker, with his thumb in his mouth, calling out, "Hi—Hi—Hi." He used only that one sound for a long time but slowly began to make progress.[3]

[3] Regina Schattner, *An Early Childhood Curriculum for Multiply Handicapped Children.* New York: The John Day Company, 1971, p. 74.

RESPONSIBILITIES OF THE PRESCHOOL TEACHER

One responsibility of the teacher is to be a good responder when children initiate, figure 13-13. Another important responsibility of the teacher is to be a good facilitator. Being a good facilitator means that the teacher makes it easy for the child to succeed. There are a number of ways that teachers can be facilitative.

- Remember that receptive language comes before expressive language.

- Keep in mind that nonverbal language often comes before verbal language (in the beginning, teachers should respond to all nonverbal efforts).

- Provide many kinds of experiences for children to talk about.

- Allow plenty of time for children to talk.

- Wait for a child's responses (prompt, if necessary, but do not answer for the child).

- Be a good listener and an alert responder. (It is important, however, that teachers do not talk too much when responding to a child.)

- Remember that children do not learn language merely by listening to it. Children learn by doing. Language is learned when the child does it.

- Include the language-deficient child in group activities with nonhandicapped children. The child then has good language models.

- Encourage children to make their needs known verbally. This means that teachers do not anticipate what a child wants. Instead, the teacher helps the child ask.

- Emphasize communication rather than correct speech.

- Ask questions that are open-ended. These allow the children to respond with something other than "yes" or "no."

- Remember that the more a language-deficient child talks, the better that child will talk.

- Use every part of the day and especially free play periods to help delayed children acquire language.

Incidental Teaching

All of the points just mentioned are important for teachers to remember. Most of the suggestions can be used with the incidental teaching procedure described in unit 10. Hart (1977) gives this example:

A four-year-old girl with delayed language stands in front of the teacher with a paint apron in her hand. The teacher says, "What do you need?" (Teacher does not anticipate the child's need by putting the apron on the child at that moment.)

If the child does not answer, the teacher tells her and gives her a prompt: "It's an apron. Can you say apron?" If the child says "apron" the teacher ties it while giving descriptive praise, "You said it right. It is an apron. I am tying your apron." The teacher's last sentence models the next verbal behavior, "Tie my apron," that the teacher will expect once the child has learned to say apron.

If the child does not say apron, the teacher ties the apron. No further comments are made at this time. The teacher must not coax, nag, or pressure the child. If each episode is kept brief and pleasant the child will contact the teacher frequently. Thus the teacher will have many opportunities for incidental teaching. If the teacher pressures the child, such incidental learning opportunities will be lost. Some children may learn to avoid the teacher. They will simply do without. Other children may learn inappropriate ways, such as whining and crying, to get what they want.[4]

Speech Therapist

Children with more severe communication problems need to receive services from a speech therapist or communications specialist. It is most important that the preschool teacher and the speech therapist act together as a team, figure 13-14. The child spends a great deal more time in the preschool or day care setting than in the therapy sessions. What is being taught in speech therapy must be integrated into the daily curriculum. It should be practiced throughout the child's day. To accomplish this, the speech therapist can be expected to do two things. One is to keep the teacher informed of the child's progress. The second is to teach the teacher what to do in the classroom to help the child use the speech behaviors being taught in

[4]Betty Hart, lecture given at University of Kansas, February, 1977.

Fig. 13-14 Teamwork is essential.

therapy. It is an artificial separation to have a therapist work on language separately from the school program.

This does not mean that teachers need to learn to be speech therapists. What is important is that the speech therapist demonstrate procedures for the teacher to carry out. For example, the teacher tries to get the initial "b" sound, if that is one of the things the therapist is working on. The therapist demonstrates how to get the "b" sound. The teacher can then do it through the day, each time the situation arises. This extends the speech therapist's treatment for each child in an important way. The same tactics should be used as those described in any incidental teaching episode. The encounter should be brief, pleasant, and nonpunishing for the child. The teacher must always be the source of positive reinforcement if children are to learn quickly and well.

SUMMARY

Learning their native language is one of the most complex developmental tasks that young children accomplish. As in every other area of development, there are sequences of development. Most young children pass through these in a fairly fixed order. A child may skip a step in the language sequence. This is not cause for alarm, however.

Most children acquire language spontaneously, without special help. For these children, the regular language part of the curriculum in the integrated preschool is usually sufficient. It is sufficient, that is, if the preschool has varied activities and a carefully planned program based on developmental theory.

Special intervention is necessary for the children whose communicative skills are not developing appropriately. The preschool teacher can be a facilitator of such intervention. Facilitation involves a three-part approach. First, the teacher must know developmental sequences in language development. Second, the teacher needs to understand the communication process as a whole. Third, the teacher needs to arrange the environment appropriately. This allows the teaching of language to be a pleasant experience which goes on throughout the day. The incidental teaching approach is one of the best ways of facilitating language development.

Many delayed or disabled children need the service of a speech therapist. In these cases the teacher and the therapist should work together closely. The therapist can demonstrate procedures to the teacher. The teacher can then carry out the therapist's program for the child in the classroom. Again the incidental teaching approach is an ideal method to use.

STUDENT ACTIVITIES

- Observe a preschool or day care class; record 25 language samples. While collecting the language samples note any child who might be of concern regarding language development. Specify your concerns.

- During the next several days collect examples of ten nonverbal behaviors which you have observed in children, classmates, or other adults.

REVIEW

A. How does the child communicate in each of the following age/stage sequences?

1. newborn (first month)
2. 2 to 4 months
3. 4 to 6 months
4. 6 to 8 months
5. 8 to 18 months
6. 18 to 27 months
7. 28 to 36 months

B. Match each term in Column I with the correct description in Column II.

Column I	Column II
1. holophrastic speech	a. errors in speech sounds such as omissions or substitutions
2. telegraphic speech	
3. syntactic development	b. holding back from unnecessarily correcting a child
4. articulation errors	
5. stuttering	c. repeating or duplicating sounds or words
6. expressive language	
7. receptive language	d. a single word to express a complex idea
8. nonverbal communication	
9. audiologist	e. what the child says
10. benevolent neglect	f. gestures, facial expressions
	g. learning the grammar of the language
	h. two-word utterances that give the full meaning
	i. a specialist who tests hearing
	j. an individual's understanding of what is said

C. List at least five answers for each of the following.

1. What kinds of questions should teachers ask themselves when observing a child's language skills in the natural environment?

2. What communication skills can teachers expect of normally developing kindergartners?

3. What should parents and teachers not do in response to articulation errors, lisping, and stuttering?

4. What should parents and teachers do to help a child with articulation errors, stuttering, or lisping?

5. What are some examples of nonverbal communication in young children?

6. How are teachers facilitators of language development?

7. How does an incidental teaching experience provide a good means for children to learn language?

8. List some examples of telegraphic speech.

9. If the child's language is developing normally, the teacher does not have to provide language intervention. However, there are some things the preschool program should include to insure normal language development. What are they?

10. List some types of preverbal communication.

D. Briefly define and give examples of the following.

1. expressive language
2. receptive language
3. inflection
4. overgeneralizations
5. language disorders
6. benevolent neglect
7. teacher as facilitator
8. native language
9. babbling
10. language samples

Unit 14 PREACADEMIC SKILLS

OBJECTIVES

After studying this unit, the student will be able to

- Discuss the relationship of preschool preacademics to successful academic performance.
- Briefly describe the most important readiness or prerequisite skills and give one example of each.
- Describe five or more ways in which the preschool teacher can help handicapped or delayed children function successfully in preacademic activities.

A preacademic period is a part of the regularly scheduled curriculum in many preschool programs, figure 14-1. What goes on during this period varies from program to program. This unit therefore does not describe a particular preacademic program. Instead, a wide range of skills related to academic learning are discussed. These are the early skills thought to be necessary if children are eventually to learn to read, write, and do arithmetic. Tasks that teach preacademic skills are found in most programs. Sometimes they are not recognized or labeled as preacademic tasks, however. This may be because of the arguments over what is work and what is play for little children.

Fig. 14-1 Preacademics is a regularly scheduled period in many preschools.

PREACADEMIC GOALS

Before describing actual preacademic activities, several reminders are in order. First, no preschool curriculum should view preparing children for kindergarten or first grade as its only goal. Today's living and learning is the important issue in the development of young children. The single most important learning for a preschool child is a sense of "I can do it." Therefore, all preacademic programs should be aimed at helping each child acquire this particular learning set. Young children who feel good about themselves have a better chance of doing well in all situations.

A second aim of the preacademic part of the preschool program should be to develop children's eagerness to learn. To promote this there must be activities to develop children's awareness and curiosity, figure 14-2. Children must want to know about the world around them. They must want to explore and experiment. It must be recognized that young children, whether handicapped or not, learn mainly through their senses. Touching, seeing, and hearing are the most common ways of learning through the senses. Taste and smell should not be ignored, however. Much can be learned through those senses, too. A good preacademic curriculum gives children a variety of firsthand experiences. Children should have objects and materials to handle and work with. This allows them to exercise their senses, to wonder, and to discover the answers to such questions as

Why does ice melt?
What makes the wind blow?
Where do rocks come from? What makes rocks hard?
How does a bird stay in the air?
Where did my shadow go?

The role of the teacher is to help children ask and discover answers to such questions. This extends children's ability to think and to ask more questions. Thus, when children enter public school they are eager to learn more and more. They want to read about, tell about,

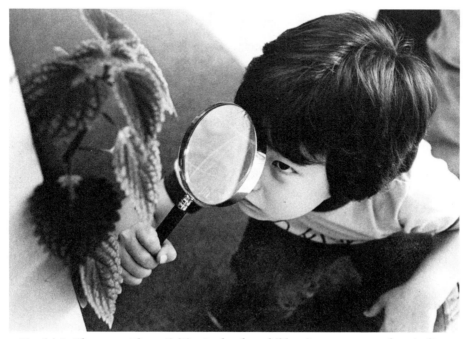

Fig. 14-2 There must be activities to develop children's awareness and curiosity.

Fig. 14-3 Motor, social, and language development are all related to preacademics.

and write about many things. This eagerness is called motivation to learn. The groundwork for such motivation is laid during the preschool years. This is true for both handicapped and nonhandicapped children.

A third aim of a sound preacademic program is to have activities that involve every area of development. Motor development, social development, and language development are all related to preacademic learnings, figure 14-3. Many preschools set aside a certain time each day as a preacademic period. This is not enough, however. Teaching concepts and skills introduced during the preacademic period should continue throughout the day. Such teaching can occur during snack time, outdoor play periods, and time spent getting ready for naps. Extensions of learning activities during these periods often appear casual. They do, however, require conscious planning on the part of teachers. The incidental teaching approach described in unit 13 is an effective way to extend and expand children's learning. It must be remembered, however, that such teaching contacts should be brief, pleasant, and fun.

PREACADEMIC SKILLS

Many different skills are involved in preacademic learning. A number of these skills are only indirectly related to reading, writing, and arithmetic. They are skills that must be learned however. They are necessary if children are to succeed in school subjects at a later time. Often these skills are referred to as readiness skills. They are also called prerequisite skills. The following is a list of some of the more important prerequisite skills:

attention span
imitation skills
instruction following
perceptual-motor skills
fine motor control
    (eye-hand-wrist coordination)
receptive and expressive language
concept formation
memory
prereading, prewriting, and premath skills

Each of these preacademic skill areas will be discussed separately, although these skills are not really separate from each other. For example, children have to be able to tell about what they saw on a trip. That is the only way a teacher can find out how much children remember about the trip, or how much they learned from it. Thus children must have expressive language. Similarly, the only way children can follow instructions is if they have receptive language. They must understand what the teacher tells them to do. A child cannot imitate a finger play if the child does not have the fine motor control.

Attention Span

Attention span is the ability to attend to an activity or a task for a reasonable length of

Fig. 14-4 Attention span is the ability to attend to a task.

time, figure 14-4. This skill is necessary for all other learning. With many young children, both handicapped and nonhandicapped, attending is a skill that needs to be taught deliberately and systematically. In most cases, it requires skillful teaching. Every child, however, can acquire this necessary prerequisite. Particular strategies for helping children to acquire attending skills will be discussed in a future unit.

Ability to Imitate

Much learning is acquired through imitation, that is, through modeling after others. When trying to learn a particular skill most individuals first watch someone else do it. Learning to jump rope, kick a football, or dive into a pool is based, in part, on watching someone else do it first. Then the individual tries to model after the person performing the act. All early learning (verbal, motor, and social) is based largely on imitation. Most infants and children imitate spontaneously. They do not have to be taught. All young children need practice in perfecting this skill, however. This is one reason for the many finger plays, action

Fig. 14-5 Action songs are an important preschool activity.

songs, and rhymes in preschool programs, figure 14-5. In the integrated preschool, imitation is important. It is one of the reasons for putting handicapped children into regular preschool classes. This gives handicapped children the opportunity to model after normal children. If a handicapped child does not learn to imitate normally developing children, an important avenue of learning is lost. Teaching children how to imitate should therefore be high on every teacher's "What to Teach" list.

Following Instructions

The ability to follow instructions and carry out requests is another important preacademic skill. For children who have difficulty carrying out instructions, teachers must first ask themselves:

- Does the child hear well enough to know what is expected?

- Does the child have the necessary vocabulary to understand the request? Does the child understand the concept "match" when the teacher instructs "Match all the blue ones"?

- Are the instructions too complicated or given too rapidly?

If a teacher has ruled out the first two possibilities, it is often the third item that gives the child trouble. It is true that many preschool children can carry out three- and four-step directions. When the teacher says, "Would you please go to the sink, wet a sponge, and wipe up the paint on the floor and table legs?" many can do it. Also, they can do it in the stated order. Some preschool children, however, cannot carry out such directions. Very young or developmentally delayed children are likely to have difficulty. The solution is quite simple. Teachers must take nothing for granted. Directions should be given one at a time. The

Fig. 14-6 Directions should be clearly stated, one at a time.

teacher should look directly at the child while giving the direction. Language should be simple and uncluttered.

"Go to the sink."

After allowing the the child time to get there, the teacher can then say,

"Find a sponge."

When the child has a sponge in hand, the teacher gives the next instruction:

"Now wet it," figure 14-6.

If the teacher does not want the child to let the sponge drip while coming across the room, an intermediate instruction should also be given:

"Squeeze the water out."

Many children would not know exactly what the teacher wants in this case. Therefore, the teacher should say, "Like this" and show the child how to squeeze the sponge until it does not drip.

Almost every child can learn to fulfill one-step directions successfully when taught in the above fashion. Teachers can then move gradually to two- and then three-step directions.

In the integrated preschool, the teacher can pair a handicapped and nonhandicapped child when giving more complex instructions. "Judi and John, will you get the chalk and slate boards and put them on the round table?" This provides the delayed child with both a model and a reminder.

Perceptual-Motor Skills

Appropriate perceptual-motor responding is an important part of preacademic skill building. Perceptual-motor skill has two parts. The first has to do with processing what is seen, heard, touched, tasted, or smelled. The second part is translating the messages into appropriate action responses.

> Example 1: A child turns at the sound of a motor, looks around, looks up, and points to a helicopter in the sky.

This child is exhibiting both auditory (hearing) and visual (seeing) perception, as well as appropriate perceptual-motor responses: turning, scanning, and pointing.

> Example 2: A child touches a hot stove and quickly pulls back.

This child has made an appropriate tactual (touch) perceptual-motor response.

> Example 3: A child picks up a bar of cocoa butter, smells it, bites off a piece, and then spits it out while making a wry face.

This child is displaying both smell and taste perceptual-motor responses. The cocoa butter smelled like candy, which led the child to take a bite. It did not taste like candy, however. It tasted more like soap. The child spit it out in distaste.

All reading, writing, and arithmetic tasks require well organized perceptual-motor systems. Almost every activity in a good preschool program promotes perceptual-motor learning. Outdoors there are such activities as running, jumping, and tricycling. Indoors there are such things as block building, painting, table toy activities, and working with clay. During music and stories there is rhyming, pantomiming, and pretending. These are but a few of the many preschool activities that help children, both handicapped and nonhandicapped, acquire perceptual-motor skills.

Fine Motor Controls

Fine motor controls are often referred to as eye-hand coordination and finger-wrist dexterity. These skills are different than perceptual-motor skills but are closely related. Most activities offered in a preschool provide practice in gaining fine motor control. The following are a few examples:

- water play - pouring, squeezing, measuring
- blocks (figure 14-7) - stacking, bridging, balancing
- artwork - painting, crayoning, pasting, working with clay, hammering and nailing, cutting
- housekeeping - dressing dolls, pouring "tea," stirring "soup"
- self-help - buttoning, zipping, lacing

Fig. 14-7 Blocks: stacking, bridging, balancing.

There is another group of materials used to promote fine motor control and perceptual-motor skills at the same time. These are often referred to as manipulative materials. Some examples are

> wooden beads and string
> puzzles
> parquetry blocks
> leggo
> kitty-in-the-barrel
> picture dominoes
> rig-a-jigs
> nesting and stacking cups
> Montessori cylinders
> pegs and pegboards

These manipulative materials and others found in well-equipped preschools are important sources of preacademic learnings. They provide nonhandicapped children with activities that make it fun to practice fine motor skills. They are also adaptable for use with handicapped children. These materials can be used successfully with children who have a variety of learning disabilities and developmental delays.

The following list suggests a few adaptations for handicapped children:

- Present the largest size wooden beads. Have the impaired child string them on a wrapped wire (such as a straightened coat hanger bound with tape) instead of the usual shoelace.

- Select puzzles with very few pieces. Each piece should be a recognizable object, figure 14-8.

- Tape down some of the inside pieces on more difficult puzzles. The child then has to do fewer pieces to complete the task; it is also an easier task, as the spaces to fit the edge pieces are usually more obvious.

- Present only the five or six largest nesting cups. Put them out, in order, in a straight line. Hand the child one at a time.

In the integrated preschool all types of children can be involved in the joint use of a manipulative material at times.

Example:

Five children are working at a table using the parquetry blocks. Billy, a cerebral palsied child, is in the group. The teacher put out only one model design, and placed

Fig. 14-8 Each piece should be a recognizable object.

Fig. 14-9 Eventually Billy learns to select the right shape and the right color by himself.

it in the middle of the table. The teacher then gave each child 6 or 8 blocks. The children take turns putting on one block at a time, building the design from the center out. Each time it is Billy's turn the teacher quietly helps him. First the teacher has him look at the design to determine the color and shape needed next. Then the child is given help in locating the approximate block in the pile. Next, with a hand over his, the teacher helps him to place the block.

Children like Billy need opportunities to learn with other children. Indirectly, through demonstrations, the teacher can involve other children in helping Billy. Eventually Billy will be able to accomplish many such tasks on his own, figure 14-9.

Receptive and Expressive Language

Language skills which include listening skills are an important aspect of preacademic learning. These skills are required at every level of schooling. Therefore they need to be worked on throughout the day. The preschool curriculum should include planned preacademic activities and incidental opportunities for increasing language skills.

Concept Formation

Concept formation may be thought of as skill in organizing one's thinking. It is the mental process that helps make sense out of the world. Forming concepts helps to bring order to the many things that children must learn about. Some of the subskills thought to be part of the concept formation process will be described.

Classification. This skill is sometimes referred to as the ability to form categories. Children learn that cats, dogs, and squirrels have certain characteristics in common. They all have fur, four legs, a tail, and so on. On the basis of these common characteristics, they can be called animals. Each category is subject to further breakdown as the child's thought processes become more developed. "Dog" becomes a category by itself as well as part of a larger category. The child eventually learns to discriminate kinds of dogs, figure 14-10, such as poodles, terriers, and collies.

Seriation and Gradation. This is the ability to order events and objects along certain dimensions:

- big, little (eventually middle-sized)
- tall, short (eventually taller, tallest)
- smooth, rough
- first, last
- left, right
- happiest, saddest
- loud, quiet

A part of this conceptual skill is the ability to tell about what happened in an orderly fashion.

Example:

"Yesterday we went to Grandma's. We played in the attic. Then we had dinner. First we had to wash our hands. After dinner, Grandpa read us a story. Then it was time to go home. I fell asleep in the car."

A favorite preschool activity is to have children arrange a series of pictures in the correct order.

Example: the first is a picture of a little girl digging up the ground. The next picture shows her planting a seed. Several pictures later she is pulling up a carrot.

Spatial Relationships. Many preschool activities are focused on helping children learn such relationships as

on	in between
in	in the corner
under	in the middle
in front of	next to
behind	at the top

Learning these relationships helps the child in reading and writing tasks later in school. Understanding these concepts seems so obvious to adults. However, young children, handicapped and nonhandicapped, often have a great deal of trouble with them. In the beginning, these concepts are best taught as children move about in play. They learn to feel their own bodies in relationship to space. Outside, for example, the teacher may comment: "Timmy, you climbed so high! You are *on top of* the box." For children having difficulty forming concepts, the teacher must do more than just comment. Immediately following the comment the teacher should ask, "Where are you, Timmy?" Then the teacher should pause so the child can respond. If the child does not respond, the teacher helps him frame the words. Then the teacher reinforces the concept, "That's right, Timmy, you said it just right! You are on *top* of the box."

Fig. 14-10 The child learns to discriminate kinds of dogs.

Discrimination.   Learning to tell how things are alike or different is another part of concept formation.   It is a skill necessary to the other concept-forming processes which have been discussed (classification, seriation, spatial relationships).   Children must be able to make very fine discriminations in order to read.   They must see and hear the difference between a and o, c and t.   Even more difficult is learning to see and hear the difference between d and b, g and p, c and e.

Many preschool activities are designed to help children learn to make a variety of discriminations.

Examples:

- At music time the teacher might introduce a song about, "Who is wearing sneakers? Sandals? Brown shoes?"

- A variety of sorting tasks can be available: yellow pegs to be put in one box, red ones in another, blue ones in still another.

- Beads can be strung in a pattern - a little round blue one; a big square red one; a long thin green one. (This task requires very complex discrimination. The beads vary in three ways - shape, color, and size.)

There are many opportunities for helping children learn to make appropriate discriminations.   For disabled and delayed children in the integrated preschool such tasks can be made very simple. The teacher might give the child a red cup, a blue cup, and only red and blue chips. The task is for the child to put the red chips in the red cup, and the blue chips in the blue cup.

Much more could be said about concept formation. The important thing for teachers of young children to remember is that it is basic to all other learning. Therefore, teachers must make conscious efforts along these lines.

They must provide every child with many experiences and opportunities to expand concept development.

Memory

The ability to remember what has been learned earlier is necessary to all new learning.   Again it is an important prerequisite to all later school learning.   Helping children to learn and practice memory skills should be a regular part of preacademic activities.   There are many times in each preschool session when the teacher can introduce memory activities. This can be done using the following ideas.

Conversational questions such as:
  What did you have for breakfast?
  What do you do when you get up in the morning?
  What kinds of fruit did we see when we went to the farm?
  What did we put in the vegetable soup we made yesterday?
  What did the caterpillar do that Jimmy brought to school?
Other kinds of memory activities:
  Remembering each other's names and the teachers' names.
  Remembering where materials are kept in order to get them out and

Fig. 14-11 Remembering where materials are kept is important.

put them away properly, figure 14-11.

Remembering the routine for various activities: keeping each paint brush in a separate container of paint when painting at the easel.

At story time, remembering the names of the characters; remembering what happened to them; retelling episodes.

At group time, telling what object has been removed in the "cover the tray" game.

Telling what happened on a special occasion, such as described under the seriation section.

Prereading, Prewriting, and Premath Skills

All of the preacademic activities which have been discussed can be viewed as prereading, prewriting, and premath skills. In addition, there are specific activities along these lines. These include such things as:

- "Reading" a series of pictures from left to right

- Counting a row of objects from left to right

Fig. 14-12 Cutting on the lines is a prewriting skill.

- Drawing lines between dots

- Tracing simple designs and coloring them in

- Grouping objects in sets of two, three, or four

- Cutting on the lines, figure 14-12

It must be remembered that these are not simple tasks. All young children, especially the disabled and delayed children in the group, need a great deal of help. For example, most young children have trouble learning to cut. Much of the difficulty is unnecessary. Teachers can adapt the task to the child's skill level. The following is an example of such an adaptation. (Note: scissors must be of good quality and must work well.)

Lonnie was a four-year-old in day care. He had a very short attention span and no skill with scissors. Each day, the teacher took him to a corner of the room, away from the other children, so he would not be distracted. First, she taught him to hold the scissors. Then she provided him with strips of firm, colored paper. These were 3/4 inch wide and about 8 inches long. At one-inch intervals, the strips of paper were marked with heavy felt-pen lines.

In the beginning, the teacher held the strip of paper for Lonnie. He held the scissors, opened. The teacher inserted the strip far back in the scissor opening. The teacher made sure that one of the heavy lines was at the point of contact. Then she said "cut." It was a simple matter for Lonnie to close the scissors successfully. A cleanly cut piece of paper came off with each crunch. This gave Lonnie immediate success. The snips of brightly colored paper went in an envelope. Lonnie could take these home to paste or to play with.

Before long Lonnie was able to hold the paper himself while cutting. Gradually the teacher made the task more difficult. She increased the width of the strips so it took 2 and then 3 snips to cut through. She made slanted lines; then curved lines; then simple shapes to be cut around. She always kept the practice time short and fun so that Lonnie did not tire of the activity.

PLANNING PREACADEMIC PERIODS

Grouping Children

A preschool class of fifteen to twenty children should be divided into two, three, or four academic groups. The number of teachers and assistants available determines the number of groups. If there are enough adults the group size should be limited. This allows each child to receive individual attention. Groups should be small enough so that children are in contact with materials at least 80 percent of the time, figure 14-13. They should not have to spend a long time waiting their turn. Waiting leads to inattention, "clowning," and other undesirable behaviors in young children.

Fig. 14-13 Children should be in contact with materials at least 80 percent of the time.

Some children may function well in a group as large as eight or ten children. These are the children with a good range of the basic skills. Less experienced children need to be in smaller groups. Children with behavior problems and developmental disorders also profit from being in a smaller group. A maximum of four is about right for such children. Some children require one-to-one attention for brief periods. This must also be provided, perhaps at odd moments during the day. Under most conditions, however, a group of five to seven preschool children seems about right. As children get close to kindergarten age, teachers should plan larger group experiences.

At the beginning of the year, children can be grouped according to age. Later, when skills have been assessed, children can be shifted into ability groups. Children who are nearest in ability may be quite different in their needs, however. Teachers must plan to individualize instruction for most of the preacademic period, figure 14-14. Also, the same child does not always perform the same way over time. Thus, teachers should reevaluate each child's placement several times each year. This is particularly necessary for children in the middle ability range. They are often overlooked because teachers tend to

Fig. 14-14 Teachers must individualize instructions.

concentrate on the brighter and the slower children.

Children also vary in their abilities depending on the task and setting. Teachers must take social behavior into account as well as preacademic skill level. For example, there may be a very shy child with good academic skills. Often a child like this profits from being placed for awhile with less academically able children. This gives the child a chance to practice social interaction in a "low-keyed" setting. Also, good friends regardless of their experience level, might be placed together. On the other hand, some teachers make sure that friends are placed in separate groups. It depends upon what the teacher hopes to accomplish for each child.

Introducing Preacademics

At the beginning of the year, some children may have difficulty at group time. It may not be easy for them to settle down. Often this is a first introduction to the more formal type of learning in groups. The teacher's first goal for the preacademic period is to help children be comfortable and interested. To make sure this transition to formal learning periods is successful, the following guidelines are given.

Start with a very short preacademic period. Three, four, or five minutes is a good start. Gradually lengthen it. By the end of the school year, most children can manage a thirty-minute preacademic period.

Clearly identify each child's work space at the table, (figure 14-15), or on the floor. This helps to promote independent work habits. A 15 x 18 inch piece of felt for each child is good for this purpose (except for writing and drawing tasks). The felt reduces noise and prevents materials from sliding around.

Fig. 14-15 Clearly define each child's work space.

Provide a neatly lettered name card for each child's place. Name cards avoid confusion and conflict about where to sit. They also help children learn to read their own names and the names of other children.

Begin with materials and activities with which children are familiar. Leggo, pegboards, beads, and crayons are examples of materials that most children enjoy. Such materials allow children to be successful and independent from the start.

When manipulative materials are used, prepare individual setups. Small baskets or low plastic boxes are good for this purpose. These reduce the likelihood of children grabbing and hoarding materials while getting used to working close together.

Note which materials children like the best. These are the materials children will be successful with. Present these materials several days in a row. Later, the teacher can use these preferred activities as a reward when

Fig. 14-16 Everything should be made ready before children arrive.

children first do a less preferred task: "After you have finished matching the circles you can do the train puzzle, John."

Know when to change tasks. If a child is not attentive or appears frustrated, the teacher should pause and observe the child. Usually the root of the problem can be spotted. The teacher can then give the child additional help or can switch to another task.

Have alternate materials at hand. These can be given to children who are having too hard a time with a planned task. They can also be for children who finish early.

Before the children arrive make sure that everything to be used is ready, figure 14-16. All materials for a preacademic session should be within the teacher's reach. This prevents the session from being broken by the teacher leaving the area. Teacher absence often prompts undesirable behavior in young children.

From the start, introduce children to holding activities. Holding activities are self-managing activities. Children can work

with such materials without supervision while waiting for the teacher and the rest of the children to join the group. Initially these are manipulative type materials presented at the beginning of the school year.

Keep interactions with each child low-keyed and positive. Show interest by well-thought-out questions and comments. Comments should describe but not label what the child is doing. Examples: "Susie, you have matched all of the animals and all of the flowers." or "You are cutting right on the lines, Jill."

Include activities which allow children to move about, figure 14-17. Young children are not expected to sit still for long periods of time. To have them do so is developmentally unsound. Therefore, especially in the beginning, alternate sitting tasks with tasks where the children can move about. Examples:

- Let children get and return materials.
- Play the "Find the Match" game. "Find something red (or something round, or smooth, or growing) somewhere in the room."

Fig. 14-17 Include activities which allow children to move about during preacademics.

Fig. 14-18 There is nothing more rewarding than to see children learn.

- Allow children to stand while working at some tasks.
- Let a child walk around the table to observe or to help another child.

MAKING PREACADEMICS FUN

It is very important for teachers to make preacademics fun. Children will then be eager to come to the session each day. They will experience success. They will grow to love learning when they are successful. Teachers will also have a good time and feel successful about their teaching. There is nothing more rewarding for teachers than to see young children learn new skills, figure 14-18.

SUMMARY

Preacademics is a main curriculum area in most preschool programs. The kinds of

activities which are included vary from program to program. Basic to every preacademic program should be readiness activities. These are activities aimed at teaching certain skills called prerequisites to reading, writing, and arithmetic. These skills range from simple attending and imitating skills to complex memory and concept-formation skills.

Successful preacademic sessions depend upon a number of things. Grouping children according to age, abilities, interests, or social development is an important consideration. How preacademics is introduced at the beginning of the year requires careful consideration. It is also important that preacademic sessions be fun for children and teacher. Only when children enjoy such activities will they love learning.

STUDENT ACTIVITIES

- Observe a preschool or day care group. Describe the preacademic period if there is one. If there is no formal period describe other activities that might qualify as preacademics.

- Follow one child in the group which you are observing - preferably choose a handicapped or delayed child. Describe any imitating or instruction-following with this child if it occurs. If it does not occur, describe other preacademic-related behaviors the child engaged in.

- List ten activities in addition to those given in this unit that would qualify as perceptual-motor or fine motor skills.

- Suggest five ways that a teacher can help a child become interested in the preacademic period.

REVIEW

A. Briefly define each of the following preacademic skills.

1. attention span
2. imitation and modeling skills
3. instruction-following
4. perceptual-motor skill
5. fine motor control

6. receptive language
7. expressive language
8. concept formation
9. memory
10. prerequisite skills

B. List four subskills of concept formation.

C. Select the three best answers from the choices offered to complete each statement.

1. Examples of spatial relationships are such words as
   a. in front.
   b. next to.
   c. hot and cold.
   d. at the top.

2. Examples of seriation and gradation are
   a. tall, taller, tallest.
   b. yesterday, today, tomorrow.
   c. cold, warm, hot.
   d. in, on, under.

3. Examples of discrimination skills are
   a. recognizing the difference between sandals, sneakers, slippers.
   b. reading pictures left to right.
   c. pointing to "d" in a "d" "p" pair.
   d. sorting objects according to size, color, or shape.

4. Examples of classification skills are
   a. grouping pictures according to content (all the cars in one pile and all the trucks in another).
   b. hearing the difference between a bugle and a drum.
   c. describing the things one does before going to bed; upon getting up in the morning.
   d. saying in what way birds are alike, or fish, or plants.

5. Examples of receptive language are
    a. shutting the door when asked.
    b. turning around when one's name is called.
    c. crying when told to stop doing something one wants to do.
    d. asking for another cookie.

D. Briefly answer each of the following.

1. What size should preschool preacademics groups be?

2. How should children be grouped?

3. How long should a preacademic period be?

4. Why should each work space have a card with the child's name lettered on it?

5. What kinds of preacademic materials should be presented early in the year?

6. Why should teachers take note of which activities children prefer?

7. What are holding materials?

8. What kind of interactions should the teacher initiate with individual children during preacademics?

9. What is the most important thing for teachers to remember in planning and conducting preacademics activities?

E. Match each item in Column I with the correct item in Column II.

Column I	Column II
1. a fine motor skill	a. withdrawing hand from a hot burner
2. a prerequisite skill	b. classification skills
3. eagerness to learn	c. motivation
4. watching, listening, and doing	d. Montessori cylinders
5. a perceptual-motor response	e. imitation
6. a manipulative material	f. prewriting skills
7. ability to form categories	g. buttoning
8. logical organization of thought	h. a prereading skill
9. seriation, gradation	i. preferred activity
10. stringing beads in a pattern	j. readiness skill
11. drawing lines between dots	k. premath skill
12. naming objects in a picture from left to right	l. a discrimination skill
13. grouping objects in sets of 2, 3, or 4	m. concept formation
14. an activity the child can manage independently before group time	n. holding activity
15. can be used as a reward	o. happy, happier, happiest

Unit 15 SELF-HELP SKILLS

OBJECTIVES

After studying this unit, the student will be able to

- List at least three self-help skills in each of the following categories: feeding, dressing, toileting, and general social.

- Discuss several reasons why the teacher should help all children, especially handicapped children, learn to take care of their own self-help needs.

- Define reverse sequencing and describe, step by step, a self-help skill that should be taught by such a procedure.

Handicapped or developmentally disabled children must learn to live as independently as possible with, and in spite of, their handicap, figure 15-1. To acquire this independence they need to have a variety of self-help skills. This means learning to care for their own needs in feeding, dressing, toileting, and other daily routines, figure 15-2. All children do not perform the behaviors at exactly the same age. Some children, both handicapped and nonhandicapped, learn self-help skills early. Some learn them later. There are developmental differences even within the same child. A child may accomplish certain self-help learnings well ahead of the average age given. Some tasks may be mastered at the average age level, and others much later.

BUILDING INDEPENDENCE

During the early years is the best time for learning self care. This is a time when all children are striving for independence. They are eager to help themselves. They work hard at it, given the opportunity to go at their own pace.

Observation of young children shows that they watch and imitate the self-help efforts of older children and adults. Furthermore, young children practice, practice,

Fig. 15-1 Handicapped children must learn to live with their handicap.

	Dressing	Feeding	Toileting and Washing	General
2 to 3 years (24 to 36 months)	Can take clothes off to put on other articles of clothing but tires easily and gives up. Generally cooperative when helped.	Can use a fork but still prefers spoon or fingers. Will feed self food that is liked. Drinks from glass.	Verbalizes toilet needs in advance. Retention span for urination lengthening—can "hold" longer.	Can open some doors with easy latches or low knobs. Goes up and down stairs, mark time fashion, usually holding rail. Can push chair or stool around to climb on and get what is wanted.
3 to 4 years (36 to 48 months)	Undresses self rapidly and well. Can put on most articles of clothing and can do some unbuttoning and zipping depending upon the size and place of buttons or zipper. Can put clothes away in drawers or hang them up given right height hooks.	Usually eats with fork; can spread with knife. Can pour from pitcher into glass with few mishaps. Enjoys eating with family but may dawdle endlessly.	May insist on washing self in tub but does it imperfectly. Very few toilet accidents. Often wakes at night and asks to be taken to toilet.	Can tell own age, sex, and first and last name. Can follow 2- and 3-step directions. Able to separate from parent—to stay at preschool by self.
4 to 5 years (48 to 60 months)	Laces shoes; some children learning to tie. Dresses and undresses with little or no assistance especially if clothes are laid out. May dawdle excessively over dressing. Can tell front from back but may still have trouble getting some garments on just right.	Uses knife, fork, and spoon appropriately; often needs help with "tough" meat. Likes to make own breakfast and lunches (dry cereal, peanut butter sandwiches, etc.)	Can bathe and dry self, at least partially. Can put self through entire toileting and hand washing and drying. May "forget" sometimes.	Plays in the neighborhood and comes home when called, most of the time. Can put play materials away but usually needs reminding. Can do many household chores: set table, empty trash, feed pets. May "forget" some steps.
5 to 6 years (60 to 72 months)	Ties own shoes. Can manage almost any article of clothing. Can assist younger brother or sister in getting dressed.	Can use all eating utensils well but often messy because always in a hurry to get back to play. Uses appropriate table manners but tends to forget.	Bathes and dries self with minimal supervision—usually does not wash own hair, but may help. Totally self-sufficient in toilet routine.	Can go to school by self. Can be trusted with small sums of money and a small list at the neighborhood store. Can make own bed, put soiled clothes in hamper. Learning to distinguish left from right.

Fig. 15-2 Examples of self-help skills for various age levels.

practice. Watch a child who has just discovered how to unlace shoes. That child takes the laces out a dozen, maybe fifteen, times a day, figure 15-3. Watch the two-year-old, pushing, pulling, and shoving a chair over to the kitchen sink. Why? The youngster wants to get a drink of water without help. Observe a three-year-old struggling, twisting, and turning in a mighty effort to get a shirt on all alone. The shirt, of course, may end up inside out or upside down. That is all right. It is part of learning this self-help skill.

SUCCESS IS IMPORTANT

The pride and joy that comes from mastery is important. Such pride can be seen

Fig. 15-3 Shoe unlacing is a big discovery.

in the glow of success when the two-year-old finally gets that drink of water. It can be heard, too, in the delighted shout of the three-year-old: "Look what I did! I got my shirt on all by myself!" or the pleasure of the five-year-old who finally learns to tie that shoe (never mind the lopsided bow or the dangling laces). It can be seen in the self-importance of the six-year-old who learns to make peanut butter sandwiches not only for himself but for his little sister as well. These are the kinds of things that help a child feel successful and confident.

The handicapped child, too, can learn these skills. That child, too, can feel good when the shirt is on, inside out or backwards. Some handicapped children may not be able to verbalize, may not be able to say, "Look what I did, all by myself!" The look on the child's face, however, tells how good the feeling is.

It is true that getting about in a wheelchair, in leg braces, or with a cane is bothersome. It does not, however, have to interfere with independence. What does interfere is the need for constant help in routine matters such as toileting, dressing, and feeding. It is a bother to ask for help all of the time. During adolescence, asking for such help can be especially embarrassing. Therefore, time and energy must be devoted to helping children acquire self-help skills while they are very young.

The preschool is a good place for all children to learn a full range of self-help skills. For the handicapped child, the preschool teacher should concentrate on step-by-step teaching of self-help skills, figure 15-4. These skills need to be practiced every day. Practice adds up to that "I can do it" feeling. Such a feeling leads to a self-confident child and eventually an independent (though handicapped) adult.

Fig. 15-4 Teachers must concentrate on step-by-step teaching of self-help skills.

LET THE CHILD DO IT

Not all adults know how to let young children learn to do things for themselves. Adults may do too much for the child. They do things which the child could do, given enough time. What happens when an adult steps in and expertly zips the zipper the child has been fumbling with so intently or reties the shoe that the child had just tied with such effort? Without meaning to, and without using words, it is as if the adult has said "You are too slow" or "You are not very good." Often, such interference sets up resistance in the child. Sometimes the opposite may happen. The child may learn to just stand there and let the adult do more and more. The child may become totally dependent, unnecessarily.

In the preschool such "helping" behavior usually comes from uncertainty on the part of the teacher. This is especially true of teachers who are just learning to work with handicapped children. They do not know what to do. They, themselves, feel helpless. By doing things for the child, the teachers feel more competent and more successful. Also, adults often feel uncomfortable, or "hard-hearted," if they let a child struggle. They feel duty-bound to help. Even kind and well-meaning help must not be pressed unnecessarily upon the child, however.

WAYS TO HELP

True kindness to handicapped children lies in quietly finding ways to help them help themselves.

- It is guiding a little boy's arm and hand so that he can reach all the way down into a shirt sleeve. It is helping him, at that point, to firmly grasp the edge of the cuff. Then it is a simple matter for him to turn the sleeve right-side out, all by himself.

- For the little girl who cannot walk, it is laying her clothes out ahead of time.

Everything she needs to dress herself is right there at her fingertips. She can then manage on her own.

- It is making sure at nap time in day care that blankets are long enough and well tucked-in at the foot of the beds. This makes it easier for children to make their beds by themselves.

Another aspect of true kindness to young handicapped children is for teachers to give positive verbal feedback as the children try to do things for themselves. This means telling the children exactly what it is they are doing right. Children then know immediately when they are successful. They know, too, that their efforts are appreciated. The following are some examples of positive feedback: "You poured your milk so nice and slow. You didn't spill a drop!" "Look at that! You already buttoned three buttons; only two to go." "You remembered to rinse the soap off your hands and to turn the water off. You are getting good at washing your hands all by yourself!"

WHEN TO HELP

There are many times when a child asks for help. Children may ask for help with tasks that they have already learned to do. Like everyone, children have off days. They have days when they are tired, upset, or not feeling well. Everyone is dependent at times, figure 15-5. Handicapped children are no exception. On these occasions it is good that a child can ask for help. Even the most independent child needs to know that there are helpful adults to turn to. In such situations, help should be given in just the right amount. The child should receive only what has been asked for. There should be the assurance, however, that more help is available if needed. Such help can often be given in a gamelike way. The child, then, is still involved, still successful, and not a passive bystander demanding to be waited upon.

HOW TO HELP

An example of such gamelike assistance is given in the following situation. Robert was a cerebral palsied child, 5 years 2 months old. He had had two years of preschool. In the left column is each step in the interaction between the teacher and the child. In the right-hand column are explanations of what the teacher did to give Robert a good learning experience.

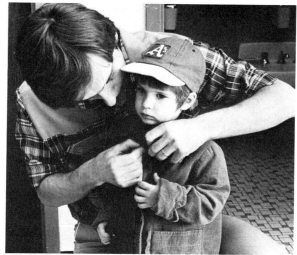

Fig. 15-5 **Even the most independent child needs help at times.**

Fig. 15-6 **First the teacher asks, "What do you need?"**

Teacher-Child Interactions	Explanation

1. Robert put his foot on the teacher's lap. His shoe was half unlaced.
   Teacher: "Hi, Robert. What do you want?" (figure 15-6)
   Robert: "Tie my shoe."

2. Teacher: "All right, but first you need to lace it."

3. Robert: "No, you lace. I don't know how."
   As he said this he looked several times toward his two special friends, who were getting ready to go outside.

4. Teacher (smiling in friendly fashion), "You are kidding me. Of course you know how to lace your shoes. I saw you do it yesterday."

5. Teacher: "But sit down here on the floor. I will help you."

6. Robert sat down. The teacher bent over and inserted the tip of one lace partly through an eyelet, and said to Robert, "Now you can pull it through." (figure 15-7)

7. Robert pulled the lace through. The teacher said, "Good, Robert, you pulled it through exactly right. Now hand me the other lace." She repeated the same process - Robert pulling the lace through and handing her the next lace - until the shoe was completely laced except for the top pair of holes.

Explanation

1. All young children need to practice using verbal language. The teacher, therefore, asked Robert to tell her what he needed. For a child with less well-developed language than Robert (or no language), the teacher might have settled for only one word or even just the gesture of putting his foot in her lap.

2. The teacher sequenced the task for Robert by stating that the shoe needed to be laced first. Another time, she may ask Robert to tell her what has to be done before the shoe can be tied. This gives the child experience in thinking a task through.

3. When Robert refused to lace the shoe, the teacher quickly appraised the whole situation. It was obvious that the child did not want to be left behind when his friends went outdoors. The teacher knew, however, that they would be gone long before Robert (with his impaired eye-hand coordination) could lace his shoe by himself. What is the best thing to do?

4. The teacher knew Robert could lace his shoe She did not want him to get away with saying "I can't." She decided to tell him, in a warm and friendly fashion, that she knew he could do it, while offering at the same time, to help him.

5. She had him sit on the floor with his back against the wall. This gave him a firm base from which to work on his shoe, without falling over. This tactic should be used with all young children. Having a child stand on one leg to tie a shoe causes him to loose his balance.

6. The teacher did the part of the task that would have been most difficult for Robert. She started the lace through the hole each time. The things he had to do he could do quickly and easily with immediate success. In other words, each time he pulled a lace through he could see that the shoe was that much closer to being laced.

7. With each step, the teacher gave Robert praise, verbal feedback, and a cue for the next step: "Good, Robert." (praise) "You pulled it through exactly right." (task feedback) "Now hand me the other lace." (cue for next step in this self-help sequence)

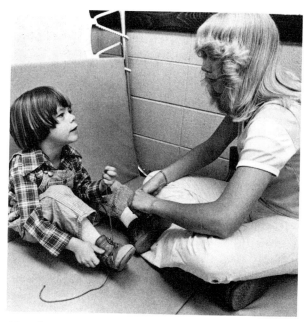

Fig. 15-7 The teacher lets the child pull the lace through.

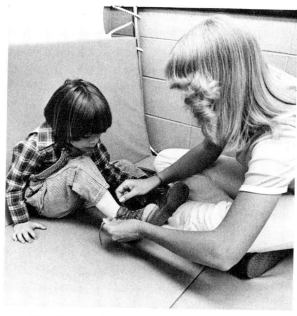

Fig. 15-8 Quickly the teacher tied the shoe.

8. Teacher: "I bet that you can do the last two all by yourself. Here, I will hand you the lace this time.
   Robert: "I know which one." He proceded to finish the last pair of holes and said, "All done."

8. Now that the job was almost done, the teacher knew it would not take Robert long to finish it. She challenged him in a friendly fashion to take that responsibility. Her motives were important. She wanted him to have the satisfaction of bringing the job to a successful conclusion all by himself.

9. Teacher: "That's right, Robert. It's all done and you finished the lacing all by yourself. Good for you. Here, let me tie your shoe for you and then you can go out and play." (figure 15-8)

9. The teacher gave Robert positive, content-focused feedback in the form of a praise statement. She said exactly what it was that he did well.

10. Then she turned around and called Robert's friends, "Can you wait a minute? Robert is almost ready to go out!"

10. The teacher made sure that Robert's hard work paid off. She asked the boys to wait for him when she saw they were about to go out. Also, she tied his shoe for him quickly so there would be no further delay.

SEQUENCING SELF-HELP TASKS

Robert was a handicapped child who had already learned a number of self-help skills. What about the children who cannot do things for themselves? There are children who cannot put on their own coat. They cannot take care of their own toileting needs. They cannot feed themselves. They cannot ask for what they want. What does the teacher do then? The first thing to do is to divide the self-help task into small steps. This sequencing strategy is described in detail in unit 11. Here are a few examples of the sequencing process.

Putting on a Coat

In helping a child learn to put on a coat the following step-by-step procedure works for most children.

1. Place the coat on a child-sized chair. Arrange it so that it looks as if a child has slipped out of the coat while sitting on the chair.
2. Have the child sit on the chair.
3. Have the child turn and look at the right (or left) armhole.
4. Guide the child's arm into the armhole.
5. Give positive, content-focused feedback and a cue as to what comes next: "Good, you have one arm in. Now look at the other sleeve."
6. Repeat this for the other arm.
7. Some children move their arms by themselves at this point so that they shrug the coat over the shoulders, figure 15-9. If this does not happen, the teacher moves the child's arms forward to make it happen.

Toileting

Learning to take care of toileting needs is a major self-help skill that all children, no matter how handicapped, can learn. The

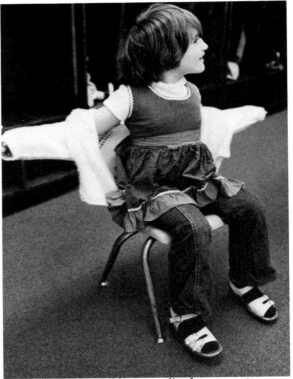

Fig. 15-9 Many children can slip the garment on over their shoulders by themselves.

sequence can be described as follows. The child

goes into bathroom
pulls pants down
gets on toilet
eliminates
uses toilet tissue
gets off toilet
flushes toilet
washes hands
gets paper towel out of dispenser
dries hands
puts towel in basket
leaves bathroom

What could be more simple? Yet, for many young children (both handicapped and nonhandicapped) most of these steps present great difficulty. The process of simply getting on and off the toilet may have to be broken down into several smaller steps. This is

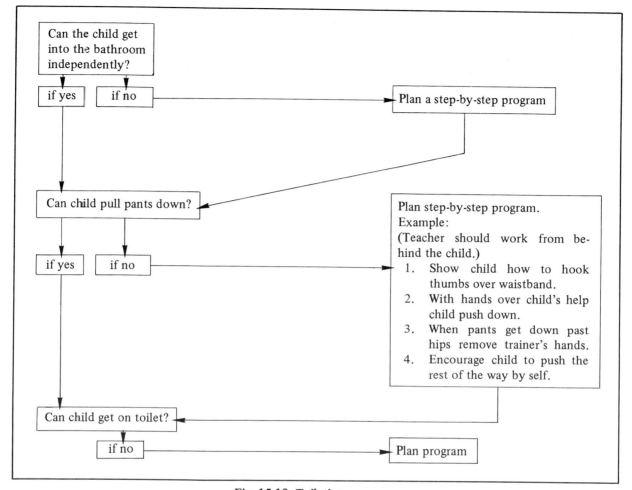

Fig. 15-10 Toileting sequence.

especially true for the very young child or the physically handicapped child. Using toilet tissue effectively is a challenge for all young children. Special training is almost always required.

Step-by-Step Planning

How does the teacher know what to do in order to provide special training? Actually, it is a fairly simple procedure. It is breaking a skill into smaller and smaller steps. To do this, the teacher turns each skill item into a question which asks if the children can do it. If the answer is yes, the teacher proceeds to a next item. If the answer is no, the teacher figures cut substeps that are appropriate

for that child at that point. The first part of a toileting sequence is shown in figure 15-10.

Backward Chaining

Some tasks can best be taught through the backward chaining procedure described in an earlier unit. Learning to zip a coat is a good example. The steps are as follows. (The adult works from behind the child.)

1. Bring both front pieces of the open coat together at the bottom.
2. Insert zipper pin into housing.
3. Seat zipper pin firmly in housing.
4. Grasp zipper tab.

5. Pull zipper tab to top, figure 15-11.
6. Push tab down firmly to lock.

In backward chaining the child first masters step six, then step five, then step four. This allows the child to move from the simplest to the more difficult parts of the task. It insures success each step of the way. For example, step four is not even attempted until steps five and six are mastered. It may take a long time to work back to steps two and one, but eventually these are mastered, too.

If a child is not learning a task, the program must be changed. The teacher must change the sequence, the size of the steps, or the task itself until the child is succeeding. Teachers must have faith that every child can learn the necessary self-help skills. Teachers must keep trying until they find a program that works for each child. Children and teachers can then feel good about themselves and about each other. Both have a feeling of success. This brings the child that much closer to independence.

SUMMARY

Young children must learn to take care of their own personal and physical needs. This is especially important for young handicapped or disabled children. They must learn to live with their handicaps and achieve independence in spite of them.

The preschool years are the best years for children to acquire self-help skills, figure 15-12. In order to accomplish this, children need the understanding and help of their preschool teachers. This help must be of a special kind and amount - not too little and not too much.

Fig. 15-11 Step 5 in backward zipper training.

Fig. 15-12 The preschool years are the best years to learn self-help skills.

The teacher must always let the children do as much for themselves as they can. To be successful at this, the teacher must know how to divide big tasks into small ones. The child then has many small successes that lead up to the big successes. With a number of such experiences, the child becomes self-confident and independent.

STUDENT ACTIVITIES

- Observe a preschool or day care center during children's arrival or departure time, during a toileting period, or at snack time. List at least six self-help tasks that children perform for themselves.

- The next time you shampoo your hair take note of the sequence of steps and write them down when you have finished. Start sequencing the steps with the decision to wash your hair. End the sequencing with your hair being in the finished state that you like it to be in.

- Select one of the major steps in the toileting sequence (or any other self-help skill). Write a six- to ten-step program for teaching it to a four-year-old deaf child who has no other physical disabilities.

- Ask a fellow student to role-play a child who cannot lace his own shoes. Teach the task in step-by-step fashion.

REVIEW

A. List the four major areas of self-help development. Give three examples of specific skills within each type.

B. Using the chart in figure 15-2, indicate the age level (2, 3, 4, or 5) a child is usually first able to accomplish each of the following skills.

1. Can bathe and dry self, at least partially.
2. Is learning to distinguish left from right.
3. Can pour liquid from a pitcher into a glass with few mishaps.
4. Laces shoes; some children learning to tie.
5. Can tell own age, sex, and first and last name.
6. Can verbalize toilet needs (asks to be taken).
7. Drinks from glass.
8. Can go up and down stairs, "mark time" fashion.
9. Can be trusted with small sums of money at the neighborhood store.
10. Likes to make own breakfast of dry cereal and lunch of peanut butter sandwiches.

C. Select the two best answers from the choices offered to complete each statement.

1. It is appropriate to expect
    a. all young children to learn a variety of self-help skills.
    b. children to refuse to help themselves; to dislike having to do things for themselves.
    c. all children to learn to bathe, dress, and feed themselves by their fifth birthday.
    d. children to work hard at learning self-help skills and to practice them over and over.

2. The handicapped child should
    a. learn self-help skills the same as any other child.
    b. enjoy the struggles required to learn to put on his own shirt just like any other young child.
    c. not be expected to learn to take care of his own toileting needs if he is in a wheelchair.
    d. not be expected to become independent when he reaches adulthood.

3. Competent preschool teachers
    a. do as much as possible for every child so that they (the teachers) can feel good.
    b. allow each child to struggle with those tasks that the child has shown he can do.
    c. see to it that the learning of self-help skills does not become a game; otherwise the child might not learn.
    d. give the child as much help as he asks for and seems to need.

4. Sequencing a self-help task for a child means that the teacher
    a. first puts the child's coat on for him, then buttons the flap at the neck.
    b. divides a task into many small, sequential steps.
    c. sometimes presents a task to the child in a reverse order of steps.
    d. decides that the child is too handicapped to learn to put his coat on if he cannot do it in the sequence that the teacher has laid out.

D. Referring to the shoe-lacing episode in the unit, briefly answer each of the following.

1. List two positive feedback statements which the teacher made to the child.
2. State why the teacher wanted the child to say what he needed.
3. Explain why the teacher had the child sit on the floor in order to help him with his shoes.
4. Describe what the teacher did to make sure the child's hard work "paid off."

E. The teacher wants a little girl to learn to zip her jacket independently. Place the following steps in an appropriate order for a backward chaining sequence.

1. Pull zipper tab to top.
2. Push tab down firmly to lock.
3. Bring both front pieces of open coat together at bottom.
4. Grasp zipper tab.
5. Insert zipper pin into housing.
6. Seat zipper pin firmly in housing.

SECTION 5
MANAGEMENT OF SPECIAL NEEDS

Unit 16 VISION AND HEARING IMPAIRED

OBJECTIVES

After studying this unit, the student will be able to

- Define residual vision and residual hearing and discuss their importance to the handicapped child's development.
- Describe five ways in which the preschool teacher can help the vision-impaired child.
- Describe five ways in which the preschool teacher can help the hearing-impaired child.

Vision and hearing are the two most important avenues of learning for young children, figure 16-1. When there is a problem in either of these areas, a child's development is affected, often seriously. Some children suffer both a severe hearing loss and a severe vision loss. These children are considered to be severely impaired or multihandicapped. Rarely are children so severely impaired enrolled in the regular preschool from the start. They require intensive special training programs in their very early years. The regular preschool cannot provide the highly specialized program.

Blind and visually impaired children can, however, be accommodated in the regular preschool. Deaf and hearing-impaired children can also be accommodated. Teachers can readily learn the necessary management skills. The important thing to remember is that the blind or deaf child is first of all a child. These children can learn in their own ways.

BLIND AND VISUALLY IMPAIRED

Total blindness means the child can see nothing at all, not even light or darkness. Most visually impaired children, though labeled blind, have at least slight vision. Sometimes they can see the general outline of things, but not the details. Some can distinguish bright colors. Residual vision is the name given to whatever amount of vision is left. This residual vision will be lost unless these children are continually encouraged to use what is left.

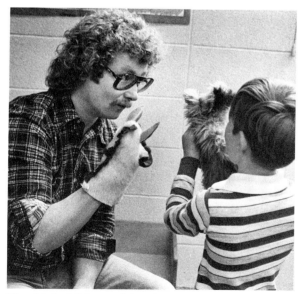

Fig. 16-1 Vision and hearing are important avenues of learning.

185

Blind and visually impaired children can function perfectly well in a regular preschool. Sighted children can be helpful. They learn to touch the blind child's shoulder or to call the blind child's name in order to get that child's attention. They learn to put things into the child's hands. They learn to describe what is going on in ways the blind child can understand.

Teachers can do many things to make the preschool a good learning experience for visually impaired children. One of the most important of these is to avoid overprotecting the child. The blind child must be allowed to explore and experiment, to bump into a wall, to fall down, to get up. The teacher must, however, make sure the environment is safe, figure 16-2. In that way, the child will not suffer unnecessary harm. Pathways must be kept clear of things the child can trip over. The blind child also needs to learn to trail the room, the halls, and the outdoor fenced play area. *Trailing* means to find one's own way by lightly keeping a hand in touch with a wall while walking.

The teacher must be careful not to speak for the child. Instead, the teacher can help blind children speak out for themselves, and defend their rights. Part of the teacher's job, then, is to follow through. The teacher must make sure that the sighted child stops ramming the tricycle, gives back the eggbeater, or does whatever else the blind child has requested.

With very little extra assistance, blind preschoolers can soon learn to manage almost all indoor and outdoor activities. There are many ways that teachers can help blind children. A number of examples are given.

Use specific words to tell the child what to do. Do not use phrases like "Come here" or "Put the book there." Use specific words to tell the child what to do. Say "Put the book on the table," or "I am sitting by the piano. Come to me."

Talk to the child about everything in the environment. Give the names over and over for chair, door, window, doll, dog. Just talking about the object is not enough, however. Talking about something called a watering can to a visually impaired child has little meaning. The child must hold one, feel what is inside, pour from it, even smell it.

Fig. 16-2 Make sure the environment is safe for the blind child to move about in.

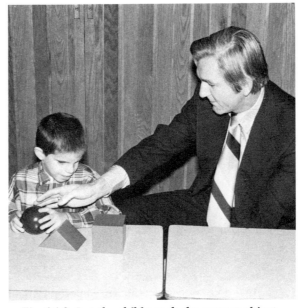

Fig. 16-3 Let the child touch the correct object.

Blind children need to learn action words. Tell the blind child what he or she is doing at the moment of action: jumping, standing, rolling, poking, laughing, frowning.

Teach blind children to listen and to sort out sounds. Tell the child what the schoolroom noises are, such as the guinea pig squeaking, the faucet dripping, and the fan whirring. Teach children the sounds of various other things such as the sound of the eggbeater, the tick of a timer, and the swish of sandpaper blocks. Play guessing games. The teacher (or another child) makes the sound. The blind child touches the correct object from a group of several items. This game is fun for sighted children, too. (So that sighted children do not guess by seeing the object, the teacher can make the noise by turning away from the group.)

Help a blind child learn which sounds are dangerous, and which need not be frightening. The lawn mower in the playground is something to stay away from. The vacuum cleaner used for quick cleanups is something the child can help push. The squeak of the swing chains warns, "Keep away." The click of the sand toys invites "Come in."

Give visually impaired children many opportunities to learn through smelling, touching, and tasting. Cooking experiences are good for all children in the preschool. These kinds of experiences are particularly valuable for the blind child. All kinds of sorting games are important, too. Shapes, sizes, textures, smells, and weights are but a few of the characteristics of objects that blind children can learn to discriminate, figure 16-3.

Teach the blind preschooler how to go from left to right on as many tasks as possible. The left-to-right skill is one the child will need when learning to read either braille or large

type. When using the pegboard, for example, have the child start in the upper left-hand corner. The child works across that entire row. The next starting place is the extreme left-hand hole in the next row down. This is a good teaching strategy for all preschool children. In order to be successful readers, children need to learn left-to-right and top-to-bottom progression.

Mannerisms of the Blind

Many visually impaired children display peculiar behaviors at times. These are sometimes referred to as *blindisms*. They may include

- rocking back and forth
- poking their fingers into their eyes
- flipping their hands back and forth in front of their eyes, figure 16-4
- spinning about
- making strange noises

It is thought that blindisms develop because blind children have "nothing better to do" as infants. Because they cannot see, they receive

Fig. 16-4 Certain mannerisms may characterize the vision-impaired child.

Fig. 16-5 Professional consultation is important.

too little appropriate stimulation. They do not learn to respond to the environment the way sighted infants do. Instead, it appears that blind babies develop their own stimulation and their own responses.

Most such mannerisms in blind children are inappropriate. They make the child stand out as different. They must be eliminated from the child's behavior patterns. These responses need to be replaced by more appropriate behaviors. The preschool is one place where more appropriate behaviors can be developed. The more interests and skills the blind child develops the less time that child spends rocking, spinning, and poking. With a little help from teachers, other children can be helpful in reducing a blind child's mannerisms: "Come Susie, let's go and get Mary and give her a ride on the back of your tricycle."

Additional Help

Parents are important resources for teachers. Parents can tell the teaching staff what kinds of things they do at home for their blind child. They can share their anxieties and their hopes with teachers. Teachers must also share with parents what is going on in the preschool.

Professional consultation is important when integrating a blind child into the preschool classroom, figure 16-5. There are many agencies that supply this kind of help. Also available are books, government pamphlets, cassette tapes, and films.

DEAF AND HEARING IMPAIRED

The child with a severe hearing impairment is handicapped in many ways. Speech and language development are usually faulty and delayed. A deaf child often develops

Fig. 16-6 Hearing aids are often prescribed.

behavior problems, too. These may be caused by loneliness and frustration. Not understanding what is going on can make children feel left out. Many deaf children have perfectly normal intellects. However, they may be labeled as mentally retarded because of how they respond. Since they cannot hear, they do not know what is expected of them.

Most children labeled as deaf have some hearing. This is referred to as *residual hearing*. As with residual vision, residual hearing must be used as much as possible. Hearing aids are often prescribed. It is felt that a hearing aid allows the greatest amount of residual hearing to be used. Very young children can be fitted with hearing aids, figure 16-6. Many hearing specialists say the earlier this is done, the better. However, there are differing opinions on this issue. There are cases where specialists may not want to prescribe amplification devices for a very young child.

Methods of Communication

Deaf children can learn to communicate in several different ways.

Speech   Many deaf children can learn to speak. Learning to speak often depends upon the degree of the hearing loss. The more severe the loss, the less intelligible the child's speech is likely to be. The age at which the hearing loss occurs is important, too.

Fingerspelling   Manual alphabet is another name for fingerspelling. Individual letters are formed by shaping the fingers in various ways. The letters so formed are put together to form words and sentences.

Lipreading   Speechreading is another word for lipreading. The child learns to "read" what a person is saying by watching that person's face, mouth, tongue placement, and throat movements.

Fig. 16-7   **Teaching through speech, signing, and lip reading.**

Sign language   This is a system for giving and receiving messages. Hand movements, body movements, and gestures represent words, thoughts, and questions. There are several signing systems.

Total communication   This is a system in which speech, fingerspelling, signing, and lipreading are combined, figure 16-7.

Preschool teachers seem to be more comfortable with deaf and hearing-impaired children than they are with some other handicapped children. One reason may be that the deaf have not been as segregated as some of the other handicapped. Even so, there are special considerations that must be kept in mind for hearing-impaired children. The following are some suggestions for teachers.

- Do not use single words or telegraphic speech. Talk in brief, but complete, sentences.

- Kneel or bend down to the child's level to talk. A deaf child needs to be talked to face-to-face.

- Do not talk in a loud or strained voice. Do not overenunciate. This makes lipreading more difficult.

- Use gestures when appropriate. Do not, however, do too much gesturing. This

Fig. 16-8 The teacher must point to what she is talking about.

may interfere with the child's efforts at lipreading.

- At group time, the child should be seated directly across from the teacher. This gives the child the best possible chance at lipreading.

- Face the light when talking to a deaf child. The light must be on the teacher's face, not the child's. If there is light glaring in the child's eyes, the child is not able to focus on the teacher's face and lips.

- When talking about something in the room, point to it, touch it, or hold it up, figure 16-8. For example, when the teacher picks up the scissors while giving the instructions the child knows what to do.

- To get a deaf child's attention, gently touch or tap the child on the hand or shoulder. Be careful not to startle the child.

- Some deaf children make strange noises. They do not hear these themselves but they bother the other children. Gently remind them to be more quiet.

- Include deaf children at music time. Let the deaf children feel the vibrations of musical instruments. Let them play the instruments. Have many clapping and rhythmic activities, such as jumping, twirling, and stretching to music.

- Include deaf children in story time. Choose books with bright, clear, colorful pictures that tell the story. Gesture when reading the story. For example, look pleased and surprised when the kittens are found in the barn. This gives the deaf child additional cues.

- Keep a regular schedule of activities each day: snack follows preacademics, and then comes music. There is security for a young child, especially a handicapped child, in knowing what comes next.

Hearing Aids

There are three common types of hearing aids worn by young children. One is strapped on or worn in a pocket close to the child's chest. Another is worn on the head, clipped to the hair or to a headband. A third type is worn behind the ear. Each type of aid is attached to cords. These plug into the child's ear through a very small insert. The insert is called an *earmold*. A hearing aid is usually comfortable when fitted properly. Minor problems may arise, however. Both teachers and parents should be alert to these possible problems. Four are mentioned here.

Improper fit or a damaged earmold. If the earmold does not fit the child's ear opening properly, it can cause discomfort. Also, if the earmold becomes chipped or cracked it may irritate the ear. A cracked earmold may also make a squealing sound. This is called feedback. It can be most annoying and uncomfortable.

Dead batteries. It is easy for parents and teachers to know when the batteries in the hearing aid are dead. The child no longer responds to sounds or to speech. Keep a supply of extra batteries on hand.

Worn cords. A hearing aid does not work if the cords are worn out, broken, or split. Cords are simple to replace. Spares should be on hand.

Sore ears. The earmold should never be inserted in a sore, cracked, or infected ear. When this condition exists, the child should be taken to the doctor.

Many young children will turn their hearing aid off when first learning to wear it. Teachers must check for that, too. Eventually, most children adapt to wearing their aid. At this point they can be taught to check the working order of the aid themselves. For the most part, however, teachers and parents need to check the child's hearing aid at least once a day, figure 16-9.

Fig. 16-9 Check the child's hearing aid at least once a day.

SUMMARY

Vision- and hearing-impaired children can usually function well in the integrated preschool. Teachers can readily learn the necessary management skills. The other children can be helpful, too. All residual vision and residual hearing must be used. Disuse causes further weakening of these senses.

Blind children need to learn to use all of their other senses. Teachers and parents should tell them about everything that is going on. The children must learn to listen and to get about by themselves. Many of the regular preschool activities can aid in these learnings. Other activities can be adapted by the preschool teacher. The important thing is to keep the blind child involved. This helps to prevent or reduce the peculiar behaviors (blindisms) that many blind children display.

Deaf children can function well in a regular preschool. These children can be taught a variety of ways to communicate. Some deaf children learn to speak. Others can "speak" and "listen" through fingerspelling, lipreading, signing, or a combination of these.

There are many things a preschool teacher can do to help the deaf child in the classroom. When talking to a child, do not stand above the child, but rather get down to the child's level. Speak directly to the child, face-to-face. Use gestures and other visual cues. However, do not use exaggerated gestures or speech. Engage the deaf child in all activities, including music and stories.

Many deaf children wear hearing aids. These aids need to be checked daily for damage or worn parts. It takes only a few moments of the teacher's time to make sure that the aid is in good working order.

STUDENT ACTIVITIES

• Play blindfold games in class. Do some of the following. Move across the room without stumbling or bumping into something. Move to a particular person based on that person's voice among several. Guess what is making certain sounds, such as a book closing, erasers clapping together, pencil sharpener, eggbeater, sand blocks, etc. Encourage students to think of other activities that will enable them to get some idea of what it is like to be without vision.

• Have a teacher of the blind come in and demonstrate various teaching materials used with blind and partially sighted children.

• Locate a person who deals with hearing aids. Ask the person to come to class and demonstrate several types. Encourage the demonstrator to let students wear one or more and then describe their reactions.

• Ask a person from your local deaf-education program to come in and demonstrate finger spelling, signing, and lipreading.

REVIEW

A. Briefly define each of the following terms.

1. total blindness
2. residual hearing
3. trailing
4. blindisms
5. amplification
6. telegraphic speech
7. earmold
8. total communication
9. overprotection
10. multihandicapped

B. Give the answers for each of the following.

1. List six things the teacher can do to help the blind child in the preschool.

2. List five examples of blindisms.

3. List five sources of help in working with blind children in the preschool.

4. List five methods of communication used by the deaf.

5. List six things the teacher can do to help the deaf child in the preschool.

C. Match each phrase in Column I with the correct item in Column II.

<table>
<tr><td colspan="2" align="center">Column I</td><td align="center">Column II</td></tr>
<tr><td>1.</td><td>two of the most important avenues of learning for young children</td><td>a. residual
b. blindisms</td></tr>
<tr><td>2.</td><td>the kind of training programs required for deaf/blind children in their very early years</td><td>c. vision and hearing
d. few</td></tr>
<tr><td>3.</td><td>the amount of children who are totally blind</td><td>e. across from (in front of)</td></tr>
<tr><td>4.</td><td>the name given to whatever vision or hearing is left</td><td>f. trail
g. intensive (special)</td></tr>
<tr><td>5.</td><td>in order to get about independently, blind children need to learn to do this on outdoor fences and the walls of the classroom and halls</td><td>h. fingerspelling
i. listening, touching, tasting, smelling</td></tr>
<tr><td>6.</td><td>visually impaired children must have many opportunities to learn by doing these things</td><td>j. hearing aid
k. overprotecting</td></tr>
<tr><td>7.</td><td>the inappropriate mannerisms of blind children</td><td>l. many</td></tr>
<tr><td>8.</td><td>amplification device</td><td>m. vibrations</td></tr>
<tr><td>9.</td><td>manual alphabet</td><td>n. deteriorates (becomes weakened even more)</td></tr>
<tr><td>10.</td><td>where the deaf child should be seated in relation to the teacher at group time</td><td>o. earmold</td></tr>
<tr><td>11.</td><td>to get a deaf child's attention, gently do this to the child's shoulder or arm</td><td>p. tap or touch</td></tr>
<tr><td>12.</td><td>let deaf children feel this effect of the musical instrument</td><td></td></tr>
<tr><td>13.</td><td>the part of the hearing aid which is inserted in the child's ear</td><td></td></tr>
<tr><td>14.</td><td>to do things for blind or deaf children that they can learn to do for themselves</td><td></td></tr>
<tr><td>15.</td><td>what happens to residual vision or hearing if not used</td><td></td></tr>
</table>

Unit 17 PHYSICAL AND HEALTH IMPAIRED

OBJECTIVES

After studying this unit, the student will be able to

- List and describe five or more physically handicapping conditions that may be encountered in the integrated preschool.
- Describe a grand mal seizure and discuss what the teacher should do.
- Suggest several adaptations to the preschool environment that will help in accommodating handicapped children.

PHYSICAL HANDICAPS

There are many different health-related and physically handicapping conditions in young children. Conditions which the teacher is most likely to encounter in the preschool are discussed in this unit. Many handicapped children have more than one handicap, figure 17-1. One condition often leads to another. These children are referred to as multihandicapped. The idea of multihandicaps must be kept in mind even though the various disabilities are studied one at a time.

Many handicapped children have retarded motor development. They crawl, stand, walk, run, and jump later than other children their age. They may stumble and fall more often. They may appear clumsy and awkward as they move about. Their motor disabilities are often caused by CNS (central nervous system) disorders. Cerebral palsied children are an example of one such combination. All motor-impaired children need help in learning basic movements such as creeping, crawling, standing, jumping, climbing, and balancing.

THE PHYSICAL THERAPIST

Most children with severe motor impairment receive physical therapy. The physical

Fig. 17-1 Many handicapped children have more than one handicap.

Fig. 17-2 **The physical therapist can train teachers in simple motor exercises.**

therapist is a person who has been trained to treat motor disabilities. If such a child is not getting this kind of help, teachers need to talk with parents. The social worker can often help the family to locate a source of physical therapy for the child.

Teachers and the physical therapist need to consult together frequently. The physical therapist can train teachers in simple motor exercises to use with children, figure 17-2. The physical therapist also needs to keep the teachers informed about what is going on in therapy sessions. Teachers can then take certain responsibilities. They can include the skills being taught in therapy into the child's classroom program. For example, the physical therapist may be teaching a child to pull up to a standing position. The teacher can plan several activities each day that motivate the child to do this. Practice through preschool games becomes fun and rewarding for that child. It also keeps the child in the mainstream.

PARENTS

Teachers of a physically disabled child also need to have an ongoing interaction with the child's parents. Parents can describe what the child can and cannot do. Parents can also

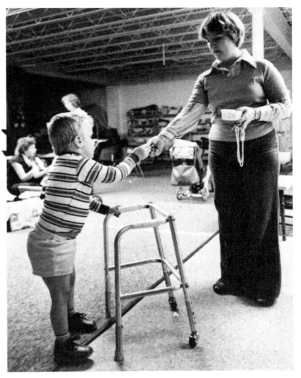

Fig. 17-3 **Some children need crutches, braces, or a walker.**

describe ways that they handle particular problems, such as what they do when the child falls, how they take the leg braces on and off, or how they help the child to transfer from wheelchair to toilet.

Parents and teachers can learn from each other. They can also maintain consistency for the child. What happens if the parent carries the child around and the teacher expects the child to walk? The child becomes confused. Together, parents and teachers can work out a program for the child, keeping expectations the same for home and school. The child learns much faster when there is consistency between programs.

LOCOMOTION PROBLEMS

Children who cannot get around easily are said to have *locomotion* problems. Some children may need braces, crutches, or a walker, figure 17-3. Other children may be totally dependent upon a wheelchair. Still others may be able to move from one activity to another on a flat, four-wheeled cart. Here, the child lies stomach-down on the cart and pushes with arms and hands. For stand-up activities, such a child can be laced into a standing board.

Children with poor locomotor skills may fall frequently. These falls often frighten the teachers more than the child. The child is probably quite used to falling. In fact, many handicapped children are given training in how to fall. They have been taught to relax to keep from hurting themselves. In order to prevent helplessness, these children must learn to get up by themselves, too. Adults must not "rush to the rescue."

Children with poor balance and poor motor control can often get around by pushing something ahead of them. Such things as a doll carriage or a large wooden box with a handlebar attached are good. Wooden "skis" can be attached to the bottom of the box for ease of pushing on carpets. If the piece of equipment is too light, it can be loaded with sandbags. The weight gives the child greater security.

PLAY AIDS

Certain toys or manipulative materials can be attached to a board. The board can then be mounted on the wall. Such an arrangement is good for children with standing and balancing problems. These materials are also good for children in wheelchairs. Wall toys allow children to grasp and play with materials they might not be able to manage otherwise.

Examples of materials that can be mounted on a playboard and hung on the walls include:

- bolts (used to lock doors)
- bicycle bells

Fig. 17-4 **Adaptive equipment for a child without arm and hand control.**

- light switches (especially ones hooked up to a dry cell battery so they light up)
- telephone dials (usually the telephone company will supply outdated equipment)

There are many things that can be done for children with poor arm and hand control, figure 17-4. Usually these consist of adapting materials already available in the regular preschool. The following are some suggested adaptations with creative materials.

- Give the child large sheets of paper. Provide large crayons, chalk, or paint-brush handles to work with. These may still be too small for the severely impaired child to grasp. If so, wrap them in several layers of taped-down paper strips.
- Push pencils, crayons, and colored pens through a sponge rubber ball. The child can hold the ball to scribble and draw.
- Tape paper to the table. This prevents the paper from slipping and sliding when the child is coloring, painting, or pasting.
- Children with very weak arm and hand muscles need special help. Provide magic markers or thick-tipped felt pens. These require much less effort than crayons.

Fig. 17-5 Flat wall-to-wall carpeting is best for children with mobility problems.

They also provide rich, bright colors with little or no pressure.

- Have fingerpaint and soft potter's clay available frequently. These materials require a minimum of fine motor control, while helping to build motor strength and control.

The classroom may need minor alterations to accommodate physically impaired children. Some examples are listed.

Railings. These should be attached to the walls at children's level. Railings help children with poor balance and coordination to move about independently. In the integrated preschool the railings have a dual purpose. They also serve as ballet and general exercise bars for nonhandicapped children.

Wheelchair accommodations. Ramps can be constructed to ease movement in and out of the building. Toileting areas must be cleared to allow enough space to accommodate the wheelchair children. There should be a rail in the toileting area, too. The child can then learn to swing from the wheelchair to the toilet seat.

Floor coverings. Flat wall-to-wall carpeting is the best floor covering for children with mobility problems, figure 17-5. If it is not possible to have carpeting, crutches must have nonskid tips. Shoes can also be made less slippery by gluing fine sandpaper or corduroy on the soles.

CEREBRAL PALSY

One of the handicapping conditions that almost always presents motor problems is cerebral palsy. CP was described briefly in an earlier unit. When working with these children, the preschool teacher needs two kinds of information. One has already been mentioned - working around the child's motor impairments. The other is how to deal with convulsive seizures (epileptic attacks) if they occur in school.

The student will recall from an earlier unit that epilepsy may take two forms. One form is the grand mal seizure. The other is the petit mal seizure.

In a grand mal seizure, the child may:

- fall to the floor
- lose consciousness for several minutes
- become rigid
- have severe jerking spasms in face, arm, and leg muscles
- drool or froth at the mouth
- lose control of urine and bowels
- breathe irregularly
- turn a pale bluish color

Petit mal seizures are quite different. They are much less severe. They usually last only a few seconds. There is often a rhythmic blinking of the eyes. Persons who do not know that the child is epileptic may think the child is daydreaming during a petit mal episode.

MANAGING THE SEIZURE

Most children with epilepsy are on anti-convulsant medication. Such medication usually controls the seizures. To insure control, the medicine must be taken regularly as prescribed by the child's physician. If an attack should occur in school, teachers need to know what to do. The following are some guidelines.

- Do not panic. There is no need to be frightened. The child will regain consciousness in a few moments.

- A child in seizure is almost sure to fall. Try to prevent injury to the child by breaking the fall or by keeping the child from falling on anything sharp such as furniture corners.

- Loosen tight clothing, especially at the neck.

- Turn the child's head to the side.

- Wipe away discharge from the mouth and nose to aid breathing.

- Never attempt to restrain the child's movement. Restraint leads to even more violent convulsing.

- Let the child rest following the seizure. Assure the child that all is well as consciousness returns.

It used to be recommended that a bar be placed between the upper and lower teeth of the convulsing child. This was thought to prevent tongue biting. Do not do this. It can cause severe damage to the child's teeth. It can also lead to the teacher getting severely bitten in attempting to insert the object.

The most important advice to the teacher is to remain calm. The teacher must appear confident. This helps both the stricken child and the other children. Children do not become alarmed if the teacher does not show alarm. In fact, the teacher's care of a child having an epileptic seizure can be valuable to all of the children. It provides a practical example in maintaining a caring human relationship for a person in trouble. All children can benefit from such modeling.

Parents should be called immediately following a child's first seizure in the classroom. Plans can then be made on how to handle future seizures that may occur. The importance of keeping the child on the prescribed regular medication schedule can also be stressed. Taking regular medication, as prescribed, is the best means of preventing seizures.

There is no need to alter the curriculum because a child has epilepsy. Unless parents or a physician gives other instructions, the epileptic child should be allowed to participate in all classroom activities. Climbing, swinging, and swimming may pose special

Fig. 17-6 Adequate supervision prevents accidents for all children in the integrated preschool.

risks at times. Adequate supervision and appropriate expectations on the part of teachers will prevent unnecessary accidents for all children, figure 17-6.

OTHER HANDICAPS RELATED TO CP

In comparison to other conditions, cerebral palsy has been given greater coverage in this unit because children with this condition are encountered frequently by teachers. Often these children are multihandicapped. As a part of their handicapped condition they may have one or more of the following:

- impaired vision
- defective speech
- impaired hearing
- specific learning problems
- mental retardation
- physical deformities
- behavioral disorders

One in three CP children may also have seizures as described earlier in the unit. Teachers who can manage CP children will be able to manage children with almost any other kind of health-related or physical impairment. Therefore, management of the other conditions that follow are discussed much more briefly. All, however, require special supervision, figure 17-7.

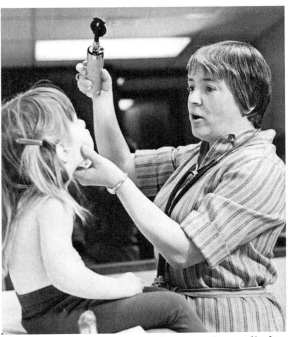

Fig. 17-7 All health problems require medical supervision.

CYSTIC FIBROSIS

Cystic fibrosis is a handicapping condition found among young children. It affects the lungs, sweat glands, and digestive system. Such children may cough a great deal. The coughing is not contagious, however. In fact, rather than spreading colds these children are highly susceptible to catching colds from others.

The child with cystic fibrosis may sweat a great deal. These children may eat more than most children, and have an excessive number of bowel movements. Cystic fibrosis children often have less stamina (that is, they tire much faster than other children). None of the characteristics of cystic fibrosis need to become serious classroom problems if treated matter-of-factly.

Most of all, children with cystic fibrosis need acceptance by other children. They may not, however, be able to play as vigorously as other children. Therefore, the teacher's first responsibility is to arrange many activities that the child can participate in. The second thing the teacher can do is to recognize and accept the child's problems without undue comment. By so doing, the other children will also be accepting.

DIABETES

Diabetes is characterized by insufficient insulin in the child's system. Insulin is a substance needed to permit passage of sugar into the cells. In the diabetic person, such passage does not happen as it should. Therefore, the diabetic child must have regular injections of insulin in order to help sugar get into the cells. Children with diabetes must also have a well-balanced diet kept free of concentrated sugars.

Diabetic children can do everything that other children do. There are no restrictions on activities. As for diet, the main restriction is to withhold candy, cake, heavily sweetened soft drinks, and similar sweets.

Occasionally the child gets too much insulin. This may lower the blood sugar too much. The result is hypoglycemia. When hypoglycemia occurs, the child may

- become irritable or drowsy
- complain of headache
- complain of hunger
- begin to sweat

The teacher must immediately give the child food with high sugar content. Orange juice, candy, a couple of sugar cubes, or cookies and milk will take care of the situation. If the child is not awake, nothing should be given by mouth; to do so may cause choking. The doctor should be consulted if the child does not recover in a few minutes.

HEART DEFECTS

Children with heart problems behave in different ways. Much depends upon the severity of the problem. It is difficult to distinguish children with a mild disability from other children. The exception is when there has been a great deal of anxiety in the home over their problem. These children may then behave as if their disability were much greater than it actually is.

Other children may have a severe heart problem. They can tolerate much less physical activity than other children. Children with such a heart condition usually know their own limits. They do not need to be restrained from everyday activities. These children may, however, need a teacher's help in adjusting to the fact that they will be left out of many activities. The teacher can help by planning quieter activities, figure 17-8, that such a child can participate in. This helps these children develop alternate skills and thus become more self-confident. As always, teachers must keep in close contact with parents.

Fig. 17-8 The teacher plans some quieter activities.

Fig. 17-9 Teachers may encounter the spina bifida child.

BLEEDING PROBLEMS

There are several kinds of bleeding disorders. The most common is hemophilia. Modern medicine provides good methods of treatment. Therefore, it is no longer necessary to take excessive precautions with a child with hemophilia. One need not fear that the child will bleed to death because of a minor injury.

To overprotect the child with a bleeding disorder may do the child emotional harm. It is important to treat the injury promptly, however. To stop a cut or other wound from bleeding, apply pressure directly on the wound. Use sterile gauze for this purpose. If the bleeding does not stop within a reasonable time call a doctor.

Injury to a joint such as an elbow or ankle may cause internal bleeding. This could be serious. Have the child lie down. Wrap the joint securely so that it does not move. Fill a plastic

bag with ice cubes and wrap it around the joint. Then call the child's parents or doctor.

Except for such emergency treatment, the teacher's role is fairly simple. It is mainly to help the child function to full potential. The child must, of course, be helped to avoid unnecessary risks. On the other hand, overprotection must be avoided. Frequent communications with parents can help a teacher be most helpful to the child.

OTHER HEALTH DISORDERS

There are a number of other disorders which the preschool teacher may encounter. Among them are cleft palate or cleft lip, spina bifida (figure 17-9), chronic asthma, and so on. In each case, the teacher needs to learn as much about the disorder as possible. Parents can supply information on how to manage the child. Most parents have had to acquire sound knowledge about their child's condition. They have also come to understand what is needed for their child's safety. Teachers can learn a great deal from parents about accommodating the child in the classroom. Likewise, parents can be helped to realize that their child can do more than they believed possible.

One word of caution is given here about medication. Any medicine that is administered must have a written order from the physician. In such cases, the bottle must be clearly labeled with the child's name. It must state how often the dosage is to be taken. All medication must be kept in a high cupboard out of the reach of all children. The cupboard should be kept locked.

SUMMARY

A variety of health problems and physical disabilities are found in young handicapped children, figure 17-10. Motor disabilities and delays are common among handicapped children. There are many ways that these children can be accommodated in the preschool, however. Most of these are simple procedures that teachers can carry out with little extra effort.

Children with cerebral palsy account for a large number of the multihandicapped children. They often present a combination of handicapping conditions ranging from mild to severe. One in every three cerebral palsied children has epileptic seizures. Teachers can learn to manage seizures within the classroom. Seizures should not be cause for undue concern to the child or to the other children if the teacher remains calm.

The preschool teacher may also encounter the child with cystic fibrosis, diabetes, heart defects, or bleeding problems. All of these can be managed within the classroom. The important thing is to let each child do as

Fig. 17-10 A variety of physical disabilities can be found among young handicapped children.

much as possible without taking unnecessary risks.

Parents can supply teachers with important information on classroom management of their handicapped child. Teachers must communicate with parents frequently and on a regular basis.

Teachers must be very cautious about giving medicine to children. Medication should only be administered upon written instruction from the child's doctor. Medication must be kept out of the reach of all children. A locked cupboard is best.

STUDENT ACTIVITIES

- Locate a physical therapist in the children's hospital or child care clinic closest to you. Invite the therapist to speak to the class on motor disabilities of young children.

- Form groups of students to make several playboards. Improvise on the ideas in the text. Be creative. See if you can make a presentation of your creative productions to local preschools.

- Contact the United Cerebral Palsy Association closest to you. Arrange to borrow a film focusing on the young cerebral palsied child to show in class.

REVIEW

A. Match each item in Column I with the correct description in Column II.

Column I	Column II
1. hemophilia	a. more than one handicap
2. locomotor problems	b. person who treats motor problems
3. hypoglycemia	c. conditions which interfere with children moving about easily
4. convulsive seizures	d. inclined surface built to accommodate wheelchairs
5. diabetes	e. severe epileptic attacks
6. medication	f. affects lungs, sweat glands, and digestive system
7. ramp	g. regular injections of insulin required
8. multihandicapped	h. to be kept in locked cupboards
9. cystic fibrosis	i. bleeding disorder
10. physical therapist	j. blood sugar too low

B. List the answers for each of the following.

1. List three characteristics of retarded motor development.

2. List five aids that help children who have locomotion problems move about.

3. List five ways to adapt art activities for the child with poor arm and hand control.

4. List three minor alterations that can be made to a classroom to accommodate physically impaired children.

5. List five characteristics of a grand mal seizure.

6. List five things a teacher should do if a child is having a grand mal seizure.

7. List four other handicaps often associated with cerebral palsy.

8. List five physical conditions that may occur with cystic fibrosis.

9. List five things that may happen to a diabetic child whose blood sugar gets too low.

10. List five emergency steps the teacher should take if a hemophilic child injures a joint.

C. Select the best answer from the choices offered to complete each statement.

1. Among handicapped children,
   a. one never finds a child with two or three different handicaps.
   b. it is rare that one finds a handicapped child with only one handicap.
   c. those with more than one handicap should not be enrolled in preschool.

2. In dealing with parents, the preschool teacher
   a. can expect to learn from parents by communicating with them frequently.
   b. should not worry the parents with a child's school problems.
   c. should never call the parent except in an emergency.

3. In managing a convulsive seizure the teacher should
   a. attempt to restrain the child's violent jerking.
   b. put a bar between the child's teeth to prevent tongue biting.
   c. demonstrate a calm and confident attitude for the other children to model.

4. Children with any kind of severe physical problems should be
   a. kept out of preschool.
   b. allowed in preschool but kept away from active play.
   c. allowed to do everything that other children do, as much as possible.

5. The child with a bleeding problem (hemophiliac)
   a. has no problem with external bleeding.
   b. may suffer emotional harm from overprotection.
   c. has no problem with internal bleeding; only external bleeding is cause for concern.

Unit 18 BEHAVIOR PROBLEMS— PART 1

OBJECTIVES

After studying this unit, the student will be able to

- List and briefly describe six common behavior problems.
- Discuss ways that preschool teachers can manage behavior problems.
- Define preventive discipline and specify why and when it should be used.

Many types of behavior problems can be found among young children. Such problems may or may not be related to other handicapping conditions affecting a child. A behavior problem can be so severe that it is considered a handicap.

Several of the most common behavior problems encountered in the preschool are discussed in this unit and in unit 19. This unit focuses on children who

- have separation problems
- are overly dependent
- are noncompliant (disobedient)
- are disruptive
- are aggressive and hostile
- cannot share and take turns

TEACHING TACTICS

There are certain teaching tactics that apply to all behavior problems, regardless of type or degree. These behavior management procedures were discussed in detail in an earlier unit. Students and teachers in the field are urged to review these procedures frequently. This is especially important whenever they have a child in class with any kind of behavior problem. The earlier the problem is brought under control the better it is for the child.

As a brief review, the basic rules in the management of behavior problems are as follows.

- Give attention to those behaviors which are appropriate and desirable in terms of the child's growth and development, figure 18-1.
- Disregard those behaviors which are damaging to the child's growth and development.

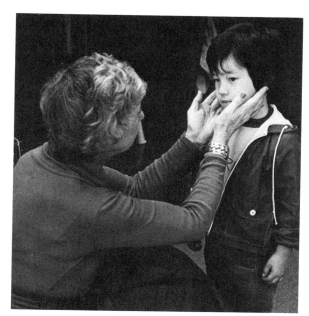

Fig. 18-1 Give attention to appropriate behavior.

- Arrange the preschool environment in such a way that the child has many opportunities to behave appropriately and to receive attention for behaving appropriately.

- Avoid using punishment except in the most extreme cases; then use it only briefly.

PROBLEM BEHAVIORS

Separation Problems

Going to preschool or day care for the first time is a big step for a child. Many young children have problems leaving their home and parents. Separation may cause problems whether or not the child is handicapped. Some handicapped children have an especially hard time, however. This is often because they have had such close, watchful attention.

Advance planning by the teaching staff can help a child be more comfortable about coming to school, figure 18-2. The first step in planning is to invite the child and parent (or parents) to visit ahead of time. The best

Fig. 18-2 Advance planning helps ease parent-child separation.

time for a visit is when the other children are not in school. This reduces confusion for the new child. It allows teachers and child (and parents) to get better acquainted. It also allows the child to explore the room, yard, toilet facilities, and play equipment without hurrying. A teacher should accompany the child on the tour and make simple comments to put the child at ease: "This is where we play with blocks. Children can play there whenever they want to. Here is where we wash our hands. Here is where we get a drink of water." Such self-evident statements help the child to be comfortable in the new environment.

For the first day or two of school, the parent can arrange to stay for awhile. Provide the parent with a chair. Ask that the parent remain as neutral as possible. The parent should not pressure the child to join activities. In most cases, the child soon moves away from the parent if not pressured to do so. The teacher moves with the child and helps the child get started in the chosen play activity.

A very anxious child may return to the parent's side several times. This is quite common and should be allowed. Soon the child moves away from the parent more often and for longer periods. It is important, however, to keep the first day of school short (about an hour at most). The child should go home while still having a good time. This promotes an eagerness to return to school the next day.

Most children let the parent go away for awhile on the second or third day. The parent should always say good-bye to the child and promise to return soon. The teacher keeps physically close to the child at the moment of separation. The parent should leave quickly but return promptly as promised. Thus, an anxious child comes to trust that the parent really will return soon, as promised. The child

Fig. 18-3 Attention-giving must be well timed.

learns, too, that teachers can be depended upon for care and understanding. Under these circumstances most young children overcome their separation anxieties within the first few weeks of school.

Overdependence

Some children may be overly dependent on teachers. Often these are the same children who had separation problems. Overly dependent children may cling to teachers. They may clutch at a teacher's clothing. They may refuse to leave a teacher's side. They may whine and complain excessively. The teacher must be careful about giving such a child too much or too little attention. Too much attention increases the child's dependency. Too little attention may make the child feel rejected and uncared for. This may make the child even more fearful of school. There are several ways that teachers can manage the overly dependent child.

- Watch for every opportunity to give the child attention when the child is *not* clinging or whining. These children need a great deal of adult attention if they are to adjust to school. Teachers must give it freely at the right times. The important thing is the timing of the attention-giving, figure 18-3.

- Refrain from responding when the child clutches or pulls at your clothing. This may not be easy at first but it can be done. One way to manage this is to put an arm around the child (or give attention in some other form) before the child begins to cling or whine.

- Tell the complaining or tattling child, "Come, I will go with you and help you tell Jimmy to let you on the jumping board."

The anxious, overly dependent child may also complain of stomachaches, headaches, or invisible minor hurts. These discomforts are usually very real to the child. When they occur day after day, it is a clue to the teacher. The child may be seeking a way to get and hold adult attention. A first step is to check with the parents to make sure the child is not really ill. The procedures for classroom management are the same as for clinging and whining. Respond only very little or not at all when the child is complaining of physical ills. At other times when the child is busily at play, give the child a lot of attention. Comment on what a good climber, builder, or painter the child is. This helps such children focus on the good times they are having.

Noncompliance

Refusing to do what the adult asks is characteristic of most young children at times. This becomes a problem, however, when it occurs all of the time, or most of the time. Such a child is often referred to as a *noncompliant* child. Examples of noncompliance noted in one child are as follows:

- The teacher said, "Michael, let's pick up the blocks," and Michael ran to the housekeeping corner.

Fig. 18-4 Give ample warning before an activity is to end.

- The teacher said, "Michael, hang up your coat." Michael said, "You do it," and refused to pick it up off the floor.

- The teacher said, "Michael, it is time to come in," and Michael climbed to the top of the jungle gym.

Preventive Discipline

Noncompliant children try teachers' patience to the utmost. Fortunately, most problems like this can be handled with preventive discipline. Through careful observation of the child the teacher can begin to anticipate the trouble spots. The teacher can then plan ways to handle problems before they develop.

First, it is important to make sure the child hears and understands the teachers' requests. Many children who have undiagnosed hearing loss have been labeled noncompliant. Children with poor receptive language skills have been called disobedient. Actually, it is almost impossible for these children to follow instructions. They do not hear or understand what was expected of them.

With children who do not have this impairment, there are guidelines for preventive discipline. This is called arranging the environment or the contingencies. Appropriate environmental contingencies help all children to comply. Contingencies are especially helpful for the noncompliant child, however. The most important of these guidelines are listed.

- Always give children ample warning before an activity ends, figure 18-4. Also, give a clue about what comes next: "Soon it will be time to come in and get ready for snack." For the child who always resists coming in, try, "Sandy, you can be the last one to come in today." Say this before the child sets up resistance.

- Make sure that children are not being overloaded with directions and expectations. Even the most compliant preschool child has trouble if there are too many rules.

- Give directions and make requests clearly, briefly, and in the order in which the child is to do them. Teachers tend to say things like, "We are getting washed for snack so go hang up your coat but first of all put your tricycle in the shed and shut the door." Such a jumble of directions can be confusing for all children, especially the noncompliant. The appropriate way to help a child through such a routine is to first give advance notice as suggested earlier. Then give the directions one at a time, starting with what comes first - in this case, it is the tricycle.

- Never say to a child, "Would you like to park your tricycle and come in now?" This gives the child a choice which (in this case) the teacher really does not intend to honor. Instead say "It is time to come indoors now. Please park your tricycle."

Fig. 18-5 **Look at and speak directly to the child when giving instruction.**

- Look at and speak directly to the child when giving an instruction, figure 18-5. Demonstrate if necessary. Use the child's name and make sure the child understands: "Jon, turn the pages one at a time, like this." Then expect the child to do it. Do not coax or nag. In some cases, it may be wise to remind the child a second time. A direction should not be stated more than twice, however.

- Be consistent, firm, and matter-of-fact when giving directions. If the teacher says, "Raoul, you must pick up your blocks before you go anywhere else to play," then Raoul must do just that. He should not be allowed to go anywhere else until the job is done. The teacher alerts the other teachers that Raoul has a job to do in the block corner before he can come into their area. If the other children are busily putting blocks away, the teacher simply pushes some blocks aside for Raoul to put away. At this point, directions can be restated clearly and simply, "Raoul, this is your share of the blocks to put away. You can go outdoors after you are finished." In many cases, the teacher offers to help the child: "As soon as you get started, I will help you get the blocks on the shelf."

The most important point in managing a noncompliant child is to be calm, firm, and consistent. Once a teacher has asked a child to do something, the child should do it and the adult must follow through. Therefore, adults need to make sure that they can hold firm. Judgment must also be used, however. If a noncompliant child is in a car pool it is unwise for a teacher to say to the child, "You must pick up your blocks before you go home." The drivers may not have time to spare. In such instances, the teacher can provide an option: "Michelle, your car

Fig. 18-6 A child may not know how to play appropriately in the sandbox.

Fig. 18-7   The child may be removed from play temporarily.

pool driver will be here in a few minutes. How about getting your blocks picked up?'' If Michelle says ''no,'' the teacher accepts it. This saves an argument which the teacher cannot win.

Whenever possible, give noncompliant children the opportunity to decide for themselves. ''Do you want to park your tricycle inside the shed or near the door?'' ''How many carrot sticks do you want, one or two?'' ''Do you want to feed the rabbit or do you want Terry to have a turn?'' Thus, hard-to-manage children do not feel that adults are always telling them what they must do.

Disruptive Children

Disruptive children are those who constantly seem to be upsetting the preschool routine. They interfere with teacher-directed activities and with other children's projects. They may upset the music period by making inappropriate noises or running around the room. They may knock down other children's block structures or stamp on sand towers, figure 18-6. At the water table other children

get splashed unnecessarily. The list of possible misdeeds is long. Every teacher, each year, encounters one or more such children.

A child who acts like this has learned that being naughty is a sure way to get attention. One way to start helping such a child is to continue giving a great deal of adult attention at the right time. Attention must be given only when the child is not misbehaving. This says two things to the child: 1) there is a reward (attention) for appropriate behavior, and 2) there is no reward for being naughty.

Often, disruptive children need to be taught how to play. They need to be ''walked through'' routines, one step at a time. At the easel they need to be shown how to keep each paintbrush in a separate pot. During the first part of such a learning task the teacher may remove all but two of the paint pots.   In this way it is easier for the child to do what is right.   It also becomes easier for the teacher to give specific, descriptive praise: ''Good for you! You remembered to put the red brush back in the red paint.''

Disruptive acts that damage the classroom, the equipment, or other children's experiences must be stopped. The teacher states the rule briefly but firmly: "I cannot let you smear paint on the walls." If the child becomes disruptive again, the child is removed from the area for a period of time. During group time, music time, or at block play, the child may be withdrawn a short distance, figure 18-7. This interrupts the disruptive behavior but allows the child to observe appropriate behavior of the other child. Disruptive children often misbehave because they do not have the skills necessary for the activity. One four-year-old boy was taken aside a few minutes each day. A teacher taught him the songs that were being sung at music time. He soon became an enthusiastic member of the music group.

AGGRESSIVE BEHAVIORS

It is difficult to deal with children who attack other children. Behaviors such as hitting, kicking, and biting may be signs that the child needs a great deal of adult attention.

As stated earlier, this attention must be given at a time when the child is neither misbehaving nor hurting other children.

Sometimes children are aggressive because they feel left out. They do not know how to get into play activities with others. Many handicapped children lack the necessary social skills. These children often lack the play skills that would make them desirable playmates. In either case, helping the child to learn these skills becomes the teacher's responsibility.

When a child hurts another child, the teacher gives full attention to the child who is hurt. The attacking child receives no adult attention at that time. It is never necessary to explain to the aggressive child (at that moment) that he or she has hurt another child. The behavior of the child who was hurt conveys that message.

The child who is frequently and severely aggressive may need to be temporarily removed from all social contact. Removal should be the consequence every time an aggressive act occurs. It is best if a second adult can remove

Fig. 18-8 Appropriate play should not go unnoticed.

the child. This allows the first adult to comfort the child who was attacked. Removal should be done with a minimum of adult attention. The teacher should say quickly but firmly, "I cannot let you hurt children." At the same time, the child is taken out of play. No further adult attention is given at this moment. Three or four minutes later the teacher should go and get the child, saying, "Let's try again. Where would you like to play?" or "There's room for you at the water table." The teacher then helps the child get started. A successful start is often the key to a successful play experience, figure 18-8. Good play usually continues if the teacher checks back frequently to make favorable comments: "Lynn, you are bathing your doll so nicely. Do you need more soap?"

Children labeled as mentally retarded or emotionally disturbed may seem to exhibit more than their share of aggressive behaviors. Some teachers tend to excuse these children, saying, "They can't help it." or "They don't know any better." This is neither fair nor appropriate, however. All young children, regardless of how retarded or disturbed, can learn basic social requirements. To allow them to do otherwise is to do them a great injustice. Other children will dislike and reject them even more. Dislike and rejection often increase the aggressive child's aggressive behaviors.

INABILITY TO SHARE AND TAKE TURNS

Learning to share and take turns is difficult for all young children, figure 18-9. It may be even more difficult for retarded, disturbed, or otherwise handicapped children. They, too, can learn these necessary skills, however. Teaching procedures are the same for all children. Having plenty of materials is one key. There should be several sets of the most popular materials. There should be several attractive centers of interest. In this way, children do not stand around waiting for a turn. The teacher can say, "You may play in housekeeping for awhile. I will call you when there is room on the bouncing board." Then the teacher must remember to call the child when there is room.

Children who constantly grab other children's toys or push children off of equipment

Fig. 18-9 Learning to share and take turns is not always easy for young children.

must be stopped. The teacher states firmly and clearly, "I cannot let you take Maria's doll," or "I cannot let you push Jerry out of the wagon." At the same time, the teacher should help the other child to hang on and to say, "That's mine. Give it back." or "It's still my turn." The teacher must then make sure the toy is returned or the place in the wagon is restored to the first child. In some cases teachers may have to physically assist in carrying out the return.

There are a number of little "tricks," too, that teachers can use to help children learn to wait and to share. These include

- Use of a kitchen timer. The teacher states the rule briefly: "When the timer rings it is your turn." or "When the timer rings, give the rolling pin to Bart." Older preschoolers can also look at the clock with the teacher: "When the big hand gets to 5 it is your turn."
- Counting turns. "Brad, you can have two more turns around. Then it's Susie's turn to have the tricycle. She has waited a long time."
- Specify a time. "I'm sorry there is no room in the block corner now. You can be the first one to go there after music."

When a teacher makes promises of this sort, they must be kept, otherwise, the only thing the child learns is to mistrust the teacher. This can increase the child's inability to share and to take turns.

SUMMARY

Behavior problems commonly found among young children include

- separation anxiety
- overdependence
- noncompliance
- disruptiveness
- aggressiveness
- inability to share

All of these problem behaviors can be managed in the preschool classroom. Specific management tactics are needed, however. The most effective management tactics are based on behavior modification principles. Teachers who have a problem child in class are urged to review these often.

Teachers must have appropriate expectations for children's behavior. There should be rules, but rules should be few. What rules there are should be obeyed by all children, even the most retarded or disturbed. Teachers must state rules and instructions briefly, clearly, and directly to the child. The teacher must then follow through, making sure the child does what is expected. Teachers must learn to be calm and consistent when handling behavior problems.

Preventive discipline is important in managing children with behavior problems. There are two steps in preventive discipline. The first is to observe the child carefully. Note what triggers the undesirable behavior. The second step is to rearrange environmental contingencies, removing the trouble spots. Most behavior problems can be avoided by using preventive discipline.

STUDENT ACTIVITIES

- Observe a teacher in a preschool or day care program for one hour. Count how many times the teacher gives a direction or instruction. Note how many of these are obeyed by the child (or children).
- During this same observation, note and describe evidence of preventive discipline. If none occurs, suggest one or more ways it might have been used to prevent a problem.

- Select a classmate to act as a child with one of the problem behaviors discussed in this unit. Role play an effective teacher management part.

REVIEW

A. Briefly define each of the following.

1. separation anxiety
2. overdependency
3. noncompliance

4. disruptiveness
5. preventive discipline

B. List the four basic behavior management principles reviewed in this unit.

C. Select the three best answers from the choices offered to complete each statement.

1. When helping a timid child stay at school
   a. have the parents stay for awhile if possible.
   b. coax the child to play with toys.
   c. plan to have the child and parents visit ahead of time.
   d. have the child stay only a short time the first few days.
   e. have the parent slip away without saying anything as soon as the child is playing.

2. The best ways to manage overly dependent children are to
   a. pick these children up and cuddle them every time they clutch and cling to the teacher.
   b. make sure that the teacher always makes other children give the overly dependent children anything they want.
   c. give such children a great deal of warm attention when they are not whining, clinging, and tattling.
   d. give very little attention to constant complaints of headaches, stomachaches, or minor hurts.
   e. make positive comments to the child when the child is playing well.

3. A noncompliant child
   a. should be expected to learn and follow the rules even if retarded or emotionally disturbed.
   b. should never be given choices.
   c. should be reminded at least four or five times about what the teacher has said to do.
   d. must have teachers who will follow through on rules.
   e. may have a language or hearing problem.

4. Disruptive children
   a. have often learned that being naughty is a sure way to get a great deal of teacher attention.
   b. often need to be taught how to play by their preschool teachers.
   c. can often be helped to learn appropriate behavior through a teacher's use of descriptive praise.
   d. should receive attention from the teacher in the form of scolding and explaining every time they misbehave.
   e. are often handicapped and cannot control the way they behave, so teachers should not expect them to behave otherwise.

5. Children who kick, hit, and bite others
   a. should not be allowed to come to preschool.
   b. often need to be taught appropriate play skills.
   c. should be removed from play temporarily when they attack a child.
   d. should not receive attention from a teacher when they have already attacked another child.
   e. should receive many explanations about the fact that hitting, kicking, and biting hurts other children.

D. Match each phrase in Column I with the correct item in Column II.

Column I	Column II
1. given to children before an activity is to end	a. the first thing the child is to do
2. directions are given one at a time, starting with this	b. cleanup
3. given to a child only when it is all right if the child does not want to do something	c. choice or option
4. use this when speaking directly to the child, such as when giving instructions	d. warning or advance notice
5. before a child starts playing in a new area, make sure the child finishes this in the first play area	e. child's name

Unit 19 BEHAVIOR PROBLEMS— PART 2

OBJECTIVES

After studying this unit, the student will be able to

- Define and suggest ways of managing each of the behavior disorders discussed.
- Specify when and why a teacher needs to seek outside help for a child with a behavior problem.
- Describe several general rules that apply to the management of behavior problems.

The behavior problems discussed in this unit are ones that are fairly common. As noted in unit 18, the problem may or may not be related to another handicapping condition. This unit discusses several disorders. As before, these are the ones that preschool teachers are most likely to encounter. Included are problems related to:

- withdrawn or isolate behavior
- hyperactivity
- temper tantrums
- self-stimulation
- perseveration
- soiling and wetting
- eating inappropriate materials

WITHDRAWING FROM OTHERS

These children seem to be constantly alone. They withdraw from play situations, figure 19-1. They withdraw from contact with other children. Such behavior can be a serious problem. Teachers are rarely as worried about these children, however, as they are about aggressive children. The quiet, withdrawn child seldom causes trouble. Yet,

the problems of a withdrawn child may be damaging to the child as an individual. The problems of the withdrawn child may be more serious than the problems of the aggressive child.

There are many reasons why children withdraw. A child may be an only child who does not know how to play or interact. Some handicapped children have not been allowed

Fig. 19-1 Some children withdraw from contact with others.

to play with other children. Parents often fear the child may get hurt. The child may be afraid of other children. Perhaps other children in the family or in the neighborhood have bullied or frightened the child. Some children are thought to have emotional problems which cause them to withdraw into themselves. Whatever the cause, pre-school teachers can help these children inter-act with others.

First, these children must be carefully observed. What activities does the child engage in when alone? What materials does the child seem to enjoy? Does the child watch certain children or certain activities more than others? When a child's preferences have been noted, a teacher can use these to help the child interact. In the beginning, this may only be done in very small ways. The following are some examples of first ap-proximations to social interaction.

Example 1. The teacher may note that the child watches housekeeping activities with great interest. Teacher and child together may deliver additional materials to the children. "Jeannie and I have brought you

Fig. 19-2 What activities does the child engage in when playing alone?

some more birthday candles. Where shall Jeannie put them?"

Example 2. The teacher says, "Yes, Jon, I will give you another rock in the rocking boat. We must let Billy in, too. Here, Billy, you can sit across from Jon." Later the teacher requests a third child to be in the rocking boat. Finally, a child must be sitting next to Jon on the same seat if Jon is to be rocked by the teacher. The chil-dren who share the rocking boat with Jon must be selected with care. Overly noisy or vigorous children may frighten him at first.

Example 3. The isolate child appears to want to use a pegboard. The teacher can say, "Here's a pegboard for you, too. There are lots of pegs in this basket. I will put the basket in the middle of the table. You and Mary can use pegs out of the same basket."

Some very shy children may focus only on one adult. They always want to sit next to that adult. They want to stay back and help the adult clean up. They engage the adult in long, exclusive conversations. For these children, teachers must plan so that the child learns to interact with other children. A child cannot do this by talking only to teachers on a one-to-one basis. The teacher should try to draw another child into the activity or conversation. If this fails, the teacher interacts with the isolate child pleasantly, but very briefly. If possible, the teacher moves to another area where there are other children. The isolate child usually follows. This increases the pos-sibility of drawing other children in.

Sometimes there is a child who does not respond to children or adults. Young children who do not interact with adults are much more difficult to work with. It is not likely that they will ever learn to interact with children unless they learn to interact with adults.

Fig. 19-3 The teacher is the source of many good things.

It is fortunate, in this case, that teachers are in charge of all of the things that a child wants in the preschool. It can be arranged that all of these good things (materials, snacks, and activities) be delivered firsthand by the teacher, figure 19-3. Thus the child comes to view the teacher favorably. The teacher can build simple but brief interactions with the child upon these wants. Thus teachers become not only the source of good material things but they also become a source of pleasurable social interaction. This positive relationship between teacher and child must be established first. The teacher can then help the child begin to relate to other children as described earlier.

HYPERACTIVITY

Young children in a preschool classroom show a wide range of activity levels. Motion is characteristic of young children. There are some children who seem to be on the move all of the time. It appears to teachers that these children seldom settle down into any activity. These children are often labeled hyperactive.

Unfortunately, the term hyperactivity is overused and misused. There are few children who are truly "hyperactive" in the medical sense of the word. Hyperactivity has become a catch-all term. It is used to refer to children who display all or some of the following behaviors:

- short attention span
- inability to sit still
- inability to wait
- impulsiveness
- distractibility
- constantly touching children and fingering objects
- repetitions and purposeless motions (drumming on the table, chair-rocking, etc.)
- unexpected shifts in mood (laughing one moment; crying the next)

Almost every so-called hyperactive child has one or two favorite activities. The child may be observed to stay with such an activity anywhere from 5 to 20 minutes. It is impor-

Fig. 19-4 Noting preferred activities is important.

Fig. 19-5 Asking "What can your thumbs do?" often expands a child's interests at finger painting.

tant that the teacher note these activities, figure 19-4, for two reasons. First, it indicates that the child is not hyperactive, medically speaking. Any child who can stay with any activity (even television) for several minutes is not hyperactive. The second reason is that noting preferred activities gives the teacher a place to start. Teachers can then praise the child for working so hard, playing so long, or doing such a good job.

Most teachers give attention to the overly active child when that child is flitting about. They attempt to stop the child. They try to get the child involved in an activity. This is exactly the wrong time to give teacher attention. Attention given at such times increases the child's "flitting."

Teachers must do just the opposite. They must be constantly on the alert for those times when the child is engaged in an activity. At those moments, they should go to the child with an interested comment or gentle challenge: "I bet you can fill that whole pail with sand. I will watch while you do it." Few children can resist staying with a task when so challenged.

The teacher can often extend the activity by asking questions. "I wonder what would

happen if we put some blue food coloring in the yellow water?" or, at finger painting, figure 19-5, "What can your thumbs do? The tips of your fingers? The backs of your hands?" Another way of extending the overly active child's interest in an activity is to offer additional materials: "Here is a kitty cookie cutter to use with your dough." or "This doll needs a bath, too." The important thing to remember is to offer suggestions and materials *before* the child leaves an activity.

With very active children, it is wise to help them plan in advance where they will play next. Noting that the child is about to leave an area, the teacher can say, "Let's decide where you will play next." If necessary, help the child decide. The teacher can offer choices, "There is room for you at blocks or at the easel." Once a choice has been made, it is best to accompany the child to the chosen area. If there is a teacher in that area the first teacher can say, "Julie has come to paint. Will you help her get started?" If there is no teacher there to receive Julie, the first teacher should get her started.

There are other ways to help overly active children. The following are some suggestions.

Fig. 19-6 Note how long a child can stay at music.

Fig. 19-7 Ignoring tantrum behavior must be carefully planned by the staff.

- Alternate active and quiet activities, large and small groups, and teacher-initiated with child-initiated activities.
- Note how long an overly active child can stay with an activity, figure 19-6. For example, Tommy can listen to music only 7 to 10 minutes. Interest him in some other activity before he becomes bored. He might, for example, assist the teacher who is setting up the snack tables. Do not allow him this special privilege if he has already left or disrupted the music group.
- Keep the classroom neat and orderly. Do not have too many materials out at once. Have children clean up each play area before they leave it. A disorderly environment encourages disorderly behavior. This is particularly true for overly active children.

Medication is sometimes prescribed for these children. It may or may not be effective. Teachers need to report to parents any behavior changes they note in the child. In turn, parents can report to the physician. It may be difficult for physicians to establish the right dosage. Determining how much medication to give depends upon the child's behavior.

Therefore the teacher can be helpful by reporting the child's activity level at school.

Even if a child is on medication a good behavior management program is still necessary. A sound preschool program is almost always beneficial to overly active children. True, these children are a challenge to teachers. They can, however, be effectively managed.

TEMPER TANTRUMS

Children who have temper tantrums find this to be a sure way of controlling adults. This does not imply that they do it consciously. Often, teachers and parents have been advised to ignore the temper tantrum. This is good advice. However, being ignored usually increases the fury of the child's tantrum. Thus, the adults become so anxious that they can no longer restrain themselves. They go to the child. This causes the child's tantrums to become longer and more violent. Thus, ignoring must be carefully planned, figure 19-7.

It is difficult to ignore tantrums in the preschool. It can be done, however. Children who tantrum should be removed to a spot where they cannot hurt themselves or destroy equipment. A small bare room is preferable. Sometimes a teacher must stay nearby for safety reasons. If so, the teacher should withhold all attention. The teacher should neither speak to nor make eye contact with the child during the course of the tantrum. If teachers withhold attention, tantrums disappear within a few days. It must be remembered, however, that a tantrum always gets worse before it gets better. Teachers must therefore be prepared for two or three severe tantrums at first.

Since the other children may become frightened during a child's tantrum, one teacher should manage the tantrum while the other teacher manages the rest of the children. The children can be gathered together to hear a special record in another part of the room. Sometimes they can be taken on a walk around the building. The children must be assured that things are all right: "Mrs. Everett is taking care of Sam. He will feel better soon."

Teachers must, of course, recognize that repeated tantrums are often a child's call for help. Such help must be given, but not at the time of the tantrum. These children usually need a great deal of caring attention. It should be given freely when a child is not tantrumming.

SELF-STIMULATING BEHAVIORS

A variety of self-stimulating behaviors can be observed in young children. The most common are

- thumb sucking or finger sucking
- hair twirling or pulling
- body rocking
- head banging
- masturbating or other handling of genitals

All young children may engage in one or more of these behaviors at some time, figure 19-8. The behaviors are never cause for concern

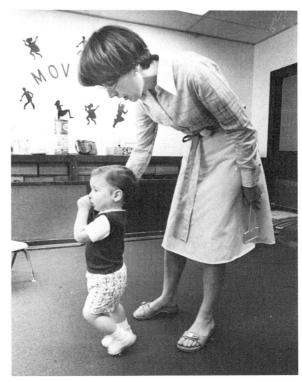

Fig. 19-8 **Thumb sucking is not cause for concern in most young children.**

unless they occur in excess. ("Excess" is when the behavior seriously interferes with the child's ability to enter into activities.)

Children with severe problems of this kind may be lonely or frightened children. They may have received very little comfort or appropriate attention from others. They are often children who feel rejected and unloved. Thus, they have learned to seek comfort in the form of self-stimulation from their own bodies.

A teacher's first job is to establish a warm and accepting relationship with the child. The teacher must find many times to sit close, giving the child physical warmth and comfort (if the child can accept it). Such attention should be given only when the child is not engaged in the self-stimulating behavior, however. Also, the teacher should note the activities which the child shows any

Fig. 19-9 Teachers may need to seek help from a clinical team.

interest in. These activities should be presented often. The child should then be given approval for engaging in the activity.

Sometimes the behavior may be so severe that the child is actually hurting himself. Children can harm themselves by their own head banging, hand chewing, and so forth. Teachers must seek help from parents and a clinical team in such cases, figure 19-9.

PERSEVERATION

Some children may perform the same act over and over. When this is done to excess it is called *perseveration*. The child is said to be perseverative. Common examples of perseverative behaviors are

- running in circles, around and around
- twirling small objects close to the eyes, at a rapid pace, for long periods at a time
- chanting the same word or phrase again and again
- drawing the same design or making the same marks with pencil or crayon, over and over

Such perseverative behaviors are often found among children who are labeled autistic. Other characteristics of the autistic child are

Fig. 19-10 The teacher may need help in selecting special programs for special children.

- severe withdrawal and inability to communicate with others
- low tolerance for noise (when the noise level in the classroom gets too high such children may scream and cover their ears)
- echolalia, or the tendency of the child to repeat back exactly what was said; these children often have no language that can be called their own; they simply echo what they hear.

Children with behavioral disorders of this type need special kinds of help. The teacher must keep in touch with parents. The child should be under the care of a clinical team. The teacher needs to work with the team, too, in planning a preschool program for the child. For example, there are special programs for dealing with the echolalic child in the classroom. The clinician can help the teacher select such a program, and programs for other handicapped children, figure 19-10.

SOILING AND WETTING

Many young handicapped children are not toilet trained. This must never be used as a reason for excluding the child from the preschool. Toilet training can usually be accomplished rapidly in the school situation. A number of good toilet training guides are available.

Some children who are toilet trained continue to wet and soil themselves occasionally. Most of these children respond well to the teacher's gentle reminders: "Run in and use the toilet. I will save your tricycle until you get back." Cues to the teacher that a child may need to use the toilet include:

- jiggling up and down

- handling genitals

- clutching self in the genital area

Children who have a toilet accident should never be shamed or made to feel guilty. They should be changed matter-of-factly. The clothing should be rinsed out and put in a plastic bag. Every child should have a change of clothing at school. Even the most conscientious young child may have a toilet accident.

At times, teachers will encounter children who continue to soil or wet themselves even though they are toilet trained. There are a number of possible reasons for this:

- Persistent wetting, especially in little girls, may occur because of a urinary tract infection.

- The child may have a recurring low-grade infection or virus which results in loose or runny bowel movements.

- The child may be fearful of using strange bathrooms.

- The child may be used to more privacy than is available in the preschool.

Sometimes all of these conditions are ruled out but the child still soils or wets. Teachers and parents usually need help if they are to help the child. Consultation with a pediatrician, nurse, or psychologist is recommended.

EATING INAPPROPRIATE MATERIALS

Preschool teachers may encounter children who constantly eat things considered inedible, such as dirt, grease, chalk, paper, fingerpaint, and so on. Persistent eating of inedible substances is called pica. It may or may not be a sign of an emotional disturbance. However, constant eating of inappropriate substances is almost sure to harm the child. Particularly harmful is the eating of flakes of paint. Lead-based paint is poisonous. It can cause severe damage to the child. If it is known that a child has eaten paint flakes, the child should be taken to the doctor. For severe pica, a pediatrician or nutritionist should be consulted.

Many young children take little tastes of materials such as play dough, fingerpaint, or paste. This is quite a different matter. It should not be confused with a case of pica. Eating these materials should, of course, be discouraged. They, too, can cause digestive upset. Usually the problem is easily solved. Removing the child from play dough or fingerpaint activities several times is all that is necessary in most cases. The teacher must remain alert, however. The child may begin sneaking bites. Often the other children will "tell on" this child. The teacher must decide the appropriateness of children's tattling, in each case.

One other point should be made about unusual eating habits in young children. Some children eat excessive amounts of certain foods. One child was known to eat whole heads of lettuce at one sitting. Other children eat very little even though they are thin, pale, and obviously underweight. All of these are symptoms of possible trouble. Teachers and parents should consult a nutritionist or related professional. The problem may have a physical base or a psychological base. Whatever the cause, these children need help.

SUMMARY

Behavior disorders that preschool teachers may encounter (in addition to those discussed in unit 18) include:

- socially withdrawn or isolate behavior
- hyperactivity
- temper tantrums
- self-stimulation
- perseveration
- soiling and wetting
- eating inappropriate materials

Children displaying any of these behaviors in excess need special help, figure 19-11. They need individualized programs. Preschool teachers can manage some of these problems without outside help. In general, children with behavior problems need a good

Fig. 19-11 The child who turns away from contact with other children needs special help.

deal of teacher attention. It is important that teachers give them the needed attention. However, it must be given when the child is not engaged in the inappropriate behaviors.

Some behavior disorders are more severe than others. They may indicate a serious underlying problem. The problem may be caused by physical, psychological, or nutritional factors. In these cases, outside professional help is required. Parents must be consulted. The most effective way to help a child with severe behavior disorders is for teachers, parents, and clinicians to work together.

Occasional episodes of any problem behavior is not cause for undue concern. All young children engage in inappropriate behaviors once in awhile. It is only when a particular behavior becomes excessive that it is considered a problem. An excessive behavior is one which interferes seriously with a child's normal activities. Children who show excessive behavior need special help. If it is not provided, serious damage can result. Often the preschool teacher must start the help-finding process.

STUDENT ACTIVITIES

- Observe in a preschool or day care setting. Note any behaviors that might be considered behavior problems. Describe what the teacher did in each case.

- Talk with preschool or day care teachers. Find out if they have children whom they consider behavior problems. Ask the teachers to describe the problems to you.

- Contact your local child care clinic. Ask if they have a person on their staff who goes into the community to talk about behavior problems in young children. Write that person a letter of invitation to speak to your class.

REVIEW

A. Briefly define each of the following.

1. isolate behavior
2. hyperactivity
3. self-stimulation
4. perseveration
5. pica

B. List at least three ways a teacher can help each child.

1. isolate child
2. overly active child
3. child who tantrums
4. child who engages in self-stimulatory behavior
5. child who soils and wets

C. Match each phrase in Column I with the correct item in Column II.

Column I	Column II
1. the problems of an isolate child may be more severe than those of this kind of child	a. behavior modification
	b. overly active
2. observe a shy child to find out this about the child's desire for certain play activities or materials	c. aggressive
	d. perseveration
	e. flitting about (changing activities)
3. an often misused term	f. preferences
4. impulsiveness, inability to wait, and distractibility are characteristics of these children	g. worse
	h. pica
	i. hyperactivity
5. when overly active children are doing this, teachers should not give attention to the children	j. additional materials
	k. excessive
	l. self-stimulating
6. extend an overly active child's engagement in an activity by providing these	m. urinary tract
	n. lead poisoning
	o. echolalia
7. even if an overly active child is on medication, this is necessary	
8. when treating temper tantrums, it can be expected that the tantrums will become this before they get better	
9. thumb sucking, body rocking, and head banging	
10. performing the same act over and over to excess	
11. children who do not speak except to repeat back what is said to them are said to have this	
12. persistent wetting may occur because of this type of infection	
13. excessive eating of inappropriate substances	
14. possible result of eating paint flakes	
15. a behavior that interferes with a child's participation in activities is called this	

SECTION 6
HOME AND COMMUNITY

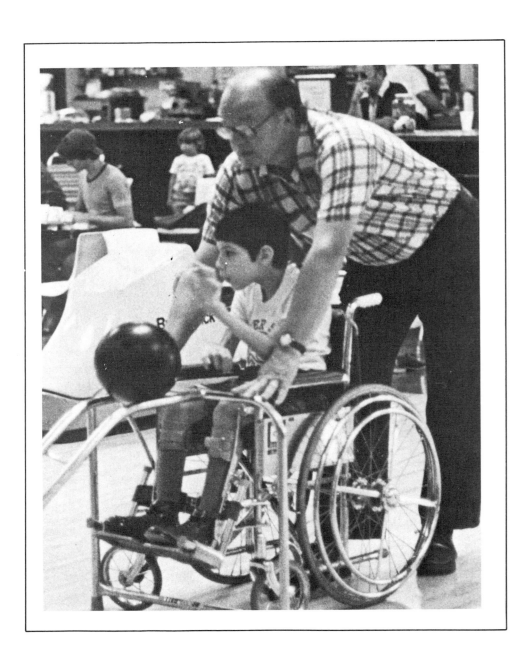

Unit 20 WORKING WITH THE FAMILY

OBJECTIVES

After studying this unit, the student will be able to

- Discuss the importance of parent involvement in early education programs for handicapped children.
- List methods of involving parents in their child's learning experiences.
- Describe ways that preschool parents can help each other.

A most important part of young children's learning environment is their family. Family groups vary. A family may consist of one or more children and a mother and father. On the other hand, a family may consist of one child and one parent. One grandparent (or grandparents) may serve as active members of the family, figure 20-1, or as the child's entire family. Sometimes children may live with a series of foster parents instead of with their natural parents. Throughout this unit, the child's principal caregivers are referred to as parents.

Parent involvement in early education programs is very important. Recently a survey was conducted of a large number of early intervention programs.[1] Some of these programs had parent participation. Others did not. The survey resulted in several important conclusions:

- The active involvement of the child's family is critical to the success of any intervention program.
- Without active family involvement, the child may slip back once the program is ended.

[1] U. Bronfenbrenner. *Is Early Intervention Effective? A Report on Longitudinal Evaluations of Preschool Programs,* Volume II. Washington, D.C.: Office of Child Development, United States Department of Health, Education, and Welfare, 1974.

- Parents who participate in early intervention programs are important in two ways:
  1. They provide an ongoing system which reinforces the effects of the program while it is in operation.
  2. They help to sustain the child's gains after the program ends.

From this it can be seen that the preschool is necessary but not sufficient for the

Fig. 20-1 Grandparents are often active members of a child's family.

Fig. 20-2 The child is at school for only a few hours each day.

education of the young child. This is particularly true where the handicapped child is concerned. Why is the parent-school partnership so important in educational programs for young handicapped children? Several reasons are given here.

- Parents know the child better than anyone else could ever get to know the child. Thus they have important information to contribute.

- The child is in school for only a few hours each day, figure 20-2. Many more hours are spent at home. Parents can help in the transfer of learnings from classroom to home, and from home to classroom.

- Teachers and parents need to expect the same things of a child. A child may become confused or resistant if the teacher expects him to put on his own coat at school, and his mother usually does it for him at home. Planned consistency between home and school expectations is therefore important.

- Handicapped children can learn specific skills almost twice as fast when parents participate in the teaching. This was a finding of a number of research studies.

There are many reasons for involving parents of a handicapped child in their child's preschool program. One is the length of time that parents need to be a part of the life of their handicapped child. The child usually requires many more years of caregiving than do other children. Furthermore, the parents of a handicapped child need special parenting and teaching skills. Other parents may not need such specialized skills.

The effect of special training for parents during their child's preschool years has additional benefits. The other children in the family are helped, too. The parenting skills are generalized from the preschool program to home.

The other benefit regarding parent involvement should also be mentioned. Parents are the source of many reinforcers for their young children, figure 20-3. Children depend upon their parents for food, warmth, caring,

Fig. 20-3 Parents are the source of many reinforcers for their children.

outings, playthings, and all else. Therefore, parents can be effective in helping their children acquire new and necessary skills. Parents can also help to decrease a child's inappropriate behaviors - ones that interfere with learning.

It can be seen that parents must be included in their handicapped child's preschool program. Early intervention is effective only to the extent that parents can be involved. A key question is how to get parents involved.

Some parents are eager to become involved. Others appear less eager, even unwilling. There may be a number of reasons for this unwillingness:

- Parents who work may have limited time and energy.

- Those who do not work often have too many personal and economic problems.

- Lack of transportation and babysitting may prevent participation.

- Many handicapped children require day and night care in the home. Parents have little energy left to cope with the child's school problems.

Fig. 20-4 There are many ways to involve parents.

- Some parents find it too painful to talk about their handicapped child. Some even feel guilty. They may blame themselves for their child's problems.

- Many parents have had very unhappy experiences with teachers and schools. They therefore avoid further contacts.

Many more reasons can be given why it may be difficult to involve parents in the preschool program. Each child is different and has individual needs. Each parent is also different. Therefore, the integrated preschool must offer a variety of ways to help parents become involved, figure 20-4. Several forms of parent partnerships are discussed.

INCIDENTAL CONTACTS

Brief, casual contacts can occur when parents deliver their child to the preschool or pick their child up. These are good starting points for building a positive relationship among parents, teachers, and school. These contacts can be used to give quick progress

Fig. 20-5 Parents can observe the kinds of preacademic experiences the teacher offers.

reports on the child: "Susie can point to red, yellow, and blue now." "Jane climbed to the top of the ladder box all by herself yesterday." "Michael has had no toilet accidents for three days!" It is well to report these good things in front of the child whenever possible. This gives the child extra social reinforcement for small gains. Do not report concerns or make negative statements in front of the child, however.

Parents should be encouraged to report brief incidents to teachers, too. "Jerry had a seizure last night. He may be a little quieter than usual today." "Sarah fell when getting out of the wheelchair onto the toilet. She wasn't hurt but she was frightened." Such information is helpful to the teacher in planning the child's day. It helps to explain why a child might appear unusually quiet, frightened, or resistant that day.

Brief "pick up and delivery" moments can also prompt contacts between parent and parent. Often the parents of a handicapped child feel left out. They need to talk with other parents. The more contacts they have the more they realize that all parents have problems. They come to realize that other parents, too, have frustrations, anxieties, needs, hopes, and desires regarding their children.

PARENT OBSERVATIONS

One of the best ways to involve parents in the preschool is by having them observe their child in the classroom. This helps parents understand what goes on at school. It is also a form of indirect parent training. Parents can watch how teachers teach certain skills. They can also see how behavior problems are managed. Parents can see that their child is not the only child with problems. This is a very comforting observation.

Frequent observations are best. An observation made once a month is ideal, or whenever the parent can find the time. The child then adapts to having the parent visit. It is often wise to provide the parent with a simple form. The parent watches and jots down answers to such questions as the following.

- What materials did your child seem to enjoy using?

- Did your child seem to avoid any particular child?

- What kinds of preacademic experiences, figure 20-5, were offered to your child? How long was your child's attention span for these tasks?

- What kinds of interactions did your child have with teachers?

Fig. 20-6 Parents feel comfortable and accepted when a friendly tone is established.

• Did you see ways that the teachers might have helped your child more?

Answering such questions helps the parent focus on the child and what is happening. It also keeps the parent busy. This helps to keep the child from seeking too much attention from the parent during a classroom visit. The parent can thus see a more normal school session. Finally, the observation sheet can be used as a takeoff point for a parent conference.

INDIVIDUAL CONFERENCES

Individual conferences can be helpful or threatening to parents. Parents often fear they will hear only bad things about their child. It is important that the teacher start out by reporting some good happenings. If the teacher reports simple, everyday accomplishments, a friendly tone is established. The parent feels comfortable and accepted when the teacher starts out on a positive note, figure 20-6. When possible, the conference should be based on a parent observation. In that way, the parents can bring up concerns

about what they actually see. This is helpful if the child has a number of negative traits. Usually the parent suggests that these behaviors be discussed. Thus the teacher does not have to point out the child's maladaptive behaviors. The risk of offending the parent is reduced. The teacher can, however, respond to the parent in ways that may be useful for the child. The teacher may describe how the problem is handled at school. The teacher can ask the parent how the situation is handled at home. The teacher may suggest working out a home-school program.

There are other points to keep in mind regarding individual conferences. The parent-teacher conference should:

• Be planned in advance.

• Allow many opportunities for parents to talk with the teacher.

• Focus on issues relevant to helping the child.

• Avoid discussion of deeply personal issues. Teachers should never assume the role of psychologist or marriage counselor.

The teacher can, however, help the parent to locate such counseling.

- In a two-parent family, include both parents if possible.

- Have a specific time limit; conferences should be short and frequent. This is better than long conferences held only once or twice a year.

PARENT-TEACHER GROUP MEETINGS

Large group parent-teacher meetings usually focus on some topic related to children's development or education. An expert is often invited to speak. A question period usually follows. Sometimes a coffee hour comes before or after the meeting. The hope is that parents and teachers, and parents and parents will get to know each other better during refreshments. An open-house hour can also come before the group meeting. Parents can visit their children's classrooms, figure 20-7. They can inspect and handle play materials and teaching materials. They can look at children's paintings, clay work, and carpentry. This is a chance for parents to talk to their child's teacher on an informal basis. Shy individuals can also talk more easily with other parents because there is something at hand to talk about. Refreshments are usually served in each individual classroom. Parents then move to the larger meeting.

Fig. 20-7 Parents can visit their child's classroom.

There are several things that help make large group parent-teacher meetings effective.

- Maintain a warm and friendly atmosphere.

- Encourage parents to assist in choosing topics, speakers, and format.

- Use films, demonstrations, and other media in addition to speakers.

- Provide long-term and short-term notice of the meeting (telephone calls, notes home with children).

- Provide baby-sitting at the place of the meeting.

- Arrange for transportation for those who do not have a way to get there.

SMALL GROUP MEETINGS

Small group meetings are usually made up of five to eight people. The participants often have some common concern, problem, interest, or need. They may be concerned about sleeping problems, toilet training, behavior disorders, or language delays in their children. They may be looking for ways to provide better services for their children. The parents in these small groups may also be searching for social and emotional support from each other.

These meetings are usually quite informal. They are often held in parents' homes. The meetings may be held as often as once a week. There is a greater opportunity for interaction available than in the large group. Shy individuals may feel freer to participate in smaller groups.

The teacher may or may not be a member of the group. Sometimes the teacher simply helps to get the group formed. At other times, the teacher may help the group to get resource people. Parents who have children with behavior problems may want to start a parent behavior modification class, for example. The teacher can help to locate a

Fig. 20-8 Demonstrations can be conducted at school or at home, with normal and handicapped children.

Fig. 20-9 A demonstration in the identification of sounds and objects.

skilled individual to serve as leader. In some situations, the teacher may serve as a regular resource person. This is time- and energy-consuming, however. Teachers who spend all day with children are usually tired by evening. They cannot do as good a job with children the next day if they have too many evening duties.

DEMONSTRATIONS[2]

Demonstrations with the handicapped child by teachers or by other parents have proven fruitful. These can be conducted in the school setting, figure 20-8, or at home. Such demonstrations focus on the development of specific skills. They are followed by actual practice by the parent with the child. One often overlooked activity is teaching the parent how to read a book to a child. During the demonstration, the teacher can point out the following to the parents.

[2]The material on demonstrations and the sample lesson plan are drawn from a paper by Merle B. Karnes and R. Reid Zehrbach, *Differential Involvement of Parents in an Educational Program for the Handicapped: Parents are Human.* #1040, 1976; Institute for Research on Exceptional Children, University of Illinois, Urbana-Champaign.

- how to hold the book
- how to direct the child's attention to specific pictures
- how to ask questions
- how to get the child to answer
- how to reinforce a child for appropriate responses

Other demonstrations might include:

- identification of objects with the sounds the object makes, figure 20-9
- learning specific meanings of prepositions
- sorting objects according to specific colors, shapes, or sizes

Specific lesson plans written for parents are useful. They can speed up parent learning of the technique or skill. Specific lesson plans often can be used by parents without demonstration. This can usually be done when the plan specifies objectives, materials to be used, and step-by-step procedures for using them. These activities can help parents view themselves as active and successful educators of

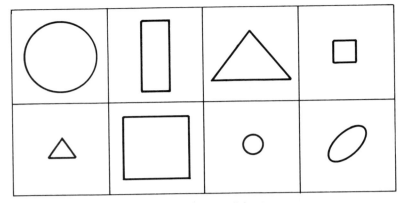

Fig. 20-10 Game card for Lotto.

their children. This increases their self-confidence and willingness to participate. The following is a sample lesson plan.

SAMPLE LESSON PLAN

Shape Lotto

The activity will help the child:

- Learn the names of basic geometric shapes.

- Match shapes that are the same.

- See form in his environment.

You will need:

> Three pieces of stiff paper or cardboard - about 12″ x 16″
> ruler, scissors, crayons
> large envelope

To make the Shape Lotto:

1. Using a black crayon and ruler, divide one piece of cardboard into eight equal spaces. Draw a shape in each space, as shown in figure 20-10.

2. Draw the same shapes on each of the other two pieces of cardboard. Cut them out. These are the individual shape pieces used in playing the game. There should be sixteen pieces.

   Note: Emphasize these words: shape, circle, square, triangle, rectangle, oval.

Other ways you can help the child:

1. Point out shapes in the environment: plates, glasses, knobs, and clocks are circles; windows and tables are squares; doors are rectangles.

2. Help the child draw and cut out shapes and make designs of the cutouts.

3. Help the child find shapes in magazine pictures.

Instructions to parents for using the Shape Lotto:

First Day. Place the game card on a table in front of your child. Say, "Look at all the shapes." Point out each shape. Help your child trace it with a finger. Talk about each one being traced: "This shape goes around and around." "This shape has corners." Ask your child to repeat the word "shape." Then, refer to one set of the individual shapes. Say, "All of these shapes have names. Let's talk about their names." Hold up a circle. "This shape is a circle. Say circle with me. Now feel the circle. Can you find a circle just like this one on the game card? Put this circle on top of it." Repeat this procedure until each shape has been named and placed on the game card. Then say, "Now, let's put the game back in the envelope. First, give me the circles." Ask for each shape by name, helping your child find the right one.

Second Day. Let your child hold the game card. Review the shape names. "Yesterday we talked about the names of these shapes. Let's see if you remember them. Show me the circle. Say, 'This is a circle.' Now, find the square." Repeat this procedure for all of the shapes. Give your child time to find the right shape but be ready to help him. After each shape has been named, give your child both sets of individual shapes. "I will watch while you play the game. Put these shapes where they belong on the game card." Show your child what you mean by selecting one of the shapes and placing it on top of the matching shape or on the game card. Encourage your child to name the shapes as he works.

Third Day. Place one set of individual shapes in front of your child. Help name them. "Let's play a new game with the shapes. First, you choose a shape, then we'll look all around the house to see how many things we can find that have the same shape." Repeat the game with the remaining shapes.

Fourth Day. Place one set of individual shapes in front of your child. Ask him to name them as you point to each one. Collect the shapes. "Let's play a guessing game with the shapes." Have your child put his hands behind his back. Put a shape in his hands and ask him to identify the shape by feeling it. After he has guessed the names of the shapes, lay them in a row on the table. "Look carefully at the shapes. In a minute I will take one away and you will have to tell me which one is missing." Ask your child to hide his eyes while you remove a shape. Repeat this activity with several other shapes.

Fifth Day. Place both sets of shapes in a pile in front of the child. "The shapes are all mixed up. Can you find all the shapes that are the same and put them together?" Show your child what you mean by finding all the circles and putting them in a group. Then put them back with the other shapes. "Now you do it by yourself." As soon as your child finishes, ask him to name the groups of shapes.

HOME VISITS

Home visits are another way to involve parents in their handicapped child's program. Preschool and day care teachers can bridge the gap between school and home by visiting a child's home. Getting to know the family helps teachers to work better with the child. Home visits can also help teachers help parents to be more effective with their own children.

Home visits require different behaviors from teachers than when they are in class. Teachers are no longer the central figure as they are in their own classroom. The parent is the central figure; the teacher is a guest. As a guest, the teacher must conform and adjust to possible social and economic differences. There may also be inconveniences, poor work space, and many interruptions. The teacher must overlook these in order to make the visits worthwhile.

In a home visit, the teacher can learn a great deal without asking, figure 20-11. Are there toys around for children to learn from? Are there books and crayons? How do the children who are not in school spend their time? Is the home especially neat or very disorganized? (Both can affect home learning.) How does the parent respond to the child? Observations of this kind enable the teacher to be of greater help to both child and parents.

Some preschool programs provide weekly home visits. Usually these are teaching-demonstration visits. The home visitor brings materials and a lesson plan already made up. One type of material might be the Shape Lotto described earlier. The teacher demonstrates the use of the material with the child. The parent then uses the material with the child. The teacher provides feedback to the parent regarding the teaching interaction. In some home-teaching programs, the parent is asked to check a simple record sheet on the child's progress. The teacher returns the next week. If progress has been good a new lesson is presented.

HOME-SCHOOL PROGRAMS

There are programs that operate jointly between home and school. The goal is for parents to carry out certain of the school activities at home. Parents are seen as the handicapped child's first and best teachers. The home is viewed as the child's most important learning environment. Daily activities are seen as the best source of learning experiences. The school serves as a supplement in such a model.

ADDITIONAL WAYS OF INVOLVING PARENTS

Staff Member

Parents can serve as volunteers or as paid aides in the classroom. They can also assist in curriculum development for their child. It is a waste to teach children skills that are not useful in their daily environment. Parents know their child best of all. They can often suggest curriculum goals, teaching techniques, and reinforcers that work for their child.

In some programs, parents are asked to assist in the classroom at least once a week. They are taught to observe, record, and carry out behavior modification projects with their child. Parents who participate on a regular basis are viewed as regular members of the teaching team.

Counselor

Parents of handicapped children can serve as counselors to the new parents coming

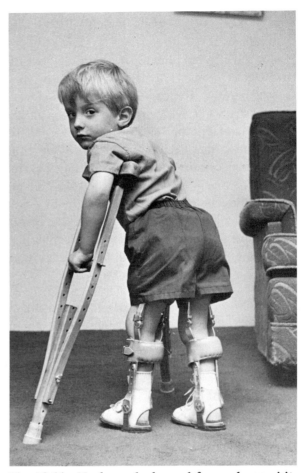

Fig. 20-11 Much can be learned from a home visit.

into the program. Putting a handicapped child into a preschool program for the first time is a big step. It can be frightening for both child and parents. Other parents who have been through the transition can help. They can offer support and guidance in helping the child to stay at school without the parent. They can share ideas that worked for them.

A parent-to-parent partnership can also be extended to help parents who have just learned that their child is handicapped. The parent who has been through such an ordeal understands. That parent has experienced the feelings of grief, distress, and guilt that result. Such a parent can help other families cope with the fact that their child is handicapped.

Fig. 20-12 Each handicapped child must be served by a child-study team.

Parents as Initiators

In some preschools, there is very little effort to involve parents. In such cases, parents, and especially parents of handicapped children, must take the first steps. What can parents do?

In order to implement Head Start legislation and PL 94-142 (see unit 4), there must be a child-study team, figure 20-12. Each handicapped child must be served by such a team. Parents must see to it that they (parents) are included on this team. It is their right, by law.

Parents should ask to see the TSP (Total Service Plan). The TSP is the written result of the child-study team meeting. It outlines what went on at the meeting, and states the plans that were made for the child. Parents should also see, and approve, the IPP (Individualized Program Plan). The IPP divides the Total Service Plan into small steps.

If the child has been tested, parents should ask for the results, figure 20-13. If the results do not make sense, parents should ask to have them explained. Parents should also make every effort to see and talk with their child's teachers. They should initiate conversations with the teacher when delivering and picking up their children. They should ask questions about the program. Parents can

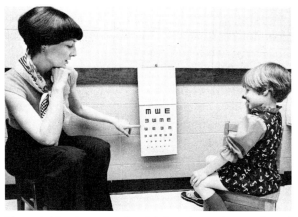

Fig. 20-13 Parents should be given the results of testing.

help to initiate a partnership if the teacher does not.

Sometimes the parents of a handicapped child have to help the preschool staff learn about a particular handicap. Parents of a blind child could invite the teacher to visit the home. The teacher can then observe, first-hand, the ways that parents manage the child. They can also see how the child gets around unaided in a familiar environment.

Parents of handicapped children are often the best people to help other parents learn about handicapping conditions. This can be done in large or small group meetings. It can also be done in casual encounters, as when delivering children. Most parents of nonhandicapped children appreciate such open discussions. It helps them to better understand handicapped children.

SUMMARY

Parents are a child's most important teachers. Ways must be found to involve parents in their child's learning experiences. Programs that include handicapped children are greatly improved when parents are involved.

A good parent program is soundly based when teachers recognize individual differences among parents. Many parents of handicapped children are under great stress. Teachers must recognize this and treat parents in a warm, friendly, and sincere fashion. Every effort must be made to involve parents as partners in their child's learning experiences.

There are many ways of involving parents. Individual conferences, incidental contact, and observations by parents in the preschool work well. There are also large and small parent-teacher group meetings. Demonstrations of methods of teaching are also useful, especially when accompanied by specific learning tasks. Another good way to involve parents in their handicapped child's learning experiences is through home visits. Coordination of home-school instructional activities is necessary. Parents can also serve as volunteers or aides in the preschool. In addition, they are often effective as counselors to other parents of handicapped children.

REVIEW

A. Select the two best answers from the choices offered to complete each statement.

1. Family groupings vary. They may consist of
   a. foster parents but never grandparents.
   b. one parent and one child.
   c. two parents and several children.

2. According to the Bronfenbrenner report, most parents
   a. can do little to sustain a child's gains once the preschool program is ended.
   b. are effective reinforcers for their children.
   c. help sustain the child's gains after the program ends.

3. Handicapped children, in contrast to nonhandicapped children, require
   a. fewer years of parent caregiving.
   b. more years of parent caregiving.
   c. parents who have learned special parenting skills.

4. Sometimes it is difficult to involve parents in their child's program because the parents
   a. are lazy and don't care.
   b. are worn out from constant care of the handicapped child.
   c. do not have transportation.

5. When the child is present, the teacher should report to the parent
   a. bad things the child does.
   b. progress the child is making.
   c. good things the child does.

6. Parents should be invited to observe in the classroom
   a. once a year.
   b. once a month.
   c. whenever the parents have time.

7. Parent conferences can
    a. be helpful to parents.
    b. be threatening to parents.
    c. have little value unless preceded by a classroom observation.
8. Parent-teacher group meetings can
    a. be combined with an open-house hour.
    b. never provide baby sitting or transportation.
    c. be preceded or followed by a refreshment period.
9. In a home visit a teacher must remember that he or she is
    a. a guest.
    b. an observer.
    c. the boss.
10. Parents may have to take the initiative in helping their children by
    a. inviting the teacher into the home.
    b. asking to see test scores.
    c. not bothering teachers by asking them to explain the child's program.

B. List four or more answers for each of the following questions.
  1. Why is a parent-teacher partnership so important in intervention programs for young handicapped children?
  2. What are some reasons why it may be difficult to involve parents in a child's program?
  3. What kinds of questions might be included in a parent observation form?
  4. What are some pointers for teachers to remember regarding individual parent conferences?
  5. What points should be remembered in planning large group parent-teacher meetings?
  6. In demonstrating to parents how to read a book to their child, the teacher may need to point out several things to the parents. List five things the teacher can point out.
  7. If the preschool staff does not involve the parents, how can the parents initiate contacts themselves?

C. Briefly define and describe the following.
  1. family
  2. incidental parent contacts
  3. parent conferences
  4. small group meetings
  5. large group parent-teacher meetings
  6. teacher-to-parent demonstrations
  7. home visits
  8. parents as aides or volunteers
  9. parents as counselors
 10. parents as initiators

Unit 21 TRANSITION TO PUBLIC SCHOOL

OBJECTIVES

After studying this unit, the student will be able to

- Determine important differences between a preschool and a kindergarten class.
- Describe a team approach for transferring a child from preschool to kindergarten.
- Name support services which could be available in the kindergarten to assist the child in adjusting to the new classroom.

School programs for children with special needs are changing rapidly. Preschool education has been involved in this change by welcoming handicapped children into its classrooms. Preschools are providing the early mainstreaming experience.

With the implementation of PL 94-142, many handicapped children are being mainstreamed into public school, figure 21-1. Teachers who have mainstreamed children successfully in preschool can help these same children in kindergarten. To accomplish this,

Fig. 21-1 With the implementation of PL 94-142, handicapped children are being mainstreamed into public schools.

communication among preschool and public school staff and parents is necessary. Such communication is the key to a handicapped child's successful transition to a mainstreamed kindergarten. Early planning is also critical. Such planning should begin the day that a handicapped child is enrolled in preschool. The following components are necessary in coordinating the handicapped child's transition from preschool to kindergarten.

- a transition coordinator
- visits to public schools
- observations in kindergarten classroom
- preschool-staff meetings
- parent meetings
- placement staffings
- transition to public school
- support services

These will be discussed as specific steps in the transition process.

STEP 1 - THE TRANSITION COORDINATOR

A preschool needs one staff member to serve as transition coordinator. This person arrranges the handicapped children's participation in special programs. Later this same person assists in transferring the children from preschool to kindergarten. The transition coordinator is sometimes the preschool director. The coordinator might also be a teacher, however.

Planning an individualized transition for each handicapped child requires time and a flexible schedule. There must be time for planning. There must be time for meetings with parents and school staffs. There must be time for visiting local kindergartens. Coordinator time is needed both before and after the child's transition into kindergarten. Continuous educational contacts between the preschool and kindergarten are important. Coordination of these contacts is necessary. Such coordination insures that the kindergarten placement builds upon the efforts of the preschool, figure 21-2.

Planning a successful transition involves several activities. The coordinator must be familiar with the kindergarten classrooms and the teachers in the community. The kindergarten teachers must also become familiar with the preschool program. Exchanges of information between the preschool staff and public school staff are important. Teachers from the kindergarten programs need to know what the children in the preschool are learning, in terms of academic and social skills. The preschool staff must also know what kindergarten teachers expect from 5-year-olds, figure 21-3. Such an exchange of information is helpful for all children. The information aids in developing an effective early education program for nonhandicapped as well as handicapped children. Preschool and kindergarten teachers who are familiar with one another's classrooms can work better together. Most importantly, their cooperation can make the transition between preschool and kindergarten a comfortable experience for all children.

STEP 2 - VISITS TO PUBLIC SCHOOLS

The coordinator should visit several kindergarten classes. It is best to visit classes of former preschoolers and classes which the current preschoolers are likely to enter. The coordinator should always observe for a full session. Only by observing a total program can the coordinator become well acquainted with the schedule, activities, and teaching style. Generally, a visit can be arranged by calling the school. Appointments should be made through the school principal, the secretary, or the classroom teacher. Many

Fig. 21-2 Kindergarten placement must build upon the efforts of the preschool.

Fig. 21-3 The preschool staff must learn what is expected of kindergartners.

school districts have an early childhood or kindergarten specialist who can help make the appointments. If the district has such a specialist, a meeting to discuss the preschool-to-kindergarten transition should be arranged. A meeting with the school principal provides helpful information, too. The principal can outline services that are available for the handicapped children already enrolled in the school.

Visitors to a public school must stop at the school office first. If the coordinator has made the appointment, the secretary or principal will be ready to meet with them. The principal or secretary can then provide introductions to the kindergarten teacher.

STEP 3 - KINDERGARTEN CLASSROOM OBSERVATIONS

The coordinator should discuss with the teacher the role of an observer in that particular classroom. Some teachers prefer that a visitor sit quietly in the back of the room. They ask that visitors do not interact with the teachers or children during the visit. Other teachers tell a visitor to move about freely. They invite the visitor to talk to the children. They encourage the visitor to ask questions at any time.

The coordinator should bring a pad and pencil to take notes during the observation. Jotting down similarities and differences between the kindergarten and preschool classes is important. In particular, differences that might create problems for the current preschoolers should be noted. The notes can be organized under the following headings:

- environment
- behavior
- academic

Environment refers to the physical arrangement of the classroom. It also refers to the number of teachers and aides, and to

Fig. 21-4 **Academic questions deal with what and how children learn.**

the daily schedule. Behavior refers to how children and teachers interact in the classroom. Academic deals with what and how children learn, figure 21-4. A form that can be used for classroom assessment is shown in figure 21-5.

Answers to the classroom assessment questions in figure 21-5 will help the coordinator to determine:

- if the handicapped child will be ready for this particular kindergarten
- what additional skills the child will need
- how the preschool can help to prepare the child
- what changes might be made in the kindergarten to help the child succeed

During the visit the coordinator often thinks of other questions. The coordinator should write these questions down. When the teacher is free, the coordinator can ask the questions. A question or comment should never be critical of the classroom. The coordinator is there as a visitor who has been invited to observe.

STEP 4 - PRESCHOOL-STAFF MEETINGS

The preschool staff should meet together after the coordinator has visited several

Teaching Staff:

1. How many teachers, aides, and volunteers work in the classroom?

2. How many children are in the classroom?

3. Do the numbers of adults and children in kindergarten differ from preschool? Figure the adult/child ratio: the number of adults to number of children. The typical preschool has 3 adults to 18 children. The typical kindergarten has 1 or 2 adults to 25 to 30 children.

Physical Arrangement:

Is the physical arrangement of the kindergarten class different from the preschool? For example:

1. Do children at group time sit on individual mats or on a group rug?

2. Do children work at tables or at desks?

3. Are work and play areas clearly separated?

4. Are play areas visible from work areas?

5. Is the bathroom next to the classroom; down a hall; elsewhere?

Daily Schedule:

1. Is the kindergarten in session longer than the preschool?

2. How many minutes do children spend:
   a) in a large group (singing, sharing, listening to stories, having snacks)?
   b) in small groups?
   c) doing academic work and fine-motor activities?
   d) in free play activities?
   e) in recess and large motor activity?
   f) moving from one scheduled activity to another (for example, lining up for recess (figure 21-7), waiting to be called from large group to a small group)?

Behavior:

1. Do children work or play in groups where no adult is present?

2. If the classroom has learning centers, do the children choose their activity? Or, does the teacher send children to activities?

3. Are the children praised frequently for appropriate social behavior? for working? for finishing work?

Self-help:

1. What self-help skills do most of the children have (for example, dressing for outdoors, shoe tying, independent toileting)?

Academics:

1. How are lessons taught:
   a) In large or small groups?
   b) On the blackboard? with worksheets? with other teaching aids?
   c) Do the children respond to questions as a group or on an individual basis?
   d) Are children grouped according to their ability?

2. What academics are taught (for example, are the children learning their alphabet and numbers, phonics, simple addition)?

3. What academic skills do most entering kindergartners have? (Ask the teacher after your visit.)

Fig. 21-5 Classroom assessment.

Fig. 21-6 Many kindergartens use a learning center approach.

Fig. 21-7 Kindergarten children are expected to be more independent.

kindergartens. They can discuss the information obtained from the visits. Attention should be directed toward the differences between the preschool and kindergartens. The following is an example:

The coordinator had observed five kindergartens in the area. Many former preschool children were enrolled in these classes. The kindergarten teachers for the most part used a learning centers approach, figure 21-6. Each day the kindergarten class was divided into four groups. Each group occupied one learning center at a time. The children were expected to stay and work at each center for 15 minutes. Then they were rotated as a group to the next center. By the end of the session, each child had been at every center. Two adults were supervising the four centers.

In the preschool the children also had three or four activities from which to choose. They did not, however, have to spend a certain amount of time in any one activity. They did not have to visit all of the activities. They could change from one activity to another at any time. The children were not grouped in the preschool. An adult was available in each activity.

Several obvious differences existed between the preschool and kindergarten. The

kindergarten children were expected to be more independent, figure 21-7. A longer attention span and greater activity involvement was required. Children transferring from a less structured preschool to this kindergarten could have difficulty. Children with learning and behavior problems would need extra teacher attention. They probably could not work independently in one activity for 15 minutes at a time.

The preschool had several children with learning and behavior problems. Some were older children who would be going to kindergarten in the fall. The preschool staff decided to make the following changes with these older children:

- to increase, slowly, the number of minutes the children spent in one activity

- to make sure that the children visited each activity
- to increase the children's independence by gradually reducing teacher attention

The staff decided not to change the younger children's program. The younger children learned more with greater adult supervision in each activity. These children often needed special help in learning to use materials appropriately. The teachers also believed that the younger children had other needs. They needed the freedom to spend extra time in new activities or favorite activities, figure 21-8.

Within a few weeks, the teachers noted that the older children were able to play more independently. These children were also more willing to change activities. Visiting all of the activities became enjoyable to them. It was no problem to convince the children in the preschool to stay in one activity for more time or less time. The larger numbers of adults in the preschool make it easy. In a larger kindergarten there would be fewer teachers. Thus less adult time would be available. The next step would be for the children to learn to stay at an activity without such convincing.

Fig. 21-8 Younger children need extra time to spend in favorite activities.

It is important to discuss how differences between preschool and kindergarten affect a child's transition. Certain differences do not cause problems. When major differences do exist, however, changes must be made. Either the preschool or kindergarten must alter their way of doing things. Each staff, as a group, should decide what and how many changes they can make. A team effort is necessary if these changes are to be successful. The preschool staff can ignore differences which do not affect a child's transition to kindergarten. Some differences will always remain, of course. The changes are not intended to make the preschool into an early kindergarten experience. The changes are meant only to prepare all children for successful later schooling.

STEP 5 - THE PARENT MEETING

The coordinator and preschool teacher should meet with the parents of the handicapped child. This meeting is in addition to the other regularly scheduled conferences. The parents, coordinator, and preschool teacher should begin planning the child's transition early. Six months before the child begins kindergarten is not too soon.

The teacher should prepare a report summarizing the child's progress. This report should also include suggestions for future goals. The summary report could be outlined as shown in figure 21-9.

The report should be discussed thoroughly with the parents. The coordinator can then talk with the parents about the child's future placement. The parents may want their child to enter kindergarten or a special class. On the other hand, they may not know what classes are available. The coordinator can help the parents contact the public school. A placement conference can be arranged.

STEP 6 - PLACEMENT STAFFINGS

Several planning meetings may be necessary. These, too, should occur several

Summary Report On:
Birthdate:
Address:
Enrollment dates:

From:

Referral:

Classroom behavior:

Academic skills to date:
(general summary)

Summary of academic tasks completed:

     1.   paper-pencil (e.g., name writing, letter writing, draw a path, draw a person, workbook skills)

     2.   classification (e.g., circle-the-same)

     3.   prereading (e.g., word match)

     4.   math

     5.   visual-manipulatives (e.g., parquetry)

Skills currently being worked on:

Future task suggestions and specific academic problems:

Social skills:

Preferred activities:

Problem behaviors and ways to deal with them:

Current impressions - child's strengths and weaknesses:

Other services to contact for information:

Fig. 21-9 Summary report form.

Fig. 21-10 Public school people must be a part of the placement meetings.

Fig. 21-11 Placement decisions are based on discussion and observations of the child.

months before the child enters kindergarten. One meeting should assess the kind of placement most appropriate for the handicapped child. Usually, public school people are part of this meeting, figure 21-10. A member of the school district's special services staff and a representative from the kindergarten committee may attend. It is often their job to meet with parents and the transition coordinator. Ideally, both of the public school people should observe the child in the preschool. This observation takes place before the placement. The group as a whole should discuss the child's current performance and future needs. Information from the summary report prepared by the preschool teacher and transition coordinator should be available. Such information is helpful during a placement meeting. A placement decision can then be made. The decision is based on the discussion and the observations of the child, figure 21-11. If the parents agree with the decision, further meetings should be arranged for planning.

The parents, transition coordinator, and preschool teacher should meet with the assigned kindergarten teacher, principal, and school psychologist. The purpose of this meeting should be to

- Discuss, again, the child's current performance, special needs, and future goals.
- Arrange for the kindergarten teacher to visit the preschool.
- Schedule a visit by the preschool teacher and transition coordinator to the kindergarten.
- Plan for the child and parents to visit the kindergarten.

It may be possible to develop an initial IEP (unit 8) at this meeting. The preschool teacher, transition coordinator, and parents are most familiar with the child. They can provide valuable suggestions to the new teacher. A team approach during these meetings is important; everyone must work together. As a team, they can combine their information about the child and about school services and facilities. With this information a smooth transition can be created for the child.

The transition coordinator should offer to meet whenever necessary with the kindergarten teacher and school personnel. Often, three or four meetings are needed to plan for the special child's needs. The transition coordinator should, of course, visit the kindergarten class. The kindergarten teacher and school psychologist should visit the preschool. As suggested earlier, differences between the two classes should be noted and discussed. Necessary changes can be considered. Everyone involved in the transition process should feel free to call upon each other for information and help. Exchange visits facilitate communication and understanding between the two schools.

An early visit to kindergarten by the child and parents also should be planned. This visit gives parents and child a chance to see what kindergarten is like. The visit should ease some of the fears all children (and many parents) face when moving to a new school.

STEP 7 - TRANSITION TO PUBLIC SCHOOL

For many handicapped children, a full kindergarten session is too much at first. Different arrangements should be made for different children. Flexibility is needed when starting a young handicapped child in a new school program. The following are some suggestions.

- The child might attend kindergarten for only an hour each day the first week or so. Then, the time in kindergarten can gradually be extended. How quickly the

Fig. 21-12 A child might be co-enrolled in preschool and kindergarten.

time is increased depends on how the child adjusts.

- The preschool teacher, coordinator, or parent might accompany the child for the first few days. When the child becomes comfortable in the new classroom, adult support could be withdrawn.

- The child might continue to attend preschool for a half-day while starting to attend kindergarten the other half of the day, figure 21-12.

- The child might immediately begin the full session of kindergarten like all other children.

The kindergarten teacher and school staff should have the final say on the child's transition and amount of time in school. Careful planning must always be done before the first day. With good planning and cooperation, the new experience can be a comfortable experience for the child.

STEP 8 - SUPPORT SERVICES

During the first weeks (or even months) of kindergarten, the handicapped child may need extra assistance. The assistance can be in the form of support services offered by the transition coordinator. The new teacher may or may not be interested in receiving extra help. Whether these services are provided will depend upon the teacher. If the teacher is interested, the coordinator should plan to maintain communications. Four possible services that can be made available to the interested teacher are described below.

Teacher Conferences

Regularly scheduled meetings can be a critical part of the support service. They provide an opportunity to follow the child's progress. Suggestions can be offered as needed. During the first days of school, the transition coordinator can provide a great deal of help. The coordinator is familiar with the child's special needs and problems. If a problem develops, the coordinator can suggest solutions based on past preschool experience. It is important to be available by phone, as problems can appear suddenly. Some teachers may want to schedule a few meetings after school. They may also want the coordinator to come and observe the class after the new child is enrolled. Sometimes the coordinator can provide the most help by listening to teachers describe their day. At times, simply talking about a problem leads to a solution. In addition, these meetings can provide an opportunity for the teachers to express their feelings. These usually include both the frustrations and joys of working with a special child.

Sharing Materials or Activity Ideas

Transition may be easier if the new classroom has materials familiar to the child, figure

Fig. 21-13 Familiar materials ease the transition for a young child.

21-13. A favorite work task or toy could be loaned to the new classroom. This would help the child during the first few weeks of school. A favorite preschool activity can also be offered in the kindergarten. Having play dough available could be one such activity. Something familiar to touch or use seems to increase a young child's sense of security. With familiar objects and activities around, the new classroom and classmates seem less strange.

Tutoring

Providing a tutor for short periods several times a week can help a teacher. The tutor can supplement the regular teaching in the classroom. This can be done whenever a child needs more intensive assistance and supervision. A tutor can work individually with the handicapped child, or with a small group containing the child. The approach chosen depends upon the classroom structure and the needs of the child. Tutors can be recruited from:

- parents and parent organizations
- community volunteer agencies
- community college or university early childhood departments

Behavior Programs

Some children, upon entering a new classroom, act out. They "test" their teachers to see what behaviors are allowable. Sometimes they push beyond the classroom limits. They may become very disruptive. These children may behave in this inappropriate way to attract more teacher attention. Some children do this even if they receive only negative attention from the teacher. They may also be disruptive to avoid certain school activities.

Typically, these behavior extremes can be controlled. The same procedures used to decrease disruptive behaviors in the preschool can be used in the kindergarten. The transition coordinator can meet with the teacher to discuss behavior management programs used previously. Such procedures work for most of the problem behaviors found among young children.

SUMMARY

For the young handicapped child, the transition from preschool to kindergarten is important. Planning for the transition should start months in advance, early in the child's preschool career.

Several things are required when planning a transition. As a starting point, a person must be appointed to serve as preschool-kindergarten coordinator. This person must be given enough time to do the job. The coordinator should visit the public schools. The coordinator can then get acquainted with programs and staff. Observing in various kindergartens is also part of this person's job. Such observations help to define kindergarten expectations. It is necessary to know how these expectations differ from what is expected of children in preschool. Kindergarten teachers should also be invited to visit the preschool. Exchange visits help to make the transition easier for everyone.

Parents need to be consulted frequently throughout the transition process. The preschool and kindergarten staff should meet together several times, too. Together, they must discuss where the child is to be placed in the public school setting. They also must discuss how the transition is to be made. Specific plans should be written up. These plans should meet with the approval of everyone - parents, administrators, and teachers.

At the time the child is actually transferred, great care is required. Moving too rapidly may be upsetting to a child with special problems. One recommendation is that the child go to the new class for only an hour or so each day at first. Sometimes the preschool coordinator or a parent can accompany the child.

After the child is enrolled in kindergarten the preschool coordinator can offer further support. Not all kindergarten teachers, however, want this service. For those who do, the following kinds of assistance can be made available:

- regularly scheduled consultations
- loans of preschool materials that the child enjoyed
- tutoring for the child
- behavior management programs

Almost every handicapped child can succeed in public school kindergarten. Mainstreaming can and should be a happy situation for all handicapped children. What is required is careful, individualized planning throughout the transition period and into the child's entire school career.

STUDENT ACTIVITIES

- Obtain permission to observe an entire preschool session; answer the questions on the classroom assessment form.

- Obtain permission to observe an entire public school kindergarten session; answer the questions on the classroom assessment form.

- Compare your preschool and kindergarten assessments. List similarities and differences.

- Write a summary report on a preschool child who will soon be entering kindergarten. Ask a kindergarten teacher how helpful such a report would be.

REVIEW

A. Briefly answer each of the following.

1. List five duties of the transition coordinator.
2. What should the coordinator look for when observing a classroom?
3. Who should be involved in planning the preschool child's transition to kindergarten?
4. Describe four ways in which a handicapped child may be introduced to kindergarten.
5. List four support services which could be provided to a handicapped child in kindergarten.

B. Select the best answer from the choices offered to complete each statement.

1. Planning for the handicapped preschooler's transition into a normal public school kindergarten should begin
   a. as a handicapped child enrolls in the preschool.
   b. the day a handicapped child enrolls in kindergarten.
   c. as soon as a handicapped child turns 5.
   d. after the public schools screen for kindergarten.
2. The coordinator's job requires extra time for
   a. planning.
   b. meeting with parents and school staff.
   c. visiting local kindergartens.
   d. all of the above.
3. When observing a classroom, a visitor should
   a. feel free to ask questions at any time.
   b. first discuss with the teacher what the visitor's role in the classroom should be.
   c. not interact with the teacher or children during the visit.
   d. make suggestions to improve the classroom.
4. If teaching methods differ a great deal between the kindergarten and the preschool
   a. the preschool staff should change their program so that the preschool experience becomes an early kindergarten experience.
   b. the preschool staff can ignore differences which will affect a child's transition into kindergarten.
   c. it is the kindergarten staff's responsibility to change their program.
   d. both the preschool and kindergarten staffs should consider ways of changing their respective programs to facilitate the handicapped child's transition.

   5. A summary report of a child's attendance in preschool
      a. should summarize the child's progress and suggest future goals.
      b. should be discussed thoroughly with the parents.
      c. should be sent to the kindergarten teacher if the parents have consented to a release of information.
      d. all of the above.

C. Fill in each blank with appropriate short answers.

   1. Frequent, open communication among preschool and public school staff and parents is the _____ to a handicapped child's successful transition.
   2. _____ are providing the early mainstreaming experience.
   3. Coordination between _____ is the best way to insure that the kindergarten placement builds upon the efforts of the preschool program.
   4. The coordinator should plan to spend a full half-day session observing a kindergarten in order to become familiar with the classroom's _____ , _____ , and _____ .
   5. When major differences exist between the preschool and kindergartens, changes must be made _____ .
   6. The summary report should include _____ .
   7. Information from the _____ will be helpful during the handicapped child's placement meeting.
   8. A _____ approach to the IEP development meeting is vital. Everyone should be working together.
   9. An early visit to kindergarten by the child and parents should ease _____ .
   10. A tutor can work _____ .

ACKNOWLEDGMENTS

The author wishes to express her appreciation to the following individuals and institutions for their contributions to this text.

Illustrations

Gary M. Mason, Erik A. Thelen, and Joe Kelley, Department of Photojournalism, University of Kansas: figures 1-1 to 1-4, 1-7 to 1-9, 2-2 to 2-4, 3-2 to 3-10, 4-2, 4-5, 5-2 to 5-5, 5-7 to 5-9, 6-4, 6-6, 6-7, 6-10, 7-1 to 7-7, 7-9, 8-1, 8-2, 8-5, 8-7 to 8-9, 8-12 to 8-14, 9-1 to 9-7, 9-9, 9-10, 9-12 to 9-14, 10-1 to 10-15, 11-1, 11-2, 11-4 to 11-12, 12-1 to 12-3, 12-5, 12-7 to 12-13, 13-1, 13-3 to 13-6, 13-11 to 13-14, 14-1 to 14-18, 15-3 to 15-9, 15-11, 15-12, 16-1, 16-2, 16-5 to 16-7, 16-9, 17-2, 17-3, 17-5, 17-6, 17-8, 18-1 to 18-5, 18-7 to 18-9, 19-1 to 19-11, 20-1 to 20-9, 20-12, 20-13, 21-1 to 21-4, 21-6 to 21-8, 21-10 to 21-13

Peter Karas: figure on page vi and figure 17-10

Frank Porter Graham Center, Chapel Hill, North Carolina: figures 1-6, 6-1, 6-3, 7-8

National March of Dimes: figures 2-6, 6-2, 17-1, 17-9, 20-11

Experimental Education Unit, College of Education and Child Development and Mental Retardation Center, University of Washington, Seattle, Washington: figures 2-7, 4-4, 6-11, 8-4, 9-11, 11-3, 13-8, 17-7

National Easter Seal Society for Crippled Children and Adults: figures 3-1, 9-8, 15-1, 17-4

National Association for Retarded Citizens (NARC): figure 4-1

University of Arkansas and the Kramer School, Little Rock, Arkansas: figure 4-3

Office of Senator Robert Dole, United States Senator from Kansas: figure 4-6

Steven M. Ennis: figures 5-1, 5-6, 12-4, 13-2, 15-11, 16-3, 16-4, 18-6

Cyrene Nassif: figures 6-5, 6-8, 6-9, 8-6

Photo Workshop, Kingston, New York: figure 8-3

Department of Speech and Drama, University of Kansas, Lawrence, Kansas: figure 13-7

Preschools, Schools, and Special Centers

Edna A. Hill Child Development Laboratory Preschool, Department of Human Development and Family Life, University of Kansas

Special Education Experimental Classes, Department of Special Education, University of Kansas

Blue Springs Deaf-Blind Center, Blue Springs, Missouri

New York School, Unified School District #497, Lawrence, Kansas

The Forum School, Waldwick, New Jersey

Grant Wood Area Education Agency, Cedar Rapids, Iowa

Acknowledgments

Individual Assistance

Susan A. Fowler, author of unit 21
Kathleen M. Sullivan, for material used in unit 4
Phyllis L. Hunter and Susan K. Bernard, for typing original manuscript material
Jane Tegeler and Ruth Ann Mowry, for assistance with classroom testing

Delmar Staff

Source Editor - Judith Barrow Thorpe
Sponsoring Editor - Barbara S. Mohan
Consultant - Jeanne Machado

The author also wishes to acknowledge the Department of Human Development and Family Life, and Bureau of Child Research, University of Kansas, for underlying support of this project.

The instructional material in this text was classroom tested at the Olathe Vocational School, Olathe, Kansas.

INDEX

1/91(OC262J)